Lov

Agnes Gonzha Boja***, ***** ***** ***** Teresa of
Calcutta, was born on 27 August 1910, of Albanian parents,
at Skopje, Yugoslavia, and at the age of 15 was inspired by
a missionary's letters to volunteer for the Bengal Mission.
In 1928 she went to Loreto Abbey, Rathfarnham, Dublin
and from there to India to begin her novitiate. From 1929
to 1948 she taught at St Mary's High School in Calcutta,
for some years being Principal of the school, as well as
being in charge of the Daughters of St Anne, the Indian
religious Order attached to the Loreto Sisters.

In September 1946 Mother Teresa asked permission to
live alone outside the cloister and to work in the Calcutta
slums. Two years later she first put on the white sari with
the blue border and cross on the shoulder which has
become so well-known. After a further two years the new
congregation of the Missionaries of Charity was approved
and instituted in Calcutta in October 1950.

Mother Teresa's work spread to many needy parts of
the world, and was recognized by various honours,
including the Pope John XXIII Peace Prize in 1971, and the
Nobel Peace Prize in 1979. She died on 5 September 1997,
and was accorded a state funeral by the government of
India as a mark of the love of the Indian people.

Love, Joy and Peace

The Love of Christ
Suffering into Joy
Contemplative in the Heart of the World

Mother Teresa

Fount
An Imprint of HarperCollins*Publishers*

Fount is an imprint of
HarperCollins*Religious*
Part of HarperCollins*Publishers*
77–85 Fulham Palace Road, London W6 8JB

This edition first published 1998
13 5 7 9 10 8 6 4 2

A catalogue record for this book is
available from the British Library

ISBN 0 00 628099 4

Printed and bound in Great Britain by
Caledonian International Book Manufacturing Ltd, Glasgow

Contents

The Love of Christ

edited by Georges Gorrée
and Jean Barbier

Contents

Introduction

Mother Teresa spoke little, published even less. Of necessity, however, she carried a large volume of correspondence. In addition, she was asked for many interviews and sometimes had to speak in public (whenever her work was recognized by a prize of one kind or another). In this varied activity, in which she was generally spontaneous and uninhibited by the fear of repetition, what she projected was the faith by which she lived and the love that impelled her.

Appearing in this work are words of Mother Teresa. Some of them have been gathered by attentive listeners. Others are drawn from her letters, or from directives to her Co-Workers, or from her commentary on the constitutions of the Missionary Sisters and Brothers of Charity. Our aim has been to reproduce her simple and straightforward language, which concentrates on the truly essential and reveals the beauty of a totally dedicated life as well as the almost unbearable realities of misery and suffering.

As an aid to the reader, some division into parts had to be made. The division, in the nature of the case, is more or less arbitrary. Mother Teresa's life, however, was not divided or compartmentalized. It was an indivisible whole, its source and strength the twofold commandment of love of God and love of neighbor.

ACKNOWLEDGMENTS

Some of the material in Parts I and II is drawn from Malcolm Muggeridge's *Something Beautiful for God* (London, Fount Paperbacks, 1972) and the authors' earlier work on Mother Teresa, *Amour sans frontière*.

The text of Parts III and IV is from unpublished material that was supplied by the Missionaries of Charity.

In addition, we have drawn upon interviews given by Mother Teresa and articles by various journalists such as Ralph Rolls and Sandro Bordignon.

PART I

God

MY LIFE, BUT NEVER MY FAITH

"Lord, give me this vision of faith, and my work will never become monotonous."

So prays Mother Teresa, in prayer both strong and confident. Ralph Rolls asked her what she would do if a country where she worked demanded that she give up her faith. She replied:*

No one can take my faith from me. If, in order to spread the love of Christ among the poor and neglected, there were no alternative but to remain in that country, I would remain—but I would not renounce my faith. I am prepared to *give up my life but never my faith.*

Voluntarily choosing this hazardous and humanly wretched life is the measure of her faith. What else explains it? Certainly not the results,

---

* Material in italics is commentary by the authors. The rest of the text is Mother Teresa's own words.

> *which, as the world counts, would have to be judged small.*

We realize that what we are accomplishing is a drop in the ocean. But if this drop were not in the ocean, it would be missed. If we did not have our schools in the quarters of the poor—they are small, primary schools, where we teach the children to like school and how to keep themselves clean—if we did not have these small schools, the thousands of children who benefit from them would be left in the streets.

It is the same with our Home for the Dying. If we did not have this home, those whom we bring in would die in the streets. I believe it is worth the trouble to have this home, if only for the comparatively few we can handle, so that they may die with some dignity and in the peace of God.

> *Another secret of Mother Teresa's life is her power of perseverance. According to the French priest-orator Lacordaire, to persevere one must be as "loving as a mother and as hard as a diamond." Mother Teresa finds the explanation in her faith:*

Faith is a gift of God. Without it there would be no life. Our work, to bear fruit, to belong only to God, to be deserving, must be built on faith.

Christ said: "I was hungry, I was naked, I was sick, I was homeless, and you did that for me."* All our work is based on faith in these words.

---

* Matthew 25:35-40: " ' For I was hungry and you gave me food, I was thirsty and you gave me drink, I was a stranger and you welcomed me, I was naked and you clothed me, I was sick and you visited me, I was in prison and you came to me.' Then the righteous will answer him, 'Lord, when did we see thee hungry and feed thee,

If faith is lacking, it is because there is too much selfishness, too much concern for personal gain. For faith to be true, it has to be generous and loving. Love and faith go together; they complete each other.

| *But she does not impose her faith.*

It is our prayer that Christ communicate His light and life to each of us and through us to the world of misery. We hope that the poor, whatever their beliefs, seeing us will be drawn to Christ and will want us to come to them, into their lives.

> *Mother Teresa's faith is something so absolute and so solid that she would rather see herself and her work destroyed than forget her faith or doubt it for a moment. The intensity of her faith is a phenomenon that is attracting the attention of the world and making history. Faith exudes from her whole being, faith that is truth.*
>
> *Though reason retains its importance in the exercise of faith and following Christ does not mean its abandonment, the young, beset with problems, sometimes forgo the reasoning process. In the case of Mother Teresa, at least, they seem to follow her implicitly.*
>
> *When she decided to join a march of seven kilometers through the streets of Milan for the purpose of arousing support for solidarity with the*

or thirsty and give thee drink? And when did we see thee a stranger and welcome thee, or naked and clothe thee? And when did we see thee sick or in prison and visit thee?' And the King will answer them, 'Truly, I say to you as you did it to one of the least of these my brethren, you did it to me.'"

> *Third World, for her, according to the French
> journalist Bordignon, it was a symbolic gesture.
> The organizers had been preoccupied with the de-
> tails of the march, but the news that she would
> participate transformed it into a procession of
> faith. Everyone was struck by the expression on
> her face, the ascetical features which, like her
> words, spoke the force of truth. Afterwards she
> was received by Cardinal Giovanni Colombo,
> archbishop of Milan, to whom she said:*

Before God we are all poor.

> *Why this march? Why would thousands of young
> people assemble at the cathedral square to begin
> with Mother Teresa this seven-kilometer march
> without fanfare, without banners? Why would the
> young march for something they did not clearly
> understand, or if they did, still hesitated to admit
> it for fear of being challenged?*

The young are the builders of tomorrow. Youth
today is in search of selflessness, and when it finds it,
is prepared to embrace it.

In Harlem a young woman of a wealthy family
came to us in a taxicab and told me: "I have given
everything to the poor and have come to follow
Christ."

Sometimes Jesus receives unusual attention. One
evening in London I had a telephone call from the
police: "Mother Teresa, there is a women in the
streets very drunk, who is calling for you." We went
to find her and on the way back she said to me:
"Mother Teresa, Christ changed water into wine so

that we would have some to drink." And she was very, very drunk!

Ralph Rolls put this question to Mother Teresa: "Is it important for you to be a Catholic?"

Yes. For me and for every individual, according to the grace God has given to each.

It matters little, then, to what part of the Christian church we belong?

No, it is important for the individual. If the individual thinks and believes that his or her way is the only way to God, if they do not know any other way, do not doubt and so do not feel the need to look elsewhere, then that is their way of salvation, the way that God comes into their life. But from the moment that a soul receives the grace to know God it must begin to seek. And if it does not seek, it moves away from the right road. But God gives to all souls that He creates a chance to meet Him and to accept Him or reject Him.

Is unity among Christians important?

Yes, because Christians represent a light for others. If we are Christians, we must resemble Christ. I believe this very deeply. Gandhi once said if Christians had lived their Christian life completely, there would be no Hindus left in India. People expect us to live our Christian life fully.

The followers of other religions, Moslems, Hindus, are they also blessed by God and does God work through them too?

God has His own means and ways of working in the hearts of people, and we do not know how close they are to Him. But in their actions we always have a clue to their attitude toward Him, whether or not they are responsive to Him. Moslem, Hindu, or Christian, the way you live your life is the measure of your belonging to God. We cannot condemn or judge, or speak words that might hurt. Perhaps a person has never heard of Christianity; if so, we do not know in what manner God appears in this soul and in what way He has this soul serve His purpose. By what right, then, can we condemn anyone?

I LOOK UPON HIM, HE LOOKS UPON ME

It is not possible to engage in the apostolate without being a soul of prayer, without consciously forgetting oneself and submitting to God's will. We must be conscious of our oneness with Christ, as He was of His oneness with His Father. Our activity is truly apostolic only to the extent that we let Christ work in us and through us, with all His power, all His desire, and all His love.

> *A soul of prayer can make progress without recourse to words, by learning to listen, to be present to Christ, and to look toward Him.*

Often we do not receive what we prayed and hoped for because we did not fix our attention and our hearts on Christ, through whom our prayers come to God. Many times a deep and fervent gaze upon Christ is the best prayer. *I look upon Him, He looks upon me* is the most perfect prayer.

| *Her prayer speaks mercy, kindness, patience.*

"Lord, grant that I may always bear in mind the very great dignity of my vocation, and all its responsibilities. Never let me dishonor it by being cold, or unkind, or impatient."

Love prayer. Feel often the need to pray, and take the trouble to pray. It is by praying often that you will pray better. Prayer enlarges the heart until it is capable of containing the gift that God makes of Himself. Ask and seek: your heart will grow capable of receiving Him and holding on to Him.

| *The need to discover Christ in the sick forms part of her daily prayer.*

"Jesus, my suffering Lord, grant that today and every day I may see You in the person of Your sick ones, and that in caring for them I may serve You. Grant also that even in the guise of the fretful, the demanding, the unreasonable, I may still recognize You and say: My suffering Jesus, how sweet it is to serve You.

"Lord, give me this vision of faith, and my work will never become monotonous. I will find joy in indulging the moods and gratifying the desires of all the poor who suffer.

"O dear sick one, how much dearer still you are to me because you represent Christ. What a privilege I have to be able to tend to you.

"O God, since You are Jesus in his suffering, deign

also to be to me a patient Jesus, overlooking my faults, seeing only my intentions, which are to love You and to serve You in the person of each of Your children who suffers. Lord, increase my faith.

"Bless my efforts and my work, now and always."

| *"How do you pray?" Bordignon asked her.*

We begin our day by seeing Christ in the consecrated bread, and throughout the day we continue to see Him in the torn bodies of our poor. We pray, that is, through our work, performing it with Jesus, for Jesus, and upon Jesus.

The poor are our prayer. They carry God in them. Prayer means praying everything, praying the work.

| *What consolation do you find in your work?*

We meet the Lord who hungers and thirsts, in the poor . . . and the poor could be you or I or any person kind enough to show us his or her love and to come to our place.

IN SILENCE, HE HEARS US, HE SPEAKS TO US

It is very hard to pray if one does not know how. We must help ourselves to learn.

The most important thing is silence. Souls of prayer are souls of deep silence. We cannot place ourselves directly in God's presence without imposing upon ourselves interior and exterior silence. That is why we must accustom ourselves to stillness of the soul, of the eyes, of the tongue.

God is the friend of silence. We need to find God, but

we cannot find Him in noise, in excitement. See how nature, the trees, the flowers, the grass grow in deep silence. See how the stars, the moon, and the sun move in silence.

Is not our mission to bring God to the poor in the streets? Not a dead God but a living God, a God of love. The apostles said: "We will devote ourselves to prayer and to the ministry of the word."

The more we receive in our silent prayer, the more we can give in our active life. Silence gives us a new way of looking at everything. We need this silence in order to touch souls. The essential thing is not what we say but what God says to us and what He says through us.

Jesus is always waiting for us in silence. *In this silence He listens to us; it is there that He speaks to our souls.* And there, we hear His voice. Interior silence is very difficult, but we must make the effort to pray. In this silence we find a new energy and a real unity. God's energy becomes ours, allowing us to perform things well. There is unity of our thoughts with His thoughts, unity of our prayers with His prayers, unity of our actions with His actions, of our life with His life.

Our words are useless unless they come from the bottom of the heart. Words that do not give the light of Christ only make the darkness worse.

Make every effort to walk in the presence of God, to see God in everyone you meet, and to live your morning meditation throughout the day. In the streets in particular, radiate the joy of belonging to God, of living with Him and being His. For this reason, in the streets, in the shelters, in your work, you should al-

ways be praying with all your heart and all your soul.
Maintain the silence that Jesus maintained for thirty
years at Nazareth, and that He still maintains in the
tabernacle, interceding for us. Pray like the Virgin
Mary, who kept all things in her heart through prayer
and meditation, and still does, as mediatrix of all
graces.

Christ's teaching is so simple that even a little
child can learn it. The apostles said: "Teach us to
pray." Jesus answered: "When you pray, say, Our
Father . . ."

ALONE, WE CAN DO NOTHING

> *Mother Teresa chooses to serve. But service she
> understands as an instrument that is more effec-
> tive the more humble it is.*

That is why we should be able to summon our courage and say in all sincerity: "I can do all things in
Him, because it is He who strengthens me."

This assertion of St. Paul should give you great
confidence in the realization of your work, or rather
God's work, in its efficacy and perfection in Jesus and
for Jesus. Be also convinced that alone, of yourself,
you can do nothing, and have nothing except sin,
weakness and misery; that all the natural gifts and
gifts of grace we have were given to us by God.

We can see the humility of Jesus in the crib, in the
Exile in Egypt and His hidden life, in the inability to
make Himself understood by people, in the abandonment by the apostles, in the hatred of His enemies

among the Jews, in all the bitter sufferings of the
Passion, and now in His acts of constant humility in
the tabernacle, where he reduces Himself to such a
small piece of bread that the priest can hold Him
between two fingers.

> *To Malcolm Muggeridge she made the request
> that his study about her work not be in the nature
> of a biography of herself:*

The life of Christ was not written during his lifetime, yet He did the greatest work on earth—He redeemed the world and taught mankind to love His
Father. The work is His work and to remain so, all of
us are but his instruments, who do our little bit and
pass by.*

Let there be no pride or vanity in the work. The
work is God's work, the poor are God's poor. Let us put
ourselves completely under the power and influence
of Jesus, so that He may think with our minds, work
with our hands, for we can do all things if His strength
is with us.

Our mission is to convey the love of God, who is not
a dead God but a living God.

> *Not a God of facile or premature solutions that
> seem reasonable but sometimes wound the sensi-
> tivity of people in distress. Not a dead God, served
> merely from a sense of duty, a burden on our con-
> science that we attempt to load onto the shoulders
> of others. But a living God, a God of mercy, of*

* Malcolm Muggeridge, *Something Beautiful for God* (New York:
Harper & Row, 1971), p. 15.

compassion, who in Jesus Christ took the form of man and became a member of the poor.

Mother Teresa teaches us that the desire to serve the poor requires that we acknowledge the misery in ourselves, our own insufficiency and radical poverty.

We must accept our vulnerability and limitations in regard to others. This is essential in gaining their confidence. We cannot expect to help others from the "outside."

Learn to be quiet so that the other can speak. Forget about rules that relegate the oppressed to the margins of society, leaving them in their isolation. Hope with the captives of unjust social conditions, who have nothing but their untold wants. Hope with "prisoners," those overwhelmed by physical, moral, or spiritual misery.

Mother Teresa permits herself to be "touched" by the untouchables, those whom we too quickly consign to the ranks of the irrecoverable, the hopeless. She permits herself to be "disarmed" by the exigent cry of people. Often it is the "marginalization," the rejection, the lack of understanding that causes people to withdraw into themselves.

It is not easy to be poor with the poor, to surrender power and the confidence in our "solutions," our "normality."

It is not easy to visit a person in his or her isolation, to break down the barriers that separate the world of the "haves" from the world of the "have-nots."

It takes a great deal of humility to acknowledge

one's limitations, one's helplessness or inadequacy.

One of Mother Teresa's favorite thoughts is:

With Jesus, everything is possible because God is love.

Despite the publicity and attention that surround her—which she does not want and tries to discourage*—Mother Teresa moves about in her unassuming manner, slight and almost unnoticed amid the others.

When one finds her, in an old building on the grounds of the Kali Temple, it is difficult to pick her out from the other Sisters. Nothing suggests that she is the founder of a congregation of religious with foundations all over the world.

She finds it painful to get ready for an interview. She confesses:

For me, it is more difficult than bathing a leper, if it comes to that.

Before a television interview she can be seen seated in a dim corner behind the curtain, fingering her large beads as she waits to speak to thousands, or millions.

---

*Mother Teresa was recently quoted to the effect that the publicity that has fallen on her since receiving the Nobel Prize was interfering with her work of service to the poor and therefore she would not "participate in any more receptions" (United News of India, 2 April 1980). Nevertheless, her work continues to be recognized. In April 1980 she received the Bharat Ratna (Jewel of India), India's highest civilian award, for her "exceptional service of charity" to the poor of India's cities.—Translator's note.

She does not put her thoughts on paper or make notes. She does not have the gift for that kind of preparation; she relies for guidance on her rosary.

GIVE ME TO DRINK

Jesus thirsts for love. This same God who says that He does not need to tell us if He is hungry did not hesitate to ask for a drink of water from the Samaritan woman. But in saying, "Give me to drink," it was the love of His creature that the Creator asked for.

"What you do to the least of my brethren, you do to me." Mother Teresa develops this thought:

When I was hungry, you gave me to eat.
When I was thirsty, you gave me to drink.

Whatsoever you do to the least of my brethren, that you do unto me.
Now enter the house of my Father.

When I was homeless, you opened your doors.
When I was naked, you gave me your coat.

When I was weary, you helped me find rest.
When I was anxious, you calmed all my fears.

When I was little, you taught me to read.
When I was lonely, you gave me your love.

When in a prison, you came to my cell.
When on a sick bed, you cared for my needs.

In a strange country, you made me at home.
Seeking employment, you found me a job.

Hurt in a battle, you bound up my wounds.
Searching for kindness, you held out your hand.

When I was Negro, or Chinese, or white, and
Mocked and insulted, you carried my cross.

When I was aged, you bothered to smile.
When I was restless, you listened and cared.

You saw me covered with spittle and blood,
You knew my features, though grimy with sweat.

When I was laughed at, you stood by my side.
When I was happy, you shared in my joy.*

We must live this life, this hard life, to be able to
continue to work among the people. The work is our
only way of expressing our love for God. Our love must
pour on someone. The people are the means of expressing our love of God.

God gives what is needed. He gives to the flowers
and the birds, and to everything that He has created
in the universe. And the little children are His life.
There can never be enough of them.

If the work is seen only through our own eyes and
our own means, obviously we are not up to the task.
But in Christ we can do all things. That is why this
work has become possible, because we are convinced
that He, Christ, works with us and through us, in the
poor and for the poor.

The work is only an expression of the love we have
for God. Loving others is an expression of our love for
God.**

* Reprinted from Muggeridge, *Something Beautiful for God*, pp.
78-79.
** Letter from Mother Teresa to Co-Workers, December, 1971.

We must all be witnesses of Christ. Christ is the vine and we are the branches. Without us, there would be no fruit. This is something to bear in mind. God is the vinedresser to all of us. Christ made no distinction between priests and brothers, sisters and laywomen, no distinction as witness-bound. We must all be witnesses of Christ's compassion, Christ's love, to our families, to our neighbors, to the towns or cities where we reside, and to the world in which we live.

Only in heaven will we know how much we owe to the poor, because on account of them we were able to love God more.*

> *For the poor, Mother Teresa renounces and empties herself. Were it not for Jesus Christ, this renunciation would seem absurd, an abdication of reason. But the poor invest it with Jesus Christ. Love of Jesus is the light that shines in her life and lends her a kind of spiritual luminosity which radiates from her in spite of herself and trails her wherever she goes. It lights up her wrinkled face and is the reason why the world is intrigued, yes, fascinated.*
>
> *Jesus is the one she wants her Co-Workers to bring to the world but especially to the poor.*

A Co-Worker must be capable of bringing Jesus to people. For that, we must remain close to God. We should have a daily holy hour of prayer and meditation. Even where we are not many, we could have it

---

* Mother Teresa, at the first national congress of Co-Workers held in Salt Lake City, Utah.

in our parish church, or wherever we are. If we truly love the poor, our first contact must be with Jesus, in the blessed sacrament. Then it will be easy to bring our love for Jesus to the poor.

> *"I am the bread of life; he who comes to me shall not hunger, and he who believes in me shall never thirst" (John 6:35).*
>
> *Mother Teresa strives to be one "body" with Jesus; her "food" is to praise His Name. To be one "body" with Jesus means to let oneself be touched and healed by His mercy, to have eyes to see,*
> *ears to hear,*
> *tongue to speak,*
> *to attack moral and physical corruption, to relieve spiritual and bodily paralysis.*
>
> *The "Body" of Christ is the prism through which she sees the body of the neighbor.*

Because we cannot see Christ, we cannot express our love to Him in person. But our neighbor we can see, and we can do for him or her what we would love to do for Jesus if He were visible.

Let us be open to God so that He can use us. Let us put love into our actions, beginning in the family, in the neighborhood, in the street. It is difficult, but there is where the work begins. We are co-workers of Christ, a fruitbearing branch of the vine.*

> *The street! With its surprises, its dens, hovels, and teeming misery! This where poverty roots. No*

---

* Mother Teresa, on receiving the Templeton Prize in London.

> *need for explanations, for big words. My brother or*
> *sister is there, waiting.*
>
> *The thoughts of the heart, does one write them*
> *down? That would be to rationalize them, to make*
> *them serve where they cannot serve. Love does not*
> *wait for explanations. It goes to work, a light, a*
> *force that finds new ways to meet the hopelessness*
> *of the old.*

We can work, but we cannot do it without God's
help. This we receive in our daily mass, when He gives
us strength through His bread.

> *She insists, to the chagrin of the world, that in*
> *dealing with the poor the tables are turned: it is*
> *not the poor who are indebted to us but we who are*
> *indebted to them.*
>
> *Mother Teresa explains what she considers to be*
> *the essential difference between the Christian and*
> *non-Christian conceptions of love.*

Non-Christians and Christians both do social work,
but non-Christians do it for something while we do it
for someone. This accounts for the respect, the love
and devotion, because we do it for God. That is why we
try to do it as beautifully as possible. We are in continual contact with Christ in His work, just as we are in
contact with Him at mass and in the blessed sacrament. There, Jesus has the appearance of bread. But
in the world of misery, in the torn bodies, in the children, it is the same Christ that we see, that we touch.

> *Accordingly, for Mother Teresa the two command-*
> *ments, love of· God and love of neighbor, are*

fulfilled together; they are in fact inseparable. Her life is a monument to these two loves which are one. How, if we do not love God, can we love our neighbor; and how, if we do not love our neighbor, can we love God?

She preaches Christ every moment of the day, by living in Him, through Him, and for Him.

In 1956 Mother Teresa introduced the daily Holy Hour for her Co-Workers.

To make a retreat, let Jesus work in you. Let there be exposition, scripture, silence.

Jesus asked his disciples to be with Him in His prayer. Finding them asleep, He said: "You can sleep now and take your rest. All is finished, the hour is come."

It is by an intuition of the heart that we are drawn to the Eucharist to come into His presence. The tabernacle is the guarantee that he has "pitched his tent" among us, perpetually.

The Eucharist is the sacrament of prayer, the source and summit of the Christian life. His presence before us hastens His cumulative presence in us. His presence imparts the Spirit to us, and lights up the shadows of our heart in deep communion.

The Holy Hour before the Eucharist should lead us to a "holy hour" with the poor, with those who will never be a human success and whose only consolation is Jesus. Our Eucharist is incomplete if it does not make us love and serve the poor. In receiving the communion of the poor, we discover our own poverty.

Every day we partake of the blessed sacrament, and

we have noticed a change come over our life. We have experienced a deeper love for Christ in the distressful appearance of the poor. We have come to a better understanding of ourselves and a better understanding of the poor—a clear sign of God's blessing.

Since we began this devotion, we have not diminished our work. We spend as much time at it as before, but now with greater understanding. People accept us more, now, because they hunger for God. Their need is not for us but for Jesus.

But how can one bring them Jesus unless oneself is intent on holiness?

I WILL

Holiness consists in doing God's will joyfully. Faithfulness makes saints. The spiritual life is a union with Jesus: the divine and the human giving themselves to each other. The only thing Jesus asks of us is to give ourselves to Him, in total poverty, and total self-forgetfulness.

The first step toward holiness is the will to become holy. Through a firm and upright will we love God, we choose God, we hasten to God, we reach Him, we have Him.

Often, under the pretext of humility, of trust, of abandonment, we can forget to use the strength of our will. Everything depends on these words: "I will" or "I will not." And into the expression "I will" I must put all my energy.

One cannot expect to become a saint without paying

the price, and the price is much renunciation, much temptation, much struggle and persecution, and all sorts of sacrifices. One cannot love God except at the cost of oneself.

If you learn the art of self-restraint and thoughtfulness, you will become more and more like Christ. His heart is all recompense, and He always thought of others. Jesus went about only doing good. At Cana, our Blessed Mother thought only of the needs of others and made them known to Jesus. The thoughtfulness of Jesus, Mary, and Joseph was so great that they made Nazareth a privileged abode of the Most High. If we had this same solicitude for one another, our communities would truly become a privileged abode of the Most High.

Mother Teresa is so closely united with God that God reveals Himself through her person. She is at once salt of the earth and light of the world. People who come to her are drawn to her in the same way that the crowds of Jerusalem were drawn to Christ.

There is a brightness, a luminosity to Mother Teresa's love which overflows her Home for the Dying and transforms repellent and irritable creatures into human beings responding to love.

A sort of "materialization" of this luminosity is reported by Malcolm Muggeridge, who was in charge of making a film about the Home for the Dying. The light inside was so dim that the cameraman said it was impossible to get a picture. It was decided to go ahead anyway. To the surprise

> *of the technicians, the processed film showed the inside of the home and the dying bathed in beautiful soft light and was some of the best footage taken! What was the explanation for this "unnatural" occurrence?*
>
> *"I myself am absolutely convinced," says Malcolm Muggeridge, "that the technically unaccountable light is, in fact, the Kindly Light Newman refers to in his well-known hymn. . . . Mother Teresa's Home for the Dying is overflowing with love, as one senses immediately on entering it. This love is luminous, like the haloes artists have seen and made visible round the heads of the saints. I find it not at all surprising that the luminosity should register on a photographic film."**

Her light restores joy. Joy is a power, and the poor followed Jesus because power dwelled in Him, "went forth" from Him, flowed from His eyes, His hands, His body, totally given, present, to God, to people.

> *Malcolm Muggeridge relates that after his television interview with Mother Teresa the response of the British public was astounding. He himself received numerous letters, all of them as much as saying: "This woman spoke to me as no one ever has, and I feel I must help her."***

---

* Muggeridge, *Something Beautiful for God*, pp. 41-44.
** Ibid., p. 31.

PART II

The Other

LOVING THE OTHER

> *Mother Teresa's love is so great that she sees the neighbor as more beautiful than the reality suggests. She believes in love and produces love where there was none.*

The poor are God's gift; they are our love. Christ will not ask how much we did but how much love we put into what we did. There are many people who are spiritually poor. The spiritual poverty found in Europe, in America, is a heavy burden to bear. In these countries it is very difficult to convey a sense of God's love.

Our spiritual life is a life of dependence on God; its fruit is our work for the poor. We try to "pray" the work, doing it for Jesus, in Jesus and to Jesus.

The poor are "hope." By their courage they truly represent the hope of the world. They have taught us a different way of loving God by making us do our utmost to help them.

> *The role of the mother in the betterment of the individual is all-important. One of them complained to Mother Teresa that her children do not listen to her and asked what she should do. Mother Teresa replied:*

Mothers are the heart of the home; they build family life by wanting, loving, and taking care of their children. One time in London I came upon a young boy who was on drugs. I said to him: "You are very young and should not be out in the street at this hour of the night." He replied: "My mother does not want me because I have long hair, and that is why I am here."

An hour later I returned to the same place and was told that the boy had taken four different drugs. He had been hurried to the hospital and very likely was already dead.

Recently, in L—, a young woman of twenty-one years, who had been scolded in the morning, attempted suicide later in the day by swallowing kerosene. Taken to the hospital, she said to the priest: "My mother chased me out of the house and I did not know where to go; so I thought the best thing would be to kill myself."

Much suffering of young people is attributable to the family, and particularly to mothers. Mothers make the home a center of love. Their role is sometimes hard, but there is the example of the Blessed Virgin, who teaches us to be good with our children. We Missionaries of Charity also have to be mothers and make our communities happy homes.

> *"Truly, I say to you, as you did it to one of the least of these my brethren, you did it to me" (Matthew 25:40).*
>   *Mother Teresa's desire is to:*

Help people recognize God in the person of the poor.*

> *Though the possibility of knowing God rests on a certain resemblance between man and the God who took a human form, there is nothing in common between the infinite nature of God and the finite nature of man.*

Let each Sister and Brother grow in resemblance to Christ, so that in the world of today He may still live His life of compassion and human kindness. Your love of Christ is so admirable! Keep the light of Christ always shining bright in your hearts. He is the Love to love.**

Love is a fruit always in season, and no limit is set. Everyone can reach this love.

Are we convinced of Christ's love for us and of our love for Him? This conviction is like the sun's rays, which cause the sap of life to flow and make the flowers of holiness blossom. This conviction is the rock on which holiness is built by serving Christ's poor and lavishing on them what we would love to do for Him in person.

If we follow this way, our faith will grow, our convic-

---

* Cf. Constitution of the International Association of Co-Workers of Mother Teresa.
** Letter, January 1973.

tion will grow, and the striving for holiness will become our daily task.

God loves those to whom He can give the most, those who expect the most from Him, who are most open to Him, those who have most need of Him and count on Him for everything.

Our works of charity are only the fruit of God's love in us. That is why those who are most united with Him love their neighbor most.

Love of Christ should be a living bond between all of us. Then the world will know that we are true missionaries of charity.

Perhaps only a smile, a little visit, or simply the fact of building a fire for someone, writing a letter for a blind person, bringing a few coals, finding a pair of shoes, reading for someone, this is only a little bit, yes, a very tiny bit, but it will be our love of God in action.

In spite of the fact that this year we might have less to show, much less in donations, if we spread and radiate love of Christ more, if we give Christ who hungers not only for bread but also our love, our presence, our contact, then 1971 could be the year of the real explosion of the love that God brings to the world.

Without God, we are human beings who have nothing to offer except sorrow and suffering.

EVERY PERSON IS UNIQUE

In serving the needs of the poor the Co-Workers should give special attention to those who are unwanted and deprived of love. For the worst disease in the world is not leprosy or tuberculosis but the feeling of being unwanted, unloved, and abandoned by everyone.

The greatest sin is the lack of love and charity, the terrible indifference to those on the fringe of the social system, who are exposed to exploitation, corruption, want, and disease. Since each member of our Society is to become a co-worker of Christ in this world of misery, each one must understand what God and the Society expect.

Let the poor, seeing the Co-Worker, be drawn to Christ and invite Him into their homes and their lives.

Let the sick and suffering find in the Co-Worker a veritable angel of comfort and consolation. And in the streets, let the little children cling to her because she reminds them of Christ who is the friend of little children.

When Mother Teresa, with only a few rupees in her pocket, went into the most wretched quarters of Calcutta to begin her work of love, we can imagine not only the courage it took but the tact and discretion. The people who confronted her were "hurt" individuals, unwanted, unloved, spurned or ignored by society, whose needs had to be prudently unearthed, sometimes with difficulty, because a hurt individual does not easily open up to a stranger but more likely masks his or her need behind suspicion, distrust, and outright antagonism. For this sort of work, Mother Teresa had to guard against having all the answers or quick and easy solutions.

> *To help, without hurt to human dignity, means not only to move through the poor but to remain among them, live among them, and be a living expression of God's love.*
>
> *If Mother Teresa's efforts on behalf of the poor had come from a sense of duty, her words and her actions would not have conveyed the feeling of God's merciful love. The poor sensed the throb of her love in each of her actions. Those whom life has treated most cruelly are not deceived. They cannot be tricked or taken in by the semblance of love, by the person who shrinks from the risks of love.*
>
> *Mother Teresa was the first person who made them feel that someone really loved them and took an interest in them.*

If sometimes our poor people have had to die, it is not because God did not take care of them but because you and I have done nothing, have not been an instrument of love in God's hands; it is because we have failed to recognize Him, Christ, when He came again in the guise of distress, of a man or woman forsaken, of a child abandoned.

Some time ago a little child came to our house about midnight. I went down and there stood this little one in tears. Upon questioning she said: "I went to my mother and she did not want me; I went to my father and he did not want me. You, do you want me?"

Here, in Melbourne, there are forlorn people who are not loved; yet these people are God's . . . and they are ours. In India, in Europe, wherever our Sisters meet Christ in this pitiable disguise, it is the same hunger. Perhaps here in Australia, and in America, it is not hunger for a piece of bread or a bit of cloth to cover themselves; but there is this great loneliness, this terrible need: the feeling of being unloved, of having no one to turn to.

In Calcutta we have given refuge to more than 27,000 persons from the street.* They come to us and we receive them, or we go out and bring them in and make them feel at home. They die so admirably ... so admirably in the peace of God. Up to now, our Sisters and I myself have never yet seen or met a man or woman who refused to ask "pardon of God," who refused to say "I love you, my God."

We have thousands of lepers. They are so brave, so admirable, disfigured as they are. Last Christmas I went to see them and said to them that they have God's care, that God loves them specially, that they are very dear to Him and their malady is not sin.

An old man who was completely disfigured came up to me and said: "Repeat that again; it does me good. I had always heard that no one loves us. It is wonderful to know that God loves us. Say it again."

We have a Home of Mercy. We have people who have no one, who roam the streets, for whom perhaps prison and the street are the only refuge.

One of them had been seriously wounded by one of his friends. Somebody asked him: "Who did that to you?" The man began to tell all sorts of lies but would not say who did it. Later, when there was no one

---

* In 1975, more than 30,000.

around, I asked him: "Why didn't you say who wounded you?" The man looked at me and said: "His suffering would not help mine."

TRUE LOVE

On receiving the Nehru Prize, Mother Teresa underscored the importance of "true love."

Love, to be true, must first be for our neighbor. This love will bring us to God. What our Sisters, our Brothers and our Co-Workers across the world try to do is to show this love of God by deeds. To help the poor we must get to know them. Some persons who came to help us with the problems of the refugees of Bangladesh said that they had received more than they gave to those whom they had served.

This is exactly what each of us experiences when we are in contact with the poorest of the poor. This contact is what our people need. They need our hands to serve them and our hearts to love them. Think of the loneliness of old people, without means, without love, with absolutely no one to care about them. There are many places where we can see this suffering, this hunger for love, which only you and I can satisfy.

Think of forsaken children. One day I saw a little child that would not eat; her mother had died. Then I found a Sister who looked like her mother and I told her just to play with the child, and the child's appetite returned.

Responding to Prince Philip, who had presented her with the Templeton Prize, Mother Teresa said:

Dear Co-Workers, let us give thanks to God that Mr. Templeton has had the courage to dispense for God's glory the wealth he received so generously from God. Giving me this prize is giving it to all who are partners with me, across the world, in the work of love.

Here in England, how many isolated individuals there are, known only by their house number. So where do we start? Do we really know if there is someone, perhaps next door to us? Perhaps there is a blind person who would be happy if someone read the paper to him or her. Perhaps there is a wealthy individual who has no one to visit him. He has much other wealth, but he is lost in it. There is no human contact, and he needs your contact. Some time ago a very wealthy man came to us and said: "See this? I want to give it to you so that someone will come and visit us. I am half blind, and my wife is depressed; our children have left us to go abroad and we are dying of loneliness."

And in Melbourne I paid a visit to an old man no one knew existed. I saw that his room was in horrible condition and I wanted to clean it up, but he stopped me: "I'm all right." I kept quiet, and finally he let me go ahead. In his room was a beautiful lamp, covered with dust. I asked: "Why don't you light the lamp?" He replied: "What for? Nobody comes to see me, and I don't need a lamp." Then I said to him: "Will you light the lamp if the Sisters come to see you?" "Yes,"

he said, "if I hear a human voice, I will light it." The
other day he sent me word: "Tell my friend that the
lamp she lit in my life burns constantly."

These are the people we must learn to know. Knowing them will bring us to love them and to love helping
them. We must not be satisfied with gifts of money.
Money is not enough. Money can be got. But they need
your hands to help them; they need your hearts to love
them.

Very often I ask for gifts other than money. I can
get these things if I want them, but I ask for them in
order to get the presence of the donor, just to touch
those to whom he or she gives, just to smile on them,
just to give them some attention. That means so much
to our people!

It is the same Jesus who met Saul on his way to
Damascus to stir up trouble and kill and destroy
Christians, and who said: "Saul, Saul, why do you
persecute me?" And to whom Saul replied: "Who are
you, Lord?" "I am Jesus whom you persecute."

And today, it is the same Christ, the same Jesus, in
our poor who are unwanted. They are of no use to
society, and nobody has time for them. It is you and
I, if our love is true, who must seek them out.

The first time I was in London I went out at night.
It was a very cold night and we met people in the
street. There was a respectable old man shivering
from the cold. With him was another old man, a black,
who had opened his coat to wrap it around the other
man against the cold. "Take me away, anywhere," the
first man said to the other; "I would like to sleep
between two sheets." He was a distinguished looking

man who must have known better days, but there he was. And we looked around, and we saw many others.

And if there had been only one, it is Jesus. And, as Scripture says: "I looked for someone to care for me and I could find none." How terrible it would be if Jesus had to say that to us today.

Without the chance to receive the message of religious thought, even the most honest and most intelligent mind is really nothing more than a bee caught in a bottle.

I want people to get involved in the actual work we do, for their own sakes and for ours. I never ask them for money, nothing like that. I only ask them to bring their love, to bring their hands to help. Then, when they meet those in need, their first reaction is to do something for them. And when they come the second time, they already are committed. After a while, they feel that they belong to the poor; they understand their need for love, who they are, and what they themselves can do for them.

> *Love must be real. The reality of love is in the tongue that is not afraid to open up, in the offer to help that makes one vulnerable to the other, in the deed that treats the poor as equals. It says to the other, "you exist."*
>
> *Every person has the right to a minimum of goods for "security," but still more to justice, to growth, to free speech. Every person has the right to be "unique," to be an individual with human dignity.* *

* International Constitution, 6.

To humor the fancies of the poor is to begin with them from where they are, to take them by the hand so they may know they are thought of, counted on, "needed."

> *There the leper stood, straight up, in his arms a small basket of cabbage. In his arms, because on his hands not a single finger was left. He said to the Father of the lepers (Father Raoul Follereau): "I have lost my fingers and my hands, but I have kept my courage. I wanted to be someone, someone who works and sings, as you have said to us. So I learned to help myself with my hands—and without hands. A hundred times the tool fell to the ground. A hundred times I got down on my knees to pick it up. I have just brought in my first vegetables. I give them to you, because it is you who taught me that I was not an unwanted."*

We shall never know all the good that a simple smile can do.

We speak of our God, good, clement, and understanding; but are we the living proof of it? Those who suffer, can they see this goodness, this forgiving God, this real understanding in us?

Never let anyone come to you without coming away better and happier. Everyone should see goodness in your face, in your eyes, in your smile.

In the dispensaries, in the slums, wherever we are, we are the light of God's goodness.

Thoughtfulness, the kindly regard for others, is the beginning of holiness. If you learn the art of being thoughtful, you will be more and more like Christ; His heart was kind and gentle, and He always thought of others. Our vocation, to be beautiful, must be full of regard for others. Jesus did good wherever He went. Our Lady at Cana thought only of the needs of others and told Jesus about them.

I AM A MAN

The Co-Workers recognize the dignity, the individuality, and the infinite value of every human being.*

> *Sandro Bordignon, the French journalist, says of Mother Teresa: "I believe that no other philosopher or humanist has such a lively sense of the humanity and the value of every human being. The presence of the mayor, the cardinal, the leper, or anyone of the poor, it makes no difference; she meets and treats them with the same respect."*
>
> *Above all else, the poor one is a person. And if works of charity are collective, charity itself is individual.*
>
> *Ladies of fashion may meet in thick-carpeted homes, draw up their monthly schedule of philanthropies, make a financial report and see the slums from afar, like the tourist viewing the city below. This is necessary but not enough. From her Co-Workers Mother Teresa demands direct contact with the poor: visiting them in person, cleaning their homes, dressing their wounds. Charity is*

* Constitution, 6.

*directed toward someone, toward a person. When
the poor "hit bottom," they can lose the idea that
they are human beings.*

*Father Raoul Follereau tells of a leper who
tried to take advantage of the revulsion his condition can inspire. One evening, seeing some women
alone, he went up to them and said: "Give me
money or I will touch your faces and you will be
lepers." Terrified, the women complied. Father
Raoul heard about it and gave him a tongue lash-
ing for his efforts. But the culprit had nothing to
say. Worse, there was no sign of remorse. Finally
the priest, beside himself, yelled out: "Yes or no,
are you a man?" The leper straightened up and,
his eyes glistening, said: "You are right. I did
wrong. I am a man." And because he had been
treated as a "man," he added: "Thanks."*

*To love one's neighbor the way Mother Teresa
does it is necessary to dismiss all thought of ine-
quality. She sees the face of Christ in the leper as
well as in the radiant beauty of a little child. And
she believes in the person-to-person relationship.*

What is important to us is the individual. To get to
love a person, there must be close contact. If we wait
for the numbers, we will be lost in the numbers, and
we will never be able to show that person the necessary love and respect. Every person is for me the only
person in the world at that moment.

I believe that people today think the poor are not
humans like them. They look down on them. But if

they had a deep respect for the poor, I am sure it would be easy for them to come closer to them, and to see that they have as much right to the things of life and to love as anybody has. In these times of development, everybody is in a hurry and rushing about, and on the way there are people falling down, people who do not have the strength to run. It is these that we want to help and take care of.

I never take care of crowds, only of a person. If I stopped to look at the crowds, I would never begin. Love is a fruit always in season.

> *To make herself accepted, Mother Teresa identifies with the poor. She eats the same food, wears the same clothes.*
>
> *At the Congress of 1973, in Melbourne, Mother Teresa spoke of Christ identifying Himself with the sick, the naked, the homeless, the hungry.*

Hungry, not only for bread but also to exist for someone; naked, not only for lack of clothing but also lack of compassion, since very few people have compassion for the nameless multitude; homeless, not only having no home of wood or stone but no friendly soul of whom one can say "I have someone."

Our little children are in this category of the rejected and unloved. Today the problem that troubles so many people is not only the fear that the world is becoming overpopulated, but more and more we hear it argued that Providence cannot take care of all the babies that will be born.

For my part, if abortion is permitted in countries

that lack for nothing, these countries are the poorest
of the poor. I would like to open in these countries
many institutions for children. We have these small
institutions all over India, and up to now we have
never had to refuse a single child. And, most wonder-
fully, God has seen to it that each of these children
that escaped death at the hands of their parents has
found a home with new parents.

In Calcutta, we have tried to combat abortion by
adoption, and we have been able to give many little
ones who were destined to die a father and a mother.
For us, in India, it is a wonderful thing, because by law
these children are untouchables.

As for countries that have enacted laws permitting
abortion as a so-called natural act, we must pray for
them, because the sin is great. It is murder.

We were invited to Bangladesh to work with girls
who had been abused by soldiers. Driven by despair
and disgrace, some committed suicide. We opened a
Home for Children for them, and had to overcome
great difficulties, as it is against Moslem and Hindu
law to take back into society girls like these who have
been abused.

But when Mujibu said that these girls were national
heroes, that they had tried to defend their purity and
had fought for their country, their own parents came
to get them. There were even young men who offered
to marry them.

And then, some persons were asked to perform
abortions on them. It was a terrible battle. I told them
that these girls had been abused, forced, and had not

wanted to sin, and that what some people wanted to do to them or help them do would be an act of murder. For the rest of their lives they would never forget that as mothers they had killed their children.

The government agreed with us, and it was announced that every child for which the mother had wanted an abortion should be brought to our home. Of the forty children we have received, more than thirty have been adopted by wonderful families. This is how we try to combat abortion.

Because our Sisters work in the slums, we have found more and more young mothers dying and children born deformed, and we could not find the reason. Looking deeper, we discovered that because of their ignorance these young women were being taken advantage of and abused. So we prayed to God to send us someone who could undertake the task of helping these women face this problem with a clean conscience, a healthy body in a happy family. We were blessed with the vocation we needed, a Sister from the Maurice Islands who had taken courses on natural family planning. We have begun the work of providing information, and today we have more than three thousand families putting it into practice, with a success rate of 95-96 percent.

When people saw what was happening in their families, they came to thank us. Some said: "Our family has remained together; our family is enjoying good health and we can have a baby when we want it."

Ralph Rolls asked Mother Teresa what she had been able to observe in England today on this subject. She replied:

England seems to be hesitant about protecting unborn children and apparently tries to get rid of them. They get rid of them by killing life; and to me, that is an obvious sign either that the country is very poor and does not have the means to take care of lives that God has created, or that it has somehow been misled.

Rolls then asked her if she preferred that abortion be illegal.

I do not say legal or illegal, but I think that no human hand should be raised to kill life, since life is God's life in us, even in an unborn child. And I think that the cry of these children who are killed before coming into the world must be heard by God.

Rolls asked how society could cope with so many children, if they all came into the world.

Jesus said that we are much more important in the eyes of His Father than the grass, the birds, and the flowers of the earth. And that if He takes care of these things, how much more He would take care of His own life in us. He cannot deceive us. Life is God's greatest gift to human beings, and humans are created in the image of God. Life belongs to God and we do not have the right to destroy it.

Our world tends toward the absurd, says Bordignon. We have created conditions of life un-

dreamed twenty years ago; we have increased many times over the capacity to produce; we have made unparalleled technological advances. In view of this, it seems madness not to be able to feed all the people in the world.

We are preoccupied with the demographic explosion and sometimes wonder what is to be gained by saving the newborn infants that Mother Teresa retrieves from the trash bins of Calcutta. But then says Bordignon, I saw how she thrilled when one of these tiny ones gave signs of life. "It lives!" she exclaimed, and that for Mother Teresa is joy.

She was also asked about the reasons for the unexpected success of her natural family planning efforts. She replied quite simply:

People understood the usefulness of self-control.

BULLDOZER OF CHRIST

Deep faith in action is love, and love in action is service.

Mother Teresa asks her Co-Workers to dedicate themselves to wholehearted free "service" to the poorest of the poor.*

I want the Co-Workers to put their hands and hearts at the service of the people. If they do not come in close contact with them, they cannot know who the poor are. That is why, especially here in Cal-

* Constitution, 5.

cutta, we have a goodly number of non-Christians and Christians working together in the Home for the Dying and other places. Some groups prepare bandages and medicine for the lepers. For example, an Australian came the other day to make a large donation. But after making the donation he said: "This is something outside of myself; now I want to give something of myself." Since then, he comes regularly to the Home for the Dying to shave the sick and talk with them. He gives not only his money but also his time. He could have spent both his money and time on himself, but he wanted to spend himself instead.

> *Mother Teresa's service is not aimless agitation, not helter-skelter activity lost in numbers. Rather, it is centered on Jesus, a single-minded service to Jesus in the guise of the poor.*
>
> *To serve, according to Mother Teresa, is to embrace and follow Christ the Servant. "I am with you as one who serves" (Luke 22:27).*
>
> *To serve is to be a servant of Christ present in the world, especially in his poor. The servant of Christ practices the compassion of Christ, which does not wait for gratitude. True compassion endures failure, conflict, thanklessness.*
>
> *To serve is to know and acknowledge the truth; to recognize the part that ignorance or innocence can play in those who fall; to give support rather than pass judgment; to be the voice of the voiceless; and never to yield to the temptation to be cross or unkind.*

To serve is to go to those who cannot render service for service, who show no gratitude, to those who are bitter, who suffer from lack of a kindly look, a smile. Mother Teresa stresses the power of a smile that communicates the joy of God.

Helping others ought to go further than the impersonal act of almsgiving. To give of our superfluity is not the same as giving of ourselves, or entering into the suffering of others.

Being rich or poor is not always a question of material possessions. Mother Teresa points out that distress, isolation, suffering can also be the lot of those who have material wealth. To serve is to take upon one's shoulders the burdens of others, to share their fears and anxieties.

Mother Teresa's service is a constant search for union with God. She serves God by serving others, children of God whose true worth she knows. Jesus bled for the poor. He wept.

Mother Teresa underlines the importance of being co-workers of Christ:

How much we ought to love our Society (the Missionaries of Charity) and show our gratitude by being what God and the Society expect of us: true co-workers of Christ. More than ever, we ought to do our work for Christ who was poor, and for the poor who are Christ's, with a humble and devoted heart.

In order to survive, love has to be nourished by sacrifices. The words of Jesus, "Love one another as I have loved you," must be not only a light to us but a flame that consumes the self in us.

Love should be as natural as living and breathing.
The Little Flower said: "When I act and think charitably, I feel it is Jesus working in me; the deeper my
union with him, the stronger my love for the residents
of Carmel."

> *Mother Teresa's congregation has experienced an
> astonishing vitality. She accounts for this by saying:*

We put our hands, our eyes, our hearts at Christ's
disposal so that he may act through us.

> *She has been called a "bulldozer of Christ," because nothing stops her. Everything is urgent.
> From Calcutta Jean Vanier writes.*
> *"I have just spent an hour with Mother Teresa.
> I was struck by her sense of urgency. She always
> seems to be returning from somewhere, New York,
> London, Rome, Gaza, the Yemen, Ethiopia,
> Amman. She spoke of Cambodia. Her acute sensitivity to the suffering in the world, which is almost an obsession, prods her to action. She was
> looking for a helicopter to bring food to the rural
> population of Ethiopia, and trying to find a way
> of helping Arabs and Israelis exchange their dead,
> as well as working out a plan to give assistance to
> the religious in Cambodia."*
> *She had seen the prime minister of Israel and
> the ruler of Gaza. She was troubled by the hatred
> in the hearts of Arabs and Jews. She spoke of the
> suffering she had seen in London, and of her
> Home for the Dying in Calcutta, which has never
> been so full.*

Could one set up a canteen at the railroad station in Saaldad for the starving?

> *Her creative talent is astonishing, always in search of solutions. Now she wants to see Madame Gandhi. Nothing is impossible. Her abandonment to God is total. Her wrinkled face shows great compassion—and fatigue; she has aged . . .*
>
> *But she is a "bulldozer of Christ." Nothing stops her. She is truly an instrument of God, and yet she is such a small woman . . .*
>
> *She does not like to speak of her community, of structures, only of the poor. One time she went to Rome for a meeting of Major Superiors and reported.*

But I said nothing. All the talk was about structures; I understood nothing. My mind was somewhere else.

> *She said this without a hint of criticism. In fact, I have never heard her make the least critical remark about anyone.*
>
> *No work is too much for Mother Teresa. Not content with washing feet, she repairs roofs damaged by the wind . . . and leads a march of seven kilometers through the streets of Milan to build solidarity with the Third World.*
>
> *She scarcely has time anymore to write to her Sisters:*

All my time is taken up by everybody; and with the Sisters it is the same. They work without interruption for the sick or the children and really do not have time to write. Tell the ailing Sisters not to be disappointed if they do not receive letters, because the work is all-consuming.*

LOVE ACCEPTS ALL AND GIVES ALL

Love and service are the key to giving.

> *"Freely have you received . . . freely give." Mother Teresa could say with one of our contemporaries: "I no longer belong to myself. Some evenings, after being worn out by others, I do not know who I am. I am someone else; I am God's."*

Love accepts all and gives all.

> *Mother Teresa's charity requires this total renunciation.*
>
> *In the constitution that governs her Co-Workers Mother Teresa declares:*

Co-Workers must recognize that all goods of this world are free gifts of God and that no one has the right to excess wealth when others are dying of hunger. Co-Workers seek to correct this grave injustice through voluntary poverty and the sacrifice of luxuries in their daily life.**

> *But Mother Teresa acknowledges that sometimes the wealthy make it a point to give.*

The wealthy, in their own way, do sometimes want to share in the misfortune of others. The pity is that

---

* Letter to Jacqueline de Decker.
** Constitution, 8.

they do not truly put themselves out. The new generation, especially the children, understand better. Children in England are making sacrifices to give a piece of bread to our children. Children of Denmark are making sacrifices to give them a glass of milk daily, and children of Germany are doing the same to give them daily vitamins. These are ways of learning to love. Children like these, when they grow up, will know what it means to give and will want to do so.

> *A beautiful display of "giving" is recounted by Sister Frederick. Students in a school in Canada went twenty-five hours without eating, in sympathy with those "who are starving." The pupils experienced what it means to go hungry and sent their impressions to Mother Teresa. Their only food was Christ, whom they received at a special Eucharist, celebrated at midnight.*
>
> *Another class arranged a "different experience," going without sleep for twenty-five hours. Like Christ, these young people bore in their flesh the cost of giving. Perhaps, through their sacrifice, somewhere in the world starving people were fed. It was their way of sharing in the suffering of others.*

We must suffer with Christ and that is why we want to share in the sufferings of the poor. Our congregation could die out in my lifetime, if the Sisters do not walk with the suffering Christ, and if the Sisters do not remain poor.

Our strict poverty is our safeguard. We do not want to begin by serving the poor and little by little end up serving the rich, like other religious orders in history. In order to understand and help those who lack everything, we must live like them. The difference is that our destitute ones are poor by force of circumstance, whereas we are by choice.

The Sisters do little things like help the children, visit the lonely, the sick, the poorest of the poor.

In one of the houses our Sisters visited, a woman living alone had been dead a long time before anyone knew it, and then they found out only because her corpse had begun to rot. Her neighbors didn't even know her name.

When someone says to me that the Sisters do not perform great tasks, that they do little things in their quiet manner, I reply that if they helped only one person, it would all be worth while.

Jesus died for one person, for one sinner.

> *Mother Teresa has no problem with culture, colonialism, or proselytism. When mass is celebrated with her poor in the pagan temple of Kali, no one takes offense. Rather, the emaciated worshippers, almost drained of life—so close are they to death—seem suffused with a sort of holiness, the holiness that is the sister of suffering and is not of this world.*

HAVING THE EXPERIENCE OF HAVING NOTHING

> *Mother Teresa exemplifies the call of Christ "not to lay up for yourselves treasures on earth, where*

*moth and rust consume and where thieves break
in and steal, but lay up for yourselves treasures in
heaven, where neither moth nor rust consume and
where thieves do not break in and steal" (Matthew
6:19).*

*In the Old Testament the prophet Isaiah directs
his maledictions against the wealthy of Jerusalem: "Woe to those who join house to house, who
add field to field, until there is no more room, and
you are made to dwell alone in the midst of the
land ... many houses shall be desolate, large and
beautiful houses, without inhabitant" (Isaiah 5:
8–9).*

*The spirit of poverty seen in the Missionaries of
Charity ought to remind the world of the prophet's
denunciations. A Mother Teresa is a standing rebuke to the mad pursuit of money.*

*For her activities on behalf of the poor she has
never accepted help from the state. She considers
her work a work of Providence.*

Even in the beginning, I never asked for money. I
wanted to serve the poor simply for love of God. I
wanted the poor to receive free what the rich get for
themselves with money.

*She regards wealth as an evil—worse than an evil,
a disaster—because it destroys generosity, closes
up the heart, suffocates. When, on occasion, she
appears in the homes of the rich, she has an un-
comfortable feeling of suffocation. When she was
invited to Washington by Senator Ted Kennedy,
the British writer St. John Stevas was present and*

> *asked her how she felt in the midst of such opu-
> lence. She replied that she was miserable, and
> that she was there, in those beautiful drawing
> rooms of Washington, only because someone had
> to plead the cause of the poor.*
>
> *But she does not condemn the rich. Instead of
> passing judgment, she says:*

Who are we that we can judge the rich? Our task is
to bring the rich and the poor together, to be their
point of contact.

> *Mother Teresa preaches revolution, but her idea
> of revolution is not confrontation. Rather it is
> the coming together, the mutually beneficial
> meeting of the rich and the poor. Already she sees
> results:*

Upper-caste families are adopting children we rescue from the streets, which is indeed revolutionary,
when one remembers the prejudice of the caste system. In this coming together the rich become better,
since they demonstrate love of God to the poor, and
the poor become better through the love they receive
from the rich.

> *Mother Teresa dignifies the poor. A journalist
> asked her who she thought was doing most for the
> Gospel today: Pope John XXIII, Martin Luther
> King, Gandhi . . .*

I believe that the most important person in the
world today is the poor person, since he or she has the
capacity to suffer and work hard.

To Mother Teresa, says Bordignon, the poor person is "the prophet of a new humanity." Perhaps we still worship the god of progress too much to appreciate the promise that her words hold for humanity.

Tender-hearted and self-effacing, Mother Teresa carries an untiring charity in her heart, on her lips, in her look, and even in the elongated fingers so accustomed to dressing wounds. A burning love impels her to follow her Lord, to recognize Him in the peeping cry of an infant, in the wailing of a lost child, in the stumps of a leper, in the poor dying in the streets. A sensitive angel of mercy, she walked through Harlem with only a rosary in her hands for protection, in a quarter where no white dared to venture alone. Back in India, she moves among the dying,

so that they may die seeing a kindly face and know there are people who love them and want to give them, at least in their final hours, a taste of human and divine love.

And also that they may have the comfort of seeing this woman bend over them and share the agony in their eyes, this woman who takes away fear and gives them a glance at the same little crucifix (the one she wears) that was kissed three times by a notorious criminal before his execution—as though in answer to the unknown prayers of St. Theresa of the Child Jesus. Of the dying she says:

They lived like animals, but here they die like angels.

> *Mother Teresa's work is immense, but in her eyes so small as to be "a drop in the ocean."*
>
> *This drop, however, would be missed if it were not in the ocean. But she does not consider it a glittering drop. As she says:*

We do not strive for spectacular actions. What counts is the gift of yourself, the degree of love you put into each of your deeds.

> *This drop is the little tear that Mother Teresa, aglow with divine love, gathers from the eyelid of one who is dying.*

NO LOVE WITHOUT FORGIVING, NO FORGIVING WITHOUT PEACE

> *This nun in a sari is so full of mercy that she attracts the poor because she is emptied of self in totally giving herself. She is not afraid to spend herself, to identify with her brother or sister in distress, or to launch into a career of mercy and forgiveness not counting the cost. She has met Christ in her work and teaches the lesson that we must forgive, since we have need to be forgiven.*

If we remember that we are sinners and have need of forgiveness, it is very easy to forgive others. If I did not understand that, it would be hard for me to say "I forgive you" to someone who comes to me.

> *Ralph Rolls asked if one had to be a Christian in order to forgive.*

Not at all, not at all. Every human being comes from the hand of God and we all know how much God loves us. Whatever our belief, we must learn to forgive if we want truly to love.

> *Have you any evidence of this forgiveness?*

Yes, I saw it in Belfast. Certain families I visited had lost members in the civil strife. These people forgave. They had neither hatred nor rancor toward those who had massacred their children.

> *The Missionary Brothers of Charity are doing wonderful work and having an influence on the lives of others. One young man had been a driver for a band of professional thieves. Seeing the work done by the Brothers in his neighborhood, he decided to change his way of life. He married a young woman who had been nursed back to health by the Brothers and now uses his leisure time to help them.*
>
> *It is a great thing to help build communities of love and goodness, which are signs of hope and strength. These signs may not be much in themselves, but they are filled with promise for peace and forgiveness in the world.*
>
> *In the encyclical* Pacem in Terris, *Pope John XXIII says: "Peace cannot reign among men unless it first reigns in each of them, that is, unless each observes in himself the order wanted by God."*

We must all work for peace. Before we can have this peace, we must learn from Jesus to be kind and humble of heart. Only humility can bring us to unity, and unity to peace. Therefore, let us help one another to draw so near to Jesus that we can learn with joy the lesson of humility.

Think of the oppressed countries. The greatest need in Bangladesh is for forgiveness. There is so much bitterness and hatred—you have no idea of what these poor people have suffered. If they could feel that someone cares about them, that they are loved, perhaps they would find it in their hearts to forgive. I believe that is the only thing that can bring peace.

We shall make this year a year of peace in a very special way. To this end we shall try to speak more to God and with God, and less to men and with men. Let us preach peace as Christ did. He went about doing good everywhere. He did not stop His works of charity because the Pharisees or others opposed Him and tried to destroy the work of His Father.

Cardinal Newman wrote: "Help me to spread your fragrance everywhere I go. Let me preach you without preaching, not by words but by my example; by the catching force, the sympathetic influence of what I do, the evident fullness of the love my heart bears to you."

SUFFERING AND JOYFULNESS

Not wanting Christ is the cause of suffering, today, in the world.

Suffering can become a "gift," says Mother Teresa.

Suffering in itself is nothing; but suffering that is sharing in the Passion of Christ is a wonderful gift, the most beautiful gift: a gift and proof of love, because in giving us his Son the Father showed that He loves the world. So, it proved that this was a gift, the greatest gift of love, because His suffering was the expiation for sin.

The suffering in Bangladesh is like an enormous Calvary, where the Body of Christ is crucified once more.

> *The barbarity of war scars the souls of people with a hatred that forgiveness, charity, and love alone can heal.*
>
> *In the appearance of those who have been "deformed" by suffering, Mother Teresa finds the outraged figure of Jesus: Jesus is present in those who are the despised and the outcasts of humanity. Jesus is transfixed in men and women of sorrow known only by their suffering, before whom we shield our eyes and flee.*
>
> *Classic outcasts from humanity, from whom we shrink and run away, lepers inevitably attracted the unfathomable love of Mother Teresa.*
>
> *Considerable progress has been made, however, in changing the attitude toward lepers. Leprosy is no longer seen as a disgrace but as a disease.*

At death we will not be judged by the amount of work we did but by the love we put into it. And this love must come from self-sacrifice and be felt until it hurts.

The heart of the work of the Missionaries of Charity

is committed to the four million lepers in the country. Leprosy is certainly a great evil, but not as great as being deprived of love or being unwanted or abandoned.

Lepers may be disfigured but they, like the poor, are wonderful people, with a great capacity for love.

Mother Teresa's love pours out on the victims of leprosy: young people and old, some of them unable to walk, reduced to crawling. She has discovered a feeling of community among them, a true comity of soul. Notwithstanding their offensive bodies, their ravaged faces, and rotting flesh, she finds in them a "hidden quality" that lends them human dignity. Working among them, she herself is so to speak transformed and becomes insensitive to the odor of the leprosarium. She forgets that she is among lepers. Appearances give way as the human person emerges. It is the person, not the leper that she knows and calls by name. She does not think of them as lepers but as individuals with their own names. Hers is a work of love, the fruit and sign of God's grace.

Those who have seen Mother Teresa and her Sisters working in a leprosarium all testify that they are joyous and would not think of giving up this work. They love these lepers and follow them through their Calvary to the cemetery—the most pathetic funeral cortege one can imagine, behind an old rattling hearse with its plumed panels of glass.

Pitiful scenes occur that tear at Mother Teresa's

heart. A woman cared for at the leprosarium was told that her little girl also was leprous. The mother was beside herself, since she already had a boy in the leprosarium. The father came to see his family. The little girl limped toward him but stopped short of clasping his knees or throwing herself in his arms despite the overwhelming urge to do so. Remembering her condition, she just stood and stared at him. Her little body was diseased; her spirit, deprived of affection, died soon after. Occurrences like this make Mother Teresa say wherever she goes that the worst disease is not leprosy but the want of affection.

Other heart-rending scenes occur when lepers suffer the emotional trauma of leaving their homes to come to the leprosarium. One five-year-old in the leprosarium was there simply because two aunts who were leprous had caressed her when she was still a little child in the crib. The day she was taken away to the leprosarium brought a painful moment when she threw herself in the arms of her grandmother and said: "Will the Sisters love me like you? Will they hear my night prayers and tuck me into bed?"*

The sick can become close Co-Workers of a Sister or Brother by offering their suffering for that Sister or Brother.**

Each Sister should have a second self who prays and suffers for her; and each can draw from this support

---

*From information supplied by the Society of Mary.
**Constitution, 19.

a new strength and their lives will be like a burning
light that burns itself out for souls.

Suffering in itself is nothing, but suffering that
shares in the Passion of Christ is a wonderful gift
. . . and a sign of love.

How good God is to give you so much suffering and
so much love. All of this is joy to me and gives me
strength on account of you. It is your life of sacrifice
that gives me strength.

| *To the sick and dying she says:*

Your prayers and sufferings are like a chalice into
which we who are working can put, can pour, our love
for the souls that we meet. For this, you are just as
necessary as we; we and you, together, can do all
things in Him who strengthens us.

The vocation of suffering Sisters is a beautiful
thing. We are bearers of God's love. We carry in our
hearts and in our souls the love of God who thirsts
for souls. You can quench His thirst, you by your
priceless suffering, and we by our hard work. You
have known, you have tasted of, the chalice of His
agony.

| *To her Sisters she says:*

Without our suffering, our work would only be social work, very good and useful, but it would not be the
work of Jesus Christ. It would not be part of the Redemption. Jesus wanted to help us by sharing our life,
our loneliness, our agony, our death. It was necessary
that he become "one" with us in order to save us. He
permits us to do the same. The afflictions of the poor,

not only their material wretchedness but also their spiritual deprivation, must be redeemed and we must share their lives, because it is only by becoming "one" with them that we can save them, that is, bring God to them and bring them to God.

When suffering overtakes us, let us accept it with a smile. This is the greatest gift of God: having the courage to accept with a smile whatever He gives us and whatever He takes from us.

| *To an ailing woman she wrote:*

Very often I am near in thought to you, and I offer up your great sufferings when mine are small or trivial. When it is going very hard for you, then let your only refuge be in the Sacred Heart, and there my heart will find with you both strength and love. You want to suffer in pure love? Say rather in the love He chooses for you. How much I thank God for having given you to me. Give more and more, until you have no more to give.

My soul is heartened by the thought of having you to pray and suffer for me; I find it easier to smile. You do the suffering, we shall do the work. Together, we hold the same chalice in our hands.

| *I slept and I dreamed*
| *that life is all joy.*
| *I woke and I saw*
| *that life is all service.*
| *I served and I saw*
| *that service is joy!*
| *(Nath Tagore)*

Mother Teresa said to an itinerant troupe called "Chant of Asia": We give joy to people by serving them; you, you give it by your performance. Your work and ours complete each other. What you do by singing and dancing, we do by scrubbing and cleaning. It is beautiful to be able to give joy to people. I am sure that thanks to you many people are comforted. And this talent you have received, only riches can deprive you of it. As long as you are willing to be empty of yourself and to be filled with God, you will keep this talent. The day that we begin to grow rich we lose something and begin to die.

Riches, material or spiritual, can suffocate you if they are not used in the right way. I praise God that you have followed your calling. Remain as "empty" as possible, so that God can fill you. Even God cannot put anything into what already is full. He does not impose Himself on us. It is you who are going to fill the world with the love God has bestowed on you. The work of moral rearmament goes on, prudently and with love. The more prudent the more effective it is. You bring it to people, and it is for them to absorb it. People are not so much interested in seeing us, but they hunger and thirst for what God wants to give them through us. We serve the same Lord. All over the globe, people hunger and thirst for God's love. In your way, you satisfy this hunger by spreading joy. In our way, we give joy by putting ourselves at the service of the sick, the dying, the rejected.

To Mother Teresa, conveying this joy is imperative. A Sister asked if she could visit the poor.

Seeing the sad expression on her face, Mother Teresa said:

Do not go. Go back to bed; we cannot meet the poor with a sad face.

Joy is "news" she wants to tell the world.

In order to spread joy, it is necessary to have joy in one's family. Peace and war begin in the home. If we really want peace in the world, let us first love one another, in the family. We shall then have the joy of Christ, our strength. It is sometimes very hard to smile at one another. It is often hard for the husband to smile on his wife, or for the wife to smile on her husband.

Once I was asked if I was married; I said yes, and I added that it is sometimes hard for me to smile on Christ.

Attempts have been made to prove that God does not exist, but God is always proving that He does exist.

Joy is a net of love by which we can capture souls. God loves the person who gives with joy. Whoever gives with joy gives more. The best way to show, our gratitude to God and to people is to accept with joy. Joy can thrive in a heart burning with love.

We wait impatiently for the paradise where God is, but we have it in our power to be in paradise with Him, right now; being happy with Him means:

To love as He loves.
To help as He helps.

To give as He gives.
To serve as He serves.

HE MAKES THE CHOICE

| *Mother Teresa was twelve years old when she experienced the first call.* *

It was in Skopje, Yugoslavia. I was only twelve years old. I was living at home with my parents. We children went to a school that was not Catholic, but we also had very good priests who helped the boys and girls to follow their vocation according to God's call. It was at that time that I knew I was called to the poor.

Between the ages of twelve and eighteen I did not want to become a nun. We were a very happy family. But at eighteen I decided to leave home for the convent, and since then, forty years ago, I have never doubted for a moment that it was the right thing for me to do. It was God's will. He made the choice.

| *It was while visiting the quarters of the poorest that she experienced a second call.*

It was a call within my vocation—a second vocation. It meant leaving the Loreto convent, where I was very happy, to go into the streets and serve the poor.

In 1946 I was going to Darjeeling to make my retreat. On the train I heard the call to give up every-

*For the beginnings of Mother Teresa's call and apostolate to the poor, see Malcolm Muggeridge's interview with her in *Something Beautiful for God,* pp. 83 ff.

thing and follow Him, to go into the slums and serve Him among the poorest of the poor.

> *Years later Bordignon asked her what had prompted her. She said simply that she didn't exactly know. And then, with a deeply human smile, as though to help him understand, she added:*

Perhaps it was a force, the Spirit of God. I knew that God wanted something . . .

> *Mother Teresa explained to Malcolm Muggeridge the steps in leaving the Loreto convent.*

First I had to apply to the archbishop of Calcutta. Then, with his approval, the Mother General of the Sisters of Loreto permitted me to write to Rome. This was the normal procedure. I was a nun; I had taken my perpetual vows, and a nun must not leave her convent. I wrote to the Holy Father, Pope Pius XII, and by return mail received an answer on April 12. He permitted me to leave and to be a non-claustral nun, that is, to live the life of a religious but under obedience to the archbishop of Calcutta. That was in 1948.

I left the convent of Loreto and went first to the Sisters in Patna to get a little medical training so that I could go into the houses of the poor. Until then, I had only done teaching. Now I had to go into the homes and see the children and the sick.

> *Mother Teresa went to look for people lying in the streets. But first she needed a place to put them.*

We needed a shelter for these most forsaken individuals. To find one, I walked, and walked, until I could walk no more. I understood then how exhausted must be the truly poor, always having to look for a little food, or some medicine, and everything. The memory of the comfort I enjoyed at the convent of Loreto then tempted me.

| *But she did not succumb.*

O God, because of my free choice and for the sake of Your love alone I want to remain here and do what Your will demands of me. No, I will not turn back. My community, they are the poor. Their security is my security; their health, my health. My home is to be with the poor, no, not the poor, but the poorest among the poorest: those who are shunned because they are infected and filthy, full of germs and crawling with vermin; those who do not go out to beg because they cannot go out naked; those who do not eat because they no longer have the strength; those who fall exhausted to the street knowing they will die, and whom the living go out of their way to avoid; those who no longer weep because they have run out of tears; the untouchables! The Lord wants me where I am. He will find a solution.

| *The first Sister to enter Mother Teresa's congregation was warned:*

You will have to renounce yourself. Your life will require constant self-denial.

| *Think it over she did, but Sister Agnes became the first Missionary of Charity. Since then, vocations*

have never stopped coming. Mother Teresa sees this as a sign of God's favor.

If God gives vocations, it is a sign that He wants us to go out to the poor.

Mother Teresa is now sure that this work is God's work and that it will continue because:

It is His, and not mine. That is why I have no fear. I know that if the work was mine, it would die with me. But I know that it is His work, that it will endure and do much good.

Does she miss the comforts of Loreto, Bordignon wanted to know.

I was the happiest Sister in that community. And it was a great sacrifice to leave the work I was doing there, but I did not leave the religious life. The change was only in the work, since the Sisters there only taught, which is an apostolate for Christ.

But my vocation, within the vocation, was for the poorest of the poor.

Asked why there are so few vocations in the world, she replied:

There is too much affluence, too much comfort, a very high standard of living, not only in families but even in the religious life.

From all parts of the world young women come to India and lead a very poor life, poorer than ours, driven by the desire to get away from their environment of riches. I believe that they really want to be a living example of the poverty of Christ. It is not enough to know the spirit of poverty; it is necessary to know poverty itself, where one literally has nothing. Today, people, even among those who come from a "good" environment, want to experience what "not having" means. The majority of vocations we have had from Europe or America asked to join our congregation, not for the work but for love of poverty.

> *One word sums up Mother Teresa: love. With the Little Flower she could say: I realized that love embodies all vocations, that love is everything, that it embraces all times and all places; in a word, that it is eternal.*

> *We do not pretend to have exhausted our subject —Mother Teresa and her work are not so easily summarized. To readers who have been touched by what they found in these pages, by Mother Teresa's appeal and example, to them we suggest that the best way to learn still more about her is by lending her not only their hearts but, in whatever way practical, a helping hand. This, among other things, is what we have tried to put across.*
> —*Editors*

> *"I am an optimist, and I am convinced that as long as there are persons like Mother Teresa, humanity can feel justified in its hope."*—GIRI, *President of India*

PART III

Mother Teresa Speaks to Her Religious

Delhi
20 September 1959

My Dear Sisters,

The seventh of October is a day of thanksgiving in our Society. It is the day when the Good God erected our little Society into being.

As the Society is the sole property of Our Lady, it was only right that on her great day she would grant us the grace of living and growing. It is for us to grow into a straight, beautiful, fruitful tree. Promise her that you will be a source of joy for her, just as she is the cause of our joy.

My dear children, there is so much in my heart to tell you but these two things are uppermost: charity and obedience. Be true co-workers of Christ; radiate and live His life. Be an angel of comfort to the sick, a friend to the little ones and love each other as God loves each of you with a special, most intense love. Be kind to each other. I prefer you to make mistakes in kindness than work miracles in unkindness.

Be kind in your words. See what the kindness and discretion of Our Lady brought to her. She never uttered a word of the angel's message to Joseph, and then God Himself intervened. She kept all things in her heart.

Try to excel in obedience. Now that we have three local Superiors, help them by your cheerful and prompt, blind and simple obedience. You may be more talented, more capable, better in many ways, even more holy, than your Superior. All these qualities are not required for you to obey. There is only one thing to remember: "She takes the place of God for you."

Be not blind, my children. The good God has given you His work. He wants you to do His work in His way. Failure or success mean nothing to Him, as long as you do His work according to His plan and His will. You are infallible when you obey. The devil tries his best to spoil the work of God and as he cannot do it directly to Him, he makes us do God's work in our way and this is where the devil gains and we lose.

In all our houses and in the noviciate God is blessing the generosity of the Sisters. Keep up this generosity. You have every reason to be happy. Keep smiling at Jesus in your Superiors, Sisters, and in your poor.

I must put all my energy into doing God's work well. 'I will,' said John Berchmans, Stanislaus, Margaret Mary and they did become saints.

What is a saint but a resolute soul, a soul that uses power plus action. Was not this what St. Paul meant when he said, "I can do all things in Him who strengthens me"?

With you, my Sisters, I will not be satisfied with your being just a good religious. I want you to be able to offer God a perfect sacrifice. Only holiness perfects the gift.

To resolve to be a saint costs much. Renunciation, temptation, struggles, persecutions and all kinds of sacrifices surround the resolute soul. One can love God only at one's own expense.

"I will be a saint" means: I will despoil myself of all that is not God; I will strip my heart and empty it of all artificial things; I will live in poverty and detachment. I will renounce my will, my inclinations, my whims, and fancies and make myself a willing slave to the will of God.

First Friday in November 1960

My Dearest Sisters,

On the 25th at 5:45 AM I am leaving by Pan Am and will be in America on the 26th at 6:30 AM. I go, but my heart and my mind and the whole of me is with you. It is the will of God that I should go, so let us therefore be happy. During my absence, Sister Mary Agnes, the Assistant General and the Council General will take all responsibility. God will take care of you all, if you remain one. Cling to the Society because in the center is Jesus.

I am not afraid to leave you, for I know the great gift God has given me in giving you to me. On my way back, that will be about the 15th of November, I shall go to Rome. I am going to try and see our Holy Father and beg him to grant us pontifical recognition. We are not worthy of this great gift, but if it is God's Holy will, we will get it.

During this time it would make me very happy if the seniors make sacrifices in obedience; juniors in charity; novices in poverty; and postulants in chastity.

Seniors: obedience that is prompt, simple, blind, cheerful; for Jesus was obedient unto death.

Juniors: charity in words, deeds, thoughts, desires, feelings; for Jesus went about doing good.

Novices: poverty in desires and attachments, in likes and dislikes; for Jesus, being rich, made Himself poor for us.

Postulants: chastity in thoughts and affections, in desires and attachments, in not listening to idle conversation; for Jesus is a jealous lover.

Be faithful in little things, for in them our strength lies. To the good God nothing is little because He is great and we so small. That is why He stoops down and takes the trouble to make those little things to give us a chance to prove our love for Him. Because He makes them, they are very great. He cannot make anything small; they are infinite.

To the feet of Christ's vicar on earth I will carry each of you, and I am sure with his fatherly love he will bless each one of you.

First Friday in January 1961

My Own Dearest Children,

Fidelity to the rule is the most precious and delicate flower of love we religious can give to Almighty God. The rule is the expression of the will of God—we must submit to it everywhere and always, down to the last breath.

We must be convinced that the slightest unjustified violation wounds the heart of Jesus and stains our conscience. When the rule becomes one of our greatest loves, then this love expends itself in free and joyful service.

Submission for someone who is in love is more than a duty. This is the secret of the saints.

Fidelity in the least things, not for their own sake; for this is the work of small minds, but for the sake of the great thing, which is the will of God and which I respect greatly in little things.

St. Augustine says: "Little things are indeed little, but to be faithful in little things is a great thing." Is not Our Lord equally the same in a small host as in a great one? The smallest rule contains the will of God as much as the big things of life. To be able to understand this truth I must have faith in the rule, that it is of divine origin. I must cling to the rule as a child clings to its mother. I must love the rule with my will and reason.

It does not matter that the rule often seems unnatural, hard and austere . . . . God has been so very wonderful to us and it is our duty to be very wonderful to God.

First Friday in February 1961

My Dearest Sisters,

We all want to do something beautiful for God. ... Try to imagine all kinds of sacrifices and mortifications. Take your rules and try to live them with greater love for Jesus and with Jesus.

St. Vincent compares the rules to "wings to fly to God." A dying Sister asked: "What should have I done to be a saint?" The priest answered: "Are you not familiar with this wonderful little book, your rule? If you had lived this rule you would have been a saint."

"Just think" says St. Alphonsus, "by the discharge of your duties you may become a saint."

St. Vincent says: "Keep your rules and you will become a saint, for they are holy in themselves, they also can make you holy."

St. Francis de Sales writes: "Walk on always in the punctual observance of your rules, and you will be blessed by God, for He Himself will lead you with great care." In the observance of the rule, you will find strength for the purity of conscience, fervor to fill your soul, and love that will inflame your heart.

Bauthier says: "The rule is to our will what the arteries are to our blood."

22 April 1961

My Dearest Sisters,

When you go to heaven, Our Lord is not going to ask you, "Was your Superior holy, clever, understanding, cheerful, and so forth?" but only one thing, "Did you obey me?" What a wasted life is ours if it is so full of self instead of Him, your spouse whose place she takes. If you cannot see Jesus in your Superior how will you see Jesus in the poor? How will you find Jesus in His distressing disguise? How will you love Jesus you cannot see, if you do not love your Superior whom you can see? When the devil is angry with the work of love of God and does not know how to spoil it, he will try to spoil the instruments and so indirectly spoil the work of God. Do not allow yourselves to be deceived. Obey fully, obey because you love Jesus. Obey, obey. It does not matter who they are and what they are, as long as they are He for whose sake you obey.

See how Our Lady obeyed the angel: "Be it done to me according to Thy word." Whose word? The angel's, because he took the place of God. She, the Queen of Heaven, obeys the angel. See how she obeyed St. Joseph. To her, St. Joseph was He whose place he took.

First Friday in June 1961

My Dearest Sisters,

Do not imagine that love to be true must be extraordinary. No, what we need in our love is the continuity to love the One we love. See how a lamp burns, by the continual consumption of the little drops of oil. If there are no more of these drops in the lamp, there will be no light, and the Bridegroom has a right to say: "I do not know you."

My children, what are these drops of oil in our lamps? They are the little things of everyday life: fidelity, punctuality, little words of kindness, just a little thought for others, those little acts of silence, of

look and thought, of word and deed. These are the
very drops of love that make our religious life burn
with so much light.

Do not search for Jesus in far off lands; He is not
there. He is in you. Just keep the lamp burning and
you will always see Him.

First Friday in July 1961

My Dearest Sisters,

I did feel very happy to be able to give the Sacred
Heart a new tabernacle in Asansol as a token of gratitude to Rev. Fr. C. Van Exem. . . . Without our suffering, our work would be just social work, very good and
helpful, but it would not be the work of Jesus Christ.
Jesus Christ wanted to help by sharing our life, our
loneliness, our agony and death, and all that in the
darkest night. . . .

All the desolation of the poor people, their material
poverty, their spiritual destitution might be redeemed
by our sharing it, by our being one with them, by
bringing God into their lives and bringing them to
God.

First Friday in August 1961

My Dearest Children,

. . . How great is our calling. How fortunate people
would think themselves if they were given a chance to
give personal service to the King of this world. And
here we are—we can touch, serve, love Christ all the
days of our lives . . .

Your work for the poor will be done better if you know the way God wants you to do it and you will know this only through obedience. Cling to your Superiors as the creeper clings. The creeper can live and grow only if it clings on something. You also will grow and live in holiness only if you cling to obedience.

First Friday in June 1962

My Dearest Children,

One day St. Margaret Mary asked Jesus: "Lord, what will Thou have me to do?"

"Give me a free hand," Jesus answered.

Let Him empty and transform you and afterwards fill the chalice of your hearts to the brim, that you in your turn, may give of your abundance. Seek Him. Knowledge will make you strong as death. Love Him trustfully without looking back, without fear. Believe that Jesus and Jesus alone is life. Serve Jesus, casting aside and forgetting all that troubles or worries you, make loved the love that is not loved.

Mother House
4 August 1962

My Dearest Children,

Let us beg Our Lady to make our hearts "meek and humble" like her Son's was. It was from her and in her that the heart of Jesus was formed. We learn humility through accepting humiliation cheerfully. We have been created for greater things; why stoop down to things that will spoil the beauty of our hearts? How

much we can learn from Our Lady! She made use of
the Almighty Power that was in her. Tell Our Lady to
tell Jesus "They have no wine," the wine of humility
and meekness, of kindness, of sweetness. . . .

First Friday in November 1962

My Dearest Children,
   The first lesson of the heart of Jesus is our examina-
tion of conscience. "Know thyself." Examen is a part-
nership between us and Jesus. We should not rest in
useless looks at our own miseries, but should lift our
hearts to God and His light. . . .
   . . . In our vow of obedience, is there no lessening of
our faith, seeing the human limitations of our Superior?
   Our obedience, by being prompt, simple, and cheerful, is the proof of our faith. If God loves a cheerful
giver how much more would He not love an obedient
giver. . . . Obey as Christ obeyed. . . . He saw the will
of His Father—in everything and everybody—so He
could say "I do the things that are pleasing to Him."
He obeyed Caiaphas and Pilate because authority was
given from "above." He submitted to them with obedience and dignity. He did not look at the human limitations of Caiaphas and Pilate.

Mother House
19 May 1963

My Dearest Children,
   The greatness of Our Lady was in her humility. No
wonder Jesus, who lived so close to her, seemed to be

so anxious that we learn from Him and her but one lesson—to be meek and humble of heart.

Humility is truth, therefore in all sincerity we must be able to look up and say: "I can do all things in Him who strengthens me." By yourself you can do nothing, have nothing but sin, weakness and misery. All the gifts of nature and grace, you have them from God. . . . Why allow temptations against your vocation?

10 November 1963

My Dearest Children,

This year we must prepare a better crib, a crib of poverty. It will be easy to fill the emptiness of the crib with charity.

We think we know ourselves enough. Our very lives are all for God, therefore why spend so much time on our spiritual life? It is not that we do not make our examen; no, we do it but do it alone. We have to do it with Christ if we want to make it real. Jesus is our co-worker.

Our souls should be like a clear glass through which God can be seen. Often this glass becomes spotted with dust and dirt. To remove this dirt and dust we make our examen, so that we become once more "clean of heart." He can, and He will help us to remove the "dirt and dust" if we allow Him to do it, with a sincere will to let Him have His way. Perhaps something has been lacking in us. Our vows, our duties, the virtues, our attitude to and our contacts with our neighbors . . . provide us with food enough for reflection. If we examine ourselves and find nothing to engage our attention, we need Jesus to help us detect our infidelities.

Our examen is after all the mirror we hold up to our nature, a poor weak human nature, no doubt, but one that needs the mirror to reflect faithfully all its deficiencies. If we undertake this work more sincerely, perhaps we shall find what we thought were stumbling blocks transformed by Him into stepping stones.

February 1964

My Dearest Children,

Our life has all the more need of humility since it is so much in the public eye. People surround us with love to guarantee the fruitfulness of our works of charity. It is beautiful to see the humility of Christ "who being in the form of God, thought it not only robbery to be equal with God, but emptied Himself, taking the form of a servant being made in the likeness of man and found in habit as a man."

. . . People do not want proud Sisters, for they are like a heavy instrument in the hands of God. The poor too want to be treated like children of God, not like slaves. . . .

It is a great virtue to practice humility without our knowing that we are humble.

March 1964

My Dearest Children,

. . . There is only one true prayer, only one substantial prayer: Christ Himself. There is only one voice

that rises above the face of the earth: the voice of
Christ. . . .

3 June 1964

My Dearest Children,
  . . . It is said that humility is truth and Jesus is the
Truth, therefore the one way that will make us most
Christlike is humility. Do not think that hiding your
gifts of God is the sign of humility. No, do and use
whatever gifts God has given you.

Mother House
15 August 1964

My Dearest Sisters,
  Today will be one of the most beautiful feasts of Our
Lady. She fulfills her role as cause of our joy. Do we
really know why we love Our Lady so much? Because
she was the spotless mirror of God's love. . . . Are we
afraid of sin? . . . How terrible sin must be, if it has the
power to kill God's life in us, for mortal sin kills, it
causes a mortal wound in the heart of God in us. Let
us die rather than ever wound God mortally.
  If venial sin is deliberately allowed to become a
daily bread, it causes moral anemia and the spiritual
life begins to crumble and fall apart. . . .
  Claude de La Colombière writes: "We see after
one, two or three years, that the cowards are still
cowardly, the irregular are still irregular, the angry
ones have acquired no gentleness, the proud no humility, the lazy no fervor, the selfish no detachment

from selfishness; that communities that ought to be
fiery furnaces, where they would unceasingly burn
for love of God and where the soul would become so
Christlike, so near to God, remain frightfully medio-
cre."

Mother House
1 November 1964

My Dearest Children,

I come again and again to the same point: silence
and charity. Silence of the tongue will teach us so
much, to speak to Christ. Silence of the eyes will always help us to see God. Our eyes are like two win-
dows through which Christ or the world comes to our
hearts? Often we need great courage to keep them
closed. . . .

The silence of the heart, like Our Lady kept all
these things in her heart.

Mother House
15 February 1965

My Dearest Sisters,

We who are wedded to Christ cannot allow any
other love into our hearts without drawing down
God's displeasure upon ourselves. God has chosen us.
He also has the right to stop choosing us, but He will
never do it of His own accord except when we force
Him to do it.

. . . Do not play with your vocation, for when you
want to preserve it, you will not find the courage to do
so. Why do we have so many broken homes? Because

of uncontrolled affections, wanting to have all the pleasures, two loves.

. . . When we left home to enter the religious life, our parents made great sacrifices to let us go and when we are unfaithful to our vocation it grieves them deeply.

"I would be happy today if her coffin had left this house," the family of a Sister who had left told me.

Mother House
27 June 1965

My Dearest Children,

The fruit of our union with Christ is the vow of charity, just as the child is the fruit of the sacrament of matrimony. . . . Just as the lamp cannot burn without oil, so the vow of charity cannot live without the vows of poverty and obedience. . . .

San Felipe
6 August 1965

My Dearest Children, Sisters and Brothers,

From Our Lady we will ask for a delicate love for God's poor. . . . Here we have real spiritual slums. . . .

Cocorote
5 July 1966

My Dearest Sisters,

. . . Smiling novices, I can hear the music of your laughter of joy right here in Venezuela.

Zealous young professed, the sound of your footsteps in search of souls must be like a sweet music for Jesus. Humble students, keep this Light of Christ, the lamp burning across your books, ever full of oil, so that you may become a true light of Christ in the slums.

Waltair
31 October 1966

My Dearest Children,

It is our emptiness and lowliness that God needs and not our plenitude. These are a few of the ways we can practice humility:

Speak as little as possible of oneself.
Mind one's own business.
Avoid curiosity.
Do not want to manage other people's affairs.
Accept contradiction and correction cheerfully.
Pass over the mistakes of others.
Accept blame when innocent.
Yield to the will of others.
Accept insults and injuries.
Accept being slighted, forgotten, and disliked.
Be kind and gentle even under provocation.
Do not seek to be specially loved and admired.
Never stand on one's dignity.
Yield in discussion even though one is right.
Choose always the hardest.

Mother House
13 June 1967

My Dearest Sisters,

Make it a special point to become God's sign in your community. We must radiate the joy of being poor but do not speak about it. Just be happy to be poor with Christ. . . .

Air India Across the Ocean
17 September 1967

My Dearest Children,

Once again I am crossing the ocean to prepare the way for you in search of God's poor.

Don Marmion says: "All you have to do is to leave yourself absolutely in His hands, like wax, for He cuts away mercilessly all the unnecessary parts." And when temptation to leave the order came to him he prostrated himself before the tabernacle and cried out: "Let me be cut to pieces rather than leave the monastery."

Are we strong enough to prefer being cut to pieces rather than give up Christ?

We do not change our profession as we change our clothes. Nowadays everything is getting looser and looser. People are trying to loosen the most sacred bindings. Are we to be guided by them or will we cling to the rock, Christ? . . .

Mother House
12 April 1968

My Dearest Children,

. . . Work without love is a slavery. The church wants "renewal." Renewal does not mean the changing of habit and a few prayers. A renewal should be faithfulness to the spirit of the Constitutions.

Mother House
18 May 1968

My Dearest Children,

We must feel the suffering of our people. To be transfigured we have to be disfigured in our own sight.

Mother House
18 July 1968

My Dearest Children,

Offer to God every word you say, every movement you make. We must more and more fall in love with God. Let it not be said that one single woman in the whole world loves her husband better than we do Christ.

Mother House
28 January 1969

My Dearest Superiors and Sisters,

See the compassion of Christ toward Judas. The Master who kept the "sacred silence" would not betray him to his companions. Jesus could have easily spoken in public and told the hidden intentions and deeds of Judas. Rather He showed mercy instead of condemning him. He called "Friend" and if Judas would have only looked into the eyes of Jesus, today Judas would have been the friend of God's mercy.

Mother House
7 May 1969

My Dearest Sisters,

These are very difficult times in the church. Do not get mixed up in gossip conversations. You hear of priests and nuns leaving and of many broken homes, but do not forget there are thousands and thousands of priests and nuns and happy families faithful unto death. This trial will purify the church of her human infirmities and she will come out of it beautiful and true.

Mother House
25 November 1969

My Dearest Children,

Next week we begin with the church the season of Advent. It is like springtime. He comes like a little child so much in need of His mother. Let us see and touch the greatness that fills the depths of their humility, Jesus' and Mary's. If we really want God to fill us we must empty ourselves through humility of all that is selfishness in us.

Mother House
19 February 1970

My Dearest Children,

The first week of Lent is nearly over. He still keeps looking for "one" to console Him. Do you try to be that "one"? Today Christ, in His vicar and the church, is being humiliated through pride in acts of disobedience and disloyalty, scourged by evil tongues.

He is thirsty for the kindness He begs from you, naked for the loyalty He hopes of you.

Today much of the suffering in the church and outside of it is caused solely by misunderstood notions of freedom and renewal. We cannot be free unless we are able to surrender our will freely to the will of God. We cannot renew unless we have the humility and the courage to acknowledge what is to be renewed in us. Therefore, be careful of people who come to you with wonderful speeches on freedom and renewal; they actually deceive and take away from you the joy and peace of Christ, the Life.

Mother House
14 March 1970

My Dearest Children,

Calcutta is really sharing in the Passion of Christ. It is sad to see so much sorrow in our beloved Calcutta. But just like Christ who after the Passion rose to live forever, so Calcutta will rise again and be the Mother of the Poor. . . . Shanti Nagar is really growing into a beautiful Town of Peace. . . .

Plane to New York
11 October 1970

My Dearest Children,

   . . . Instead of spending their days in fear and trembling, our Sisters in Amman prayed the rosary continuously and the result was that on the ninth day the troops stopped near our place—peace has been proclaimed. . . .

   . . . Today in the words of our Holy Father every Missionary of Charity must be able "to cleanse what is dark." . . .

Mother House
17 January 1971

My Dearest Children,

   . . . The award* was most unexpected and so I had no chance to let you know in time as I knew only on the 23rd when I returned from Amman.

   . . . Jesus wants to live the Truth in us and through us. . . . Speak the truth, think the truth, act the truth with God, with His church, with each other and with yourselves. Do not be surprised at each other's failure. . . . Try to see and accept that every Sister is a branch in Christ the Vine. The same life-giving sap that flows from the Vine (Jesus) through each of the branches (Sisters) is the same.

*The Pope John XXIII Peace Prize.

7 March 1971

My Dearest Children,

Sacrifice, to be real, must empty us of self. We often pray "Let me share with you Your pain" and yet when a little spittle or thorn of thoughtlessness is given to us, how we forget that this is the time to share with Him His shame and pain.

If we could but remember that it is Jesus who gives us the chance through that certain person or circumstance to do something beautiful for His Father.

Superiors: try to look and see Jesus in your Sisters. Your Sisters are His in a special way because He has chosen them and given them to you to take care of and lead them through holiness to His heart. Love them as you love Christ.

Sisters: look up and see Jesus in your Superiors. Your superior is the vine and you are a branch, and unless you and they are one and allow His Father, the Gardner, to prune you, through suffering and trials, through bearing each other's burdens, neither of you will be able to bring any fruit.

The tenth of September will be the twenty-fifth anniversary of our Society. You could not show deeper gratitude than by thinking and speaking of the goodness of each other—appreciating the good your Sisters are doing, accepting each other as you are and always meeting each other with a smile.

**Mother House
29 April 1971**

My Dearest Children,

The news of Bangladesh seems to become worse day by day. Hatred and selfishness are destroying a whole nation.

Today when our people are being tortured and suffer untold pain, let us reflect and avoid anything that may cause deep wounds in the hearts of the poor.

We have no right to use what belongs to the poor. We eat nothing in the houses of the rich so as to be able to tell the poor when they offer us a drink: "We do not take anything outside . . ."

They love to see the Sisters in the company of Mary, rosary in hand, always making haste to bring the good news.

10 August 1971

My Dearest Children,

. . . May our Mother be a mother to each one of us and so the cause of our joy. And may each one of us be Jesus to her and so become the cause of her joy. No one learned the lesson of humility as well as Mary did. She was the handmaiden. To be a handmaiden is to be at someone's disposal—to be used according to someone's wish—with full trust and joy. Cheerfulness and joy were Our Lady's strength. Only joy could have given her the strength to go in haste over the hills of Judea to do the work of handmaiden to her cousin. So let us go in haste over the hills of difficulties.

> Franciscan Handmaids of Mary Convent
> 15 West 124th Street, New York
> 15 October 1971

My Dearest Children,

The Negro Sisters have given us a separate part of their building and this will be our convent with a lovely chapel. . . .

The news of Calcutta's cyclone is so hard to accept. Our poor people are becoming poorer day by day. Be kind to them, be a comfort to the poor and take every trouble to help them. Open your eyes to the needs of the poor.

P.S. (By Sister Andrea).—The prize our Mother received was a big heavy glass vase with a silver foot and these words engraved on it:

"The Great Seraph RAPHAEL, Mightiest of Angels, Patron of Science and Healing, whose hand stirred the waters of the Pool at Bethsaida, Protector of the Young Tobias, Helper of the Patriarch Abraham, Paragon of Knowledge and Love.

To Mother Teresa, whose struggles have shaped Something Beautiful for God.

1971 Kennedy International Award."

> Mother House
> 3 December 1971

My Dearest Children,

Love begins at home. Do not be afraid to love until it hurts.

Love your Superiors. The Society will be what you

together with your Superior make it: a fervent or a tepid, a fruitful or a dry branch.

> Mother House
> 26 February 1972

My Dearest Children,

We have been asked by the government of Bangladesh to take care of the girls who have been misused. I want to draw your attention to the sentence Mujibur Rahman said on behalf of these girls: "They will be treated as heroines of the country because they suffered so much to protect their purity." These girls, Hindu and Muslim, out of their natural love for purity fought to protect themselves. Many committed suicide rather than lose the beautiful virtue of womanhood.

We religious who have a chance to consecrate that beautiful gift to God in loving Him with undivided love, do we really take all the trouble to protect it and make it grow in beauty and strength?

. . . During this Lenten season we will take as a special point: Forgiveness. If we do not forgive then it is a sign that we have not been forgiven.

Sister M. Francis Xavier met with a terrible car accident but thank God, as she says: "Our Lady took care of me." She was saying the rosary and had the rosary in hand when she gained consciousness.

Mother House
19 March 1972

My Dearest Children,

Today when everything is questioned and changed,
let us go back to Nazareth. How strange that Jesus
should spend thirty years doing nothing, wasting His
time, not giving His personality or His gifts a chance!
We know that at the age of twelve He silenced the
learned priests of the Temple, who knew so much and
so well. Then for thirty years we hear no more of Him.
No wonder the people were surprised when He came
in public to preach; He was known only as a carpenter's son.

We hear so much of "personality," of "maturity,"
of "maternalism," and so forth, . . . and yet the
Gospel is so full of words such as "little children"
used by Jesus when addressing His grown-up apostles.

Mother House
28 June 1972

My Dearest Children,

Let us ask the Sacred Heart for one very special
grace: love for Our Lady. Ask Him to give and deepen
our love and make it more personal and intimate for
her:

To love her as He loved her.
To be a cause of joy to her as He was.
To keep close to her as He kept.
To share with her everything, even the cross.

Each one of us has our cross to bear, for this is the sign that we are His. Therefore we need her to share it with us. . . .

. . . Holiness is not a luxury but a simple duty for you and me. Very great holiness becomes very simple if we belong fully to Our Lady. . . .

. . . I am sure each one of us has much to thank God:

For all the tiring journeys we have made by road, by train, by plane, by cycle in search of souls.
For all the joy we have tried to spread throughout the world.
For letting us give Our Lady full liberty to use us.

Mother House
15 August 1972

My Dearest Children,

This is my feastday greeting to each one of you: that you may know each other at the breaking of bread and love each other in the eating of this Bread of Life.

When communicating with Christ in your heart during the partaking of the Living Bread, remember what Our Lady must have felt when the Holy Spirit overpowered her and she became full with the Body of Christ. The Spirit in her was so strong that immediately she "rose in haste" to go and serve.

At the breaking of bread they recognized Him. Do I recognize the beauty of my Sisters, the spouses of Christ? Our Lady was full of God because she lived for God alone, and yet she thought of herself only as the handmaiden of the Lord. Let us do the same.

Mother House
13 December 1972

My Dearest Children,

Let us all be very much aware of the responsibility we must share together in building up our Society as a living and fruitful branch of the Body of Christ. . . .

Jesus has warned us already: "Woe to the world because of scandals. For ` it must needs be that scandals come; but nevertheless woe to the one by whom the scandal comes" (Matthew 18:7).

Woe to her through whom scandals are made, wrong attitudes and worldliness being very much contrary to the poverty and obedience of Christ we have chosen. It would be a shame for us to be richer than Christ, Who being rich became poor and was "subject to them."

August 1973

My Dearest Children,

I wish you the joy of Our Lady, who because she was humble of heart could hold Jesus for nine months in her bosom. What a long Holy Communion!

Rome
24 October 1973

My Dearest Children,

So many of our Sisters' parents, brothers and sisters have gone home to God during these years. I am sure they are making a new group of Co-Workers in Heaven. . . .

. . . In Ostia, there is a terrible poverty, not hunger for food but for God. People are starving for the knowledge of God.

In Yemen, our Sisters have their hands full in spite of not yet knowing the language. One of the government officials wrote: "A new era of light and love has started in Yemen."

Mother House
14 December 1973

My Dearest Children,

Our Holy Father has proclaimed the Holy Year as Year of Reconciliation. Reconciliation begins not first with others but with ourselves. It starts by having a clean heart within. A clean heart is able to see God in others. The tongue, the part of our body that comes in such close contact with the Body of Christ can become an instrument of peace and joy or of sorrow and pain. . . . Forgive and ask to be forgiven; excuse rather than accuse. . . .

25 February 1974

My Dearest Children,

Our lives should be more and more pervaded by a profound faith in Jesus, the Bread of Life, which we should partake of with and for the poor. . . .

The Sisters assure you all of their overflowing love: from Yemen, Ostia, Addis Ababa, Lima, Gaza, Coimbatore, Vijayawada, Shivpur, Tiljala, Takda, all the new homes send you their prayers. . . .

Are we truly attempting to be the poorest of the poor? In poverty which is liberty, charity increases.

Easter, 1974

My Dearest Children,

Jesus has chosen each and every one of you to be His love and His light in the world. . . .

The spirit of sacrifice will always be the salt of our Society. . . .

PART IV

Living with the Poor and Like the Poor

Mother Teresa's Commentary on the Constitution of the Missionaries of Charity (Unpublished Documents)

"I thirst," Jesus said on the Cross. He spoke of His thirst not for water but for love.

Our aim is to quench this infinite thirst of God made man.

So the Sisters, using the four vows of chastity, poverty, obedience and wholehearted free service to the poorest of the poor, ceaselessly quench that thirsting of God.

"Nothing common" wrote St. Ignatius to the scholastics, "can satisfy the obligations by which you have bound yourselves to striving after perfection. Consider your vocation, of what character it is, and you will see what might be satisfactory in others is not so in your case."

Let us remember the words of St. Theresa of Lisieux: "How shall I show my love, since love shows itself by deeds?" Well, the little child Theresa will strew flowers: "I will let no tiny sacrifice pass, no look, no word. I wish to profit by the smallest actions and to do them for love. . . . I will sing always even if my roses must be gathered from amidst thorns and the longer and sharper the thorns, the sweeter shall be my song."

"Our Lord," she said, "has need of our love; He has no need of our works."

The same God who declares that He has no need to tell us if He be hungry did not disdain to beg a little water from the Samaritan woman. He was thirsty, but when He said "Give me to drink," He, the Creator of the Universe, was asking for the love of His creatures.

To become a saint, one must suffer much. Suffering begets love . . . and life among the souls.

For us, the carriers of God's love, how full of love we must be in order to be true to our name.

Let us always remain with Mary our Mother near our crucified Jesus, with our chalice made of the four vows and filled with the wine of self-sacrifice.

All our actions, therefore, must tend to advance our own and our neighbor's perfection by nursing the sick and dying, by gathering and teaching little street children, by visiting and caring for beggars and their children, and by giving shelter to the abandoned.

To labor at the conversion and sanctification of the poor in the slums means hard ceaseless toil, without counting the results or the cost.

To convert is to bring to God. To sanctify is to fill with God. To convert and sanctify is the work of God, but God has chosen in His great mercy the Missionaries of Charity to help Him in His own work. It is a special grace granted to the Missionaries of Charity with no merit on their part to carry the light of Christ into the dark holes and slums.

Those, therefore, who join the Institute are resolved to spend themselves unremittingly in seeking out in towns and villages, even amid squalid surroundings, the poor, the abandoned, the sick, the infirm, the dying.

Zeal for souls is the effect and the proof of true love of God. We cannot but be consumed with the desire for saving souls. Zeal is the test of love and the test of zeal is devotedness to His cause, spending life and energy in the work of souls. . . .

It cannot be denied that the active life is full of dangers, because of the numerous occasions of sin to which it gives rise, but let us be sure of God's special protection in all our works assumed under obedience. To hesitate when obedience calls us to action would be to deserve the rebuke Peter merited, "O thou of little faith, why didst thou doubt . . ."

Our Lady arose and went with haste to the hill country . . . and Mary remained about three months to do the work of a servant for her old cousin. . . . We must possess before we can give. She who has the mission to distribute must first increase in the knowledge of God and fill herself with the knowledge God wishes to grant to souls through her agency.

"Before allowing his tongue to speak, the apostle

ought to raise his thirsting soul to God and then give forth what he has drunk in, and pour forth what he has been filled with," says St. Augustine.

St. Thomas tells us: "Those who are called to the works of the active life would be wrong in thinking that their duty exempts them from the contemplative life." This duty adds to it. Thus these two lives, instead of excluding each other, call for each other's help, implement and complete each other. Action to be productive has need of contemplation. The latter, when it gets to a certain degree of intensity diffuses some of its excess on the first.

. . . When there is need of speaking, we must not be afraid. He will tell us what and how to say the things He wants us to say.

Christ must be preached to pagans that they may know him, to heretics and schismatics that they may return to His fold; to bad Catholics that they may be drawn by His mercy; to the good and the pious that they may in His love be consumed and live His life.

Mary, under her divine Son, has sovereign dominion in the administration of supernatural graces and benefits of God's kingdom. She is our Mother because in her love she cooperated in our spiritual rebirth. She continues to be our Mother by nourishing the life of Christ in us.

Holiness increases in proportion to the devotion that one professes for Mary. The way back to God is through sinlessness and purity of life. Mary the Immaculate One is the way. She, "our life, our sweetness and our hope," is the way to peace. Pope Pius XII first consecrated the world to the Immaculate Heart of Mary on 31 October 1942. "There will be peace if the devotion to the Immaculate Heart of Mary is established throughout the world." This Our Lady promised to the three children of Fatima.

Charity must not remain shut up in the depth of the heart, for "no man lighteth a candle and putteth it under a bushel, but on a candlestick, that it may shine for all that are in the house."

A Missionary is a carrier of God's love, a burning light that gives light to all; the salt of the earth. It is said of St. Francis Xavier that "he stood up as a fire, and his words burnt like a torch." We have to carry Our Lord in places where He has not walked before. The Sisters must be consumed with one desire: Jesus. We must not be afraid to do the things He did—to go fearlessly through death and danger with Him and for Him.

A Missionary carries the interest of Christ continually in her heart and mind. In her heart there must be the fire of divine love and zeal for God's glory. This love makes her spend herself without ceasing. This becomes her real object in life and her joy. When Brother Lievens, S. J., was told to make his fire "a lasting one" he replied "No, I must make it a burning one." He spent himself in ten years' time. Jesus says: "Amen, unless the grain of wheat falls to the ground and dies, itself remaineth alone. But if it dies it brings forth much fruit". The Missionary must die daily if she wants to bring souls to God. The title "Missionary Religious" should humble us, for we are unworthy.

Our holy faith is nothing but a Gospel of love, revealing to us God's love for men and claiming in return man's love for God.

Let us "act" Christ's love among men, remembering the words of the Imitation, "love feels no burden, values no labors, would willingly do more than it can. It complains not of impossibilities, because it conceives that it may and can do all things; when weary is not tired; when straitened is not constrained; when frightened is not disturbed; but like a living flame and a torch all on fire, it mounts upwards and securely passes through all opposition."

Charity is patient, is kind, feels no envy, is never perverse or proud or insolent; it has no selfish aims, cannot be provoked, does not brood over an injury; it takes no pleasure in wrong-doing but rejoices over the victory of the truth; it sustains, believes, hopes, endures to the last. Love has a hem to her garment that reaches the very dust. It sweeps the stains from the streets and lanes, and because it can, it must. The Missionary of Charity, in order to be true to her name, must be full of charity in her own soul and spread that same charity to the souls of others, Christians and pagans alike.

Total surrender consists in giving ourselves completely to God, because God has given Himself to us. If God owes nothing to us and is ready to impart to us no less than Himself, shall we answer with just a fraction of ourselves? I give up my own self and in this way induce God to live for me. Therefore to possess God we must allow Him to possess our souls. How poor we would be if God had not given us the power of giving ourselves to Him. How rich we are now. How easy it is to conquer God. We give ourselves to Him, then God is ours, and there can be nothing more ours than God. The money with which God repays our surrender is Himself.

To surrender means to offer Him my free will, my reason, my own life in pure faith. My soul may be in darkness. Trial is the surest way of my blind surrender.

Surrender is also true love. The more we surrender, the more we love God and souls. If we really love souls, we must be ready to take their place, to take their sins upon us and expiate them. We must be living holocausts, for the souls need us as such.

There is no limit to God's love. It is without measure and its depth cannot be sounded. "I will not leave you orphans."

Now reverse the picture. There must be no limit to the love that prompts us to give ourselves to God, to be the victims of His unwanted love. We cannot be pleased with the common. What is good for others is not sufficient for us. We have to satiate the thirst of an infinite God dying of love. We cannot be content with the common lot, but with undaunted courage and fearlessness meet all perils and dangers with equanimity of soul, ever ready to make any sacrifice, to undertake any toil and labor. A Missionary of Charity must always push forward until she comes close to the King dying of thirst.

Loving trust. One thing Jesus asks of me is that I lean upon Him; that in Him alone I put complete trust; that I surrender myself to Him unreservedly. I need to give up my own desires in the work of my perfection. Even when I feel as if I were a ship without a compass, I must give myself completely to Him. I must not attempt to control God's actions. I must not desire a clear perception of my advance along the road, nor know precisely where I am on the way of holiness. I ask Him to make a saint of me, yet I must leave to Him the choice of that saintliness itself and still more the choice of the means that lead to it.

Cheerfulness should be one of the main points of our religious life. A cheerful religious is like sunshine in a community. Cheerfulness is a sign of a generous person. It is often a cloak that hides a life of sacrifice. A person who has this gift of cheerfulness often reaches great heights of perfection. Let the sick and suffering find us real angels of comfort and consolation. Why has the work in the slums been blessed by God? Not on account of any personal qualities but on account of the joy the Sisters radiate. What we have, faith and the conviction that we are the beloved children of God, people in the world have not got, much less the people in the slums. The surest way to preach Christianity to the pagan is by our cheerfulness. What would our life be if the Sisters were unhappy? Slavery and nothing else. We would do the work but we would attract nobody. This moodiness, heaviness, sadness, is a very easy way to tepidity, the mother of all evil.

If you are cheerful, have no fear of tepidity. Joy shines in the eyes, comes out in the speech and walk.

You cannot keep it in for it bubbles out. When people see the habitual happiness in your eyes, it will make them realize they are the loved children of God. Every holy soul at times has great interior trials and darkness, but if we want others to realize that Jesus is there, we must be convinced of it ourselves. Just imagine a Sister going to the slums with a sad face and heavy step. What would her presence bring to these people? Only greater depression.

Joy is very infectious; therefore, be always full of joy when you go among the poor. That cheerfulness, according to St. Bonaventure, has been given to man that he may rejoice in God in the hope of eternal good and at the sight of God's benefits; that he may rejoice in his neighbor's prosperity, take a delight in praising God and doing good works and feel disgust for all vain and useless things.

"It would be equally extraordinary," says St. Ignatius, "to see a religious who seeks nothing but God sad, as to see one who seeks everything but God happy."

Nationalism is inconsistent with our Constitution. Hence we should never fasten an unfavorable opinion on to people belonging to a nation other than ours. We must not defend politicians, nor should we make war and strife the subject of our conversation if mentioning them harms charity. . . . Nationalism is contrary to "Go therefore, and teach all nations" (Matthew 28:19). "Their sound hath gone forth to all the earth," St. Chrysostom says of St. Paul. "The heart of Paul is the heart of the whole world." Would that the same could be said of us. Girls of any nationality are welcome in our society.

Poverty. One loses touch with God when one takes hold of money. God preserve us. It is better to die. What would one do with surplus money? Bank it? We must never get into the habit of being preoccupied with the future. There is no reason to do so: God is there. Once the longing for money comes, the longing also comes for what money can give: superfluous things, nice rooms, luxuries at the table, more clothes, fans, and so on. Our needs will increase, for one thing leads to another, and the result will be endless dissatisfaction.

If you ever have to get things, you must buy things of cheaper quality. We must be proud of being poor. Pay attention to the little fox that sneaks in after us. We may carry water upstairs for a bath and find three buckets already full in the bathing room. Then the temptation comes to use all the water. . . .

If you have to sleep in a corner where there is no breeze, do not gasp and pant to show how much you feel it. In these little things one can practice poverty. Poverty makes us free. That is why we can joke and smile and keep a happy heart for Jesus. . . .

Some Sisters seem to be in a continual, feverish excitement about money for their work. Never give the impression to people when you beg that you are out to gather money. Let your work speak. Let your love for the people enkindle the rich people's hearts. They will give if you don't grab. Even if you have to beg, show that your heart is detached by being at ease, both when they refuse you and when they give.

A rich man of Delhi said: "How wonderful it is to see Sisters so free from the world, in the twentieth century when one thinks everything is old-fashioned but the present day."

Keep to the simple ways of poverty, of repairing your own shoes, and so forth, in short, of loving poverty as you love your mother. Our Society will live as long as that real poverty exists. The institutes where poverty is faithfully practiced are fervent and need not fear decay. We must always try to be poorer still and discover new ways to live our vows of poverty. We must think ourselves very fortunate if we get a few chances in life to practice this wonderful poverty. . . . To rejoice that others are more fortunate than we takes much virtue. . . .

When St. Francis of Assisi heard that a new rich house had been built for the brethren, he refused to enter the city. . . . We must not spend time and energy on the house by making it look attractive and beautiful. God save us from such convents where the poor would be afraid to enter lest their misery be a cause of shame to them.

When we dress ourselves we should with devotion remember what each article of the religious habit means to us: the sari with its blue band is a sign of Mary's modesty; the girdle made of rope is the sign of Mary's angelic purity; sandals are a sign of our own free choice; and the crucifix is a sign of love.

. . . Sisters shall live by begging alms. We depend entirely on the charity of the people. The Sisters should not be ashamed to beg from door to door if necessary. Our Lord Himself has promised a reward even for a cup of water given in His name. It is for His sake that we become beggars.

In fact He often endured real want, as the stories of the multiplication of the loaves and fishes and the plucking of the ears of corn on walks through the fields teach us. The thought of these instances should be salutary reminders whenever in the mission or at home our meals are meagre. . . . Our Lord on the cross possessed nothing. . . . He was on the cross that was given by Pilate. The nails and the crown were given by the soldiers. He was naked and when He died, cross, nails, and crown were taken away from Him. He was wrapped in a shroud given by a kind heart, and buried in a tomb that was not His. Yet Jesus could have died as a king and He could have risen from the dead as king. He chose poverty because He knew in His infinite knowledge and wisdom that it is the real means of possessing God, of conquering His heart, of bringing His love down to this earth.

Wholehearted free service. "What so ever you do to the least of my brethren, you do it to me. This is my commandment that you love one another." Suppress this commandment and the whole grand work of the church of Christ falls in ruins. . . .

Charity for the poor must be a burning flame in our Society. And just as when a fire ceases to burn, it is no longer useful and gives no more heat, so the day the Society loses its charity toward the poor, it will lose its usefulness and there will be no life.

Charity for the poor is like a living flame. The drier the fuel, the brighter it burns; that is, when our hearts are separated from earthly motives and completely united to the will of God, we shall be able to give free service. . . . . The more united we are to God, the greater will be our love and readiness to serve the poor wholeheartedly. The more repugnant the work or the person, the greater also must be a Sister's faith, love, and cheerful devotion in ministering to Our Lord in this distressing disguise. . . .

When we recollect that in the morning we have held in our hands an all-holy God, we are more ready to abstain from whatever could soil their purity. Hence we should have deep reverence for our own person and reverence for others, treat all with accepted marks of courtesy, but abstain from sentimental feeling or ill-ordered affections. When we handle the sick and the needy we touch the suffering Body of Christ and this touch will make us heroic; it will make us forget the repugnance.

We need the eyes of deep faith to see Christ in the broken body and dirty clothes under which the most beautiful One among the sons of men hides. We shall need the hands of Christ to touch those bodies wounded by pain and suffering.

How pure our hands must be if we have to touch Christ's Body as the priest touches Him in the appearance of bread at the altar. With what love and devotion and faith he lifts the sacred host! These same feelings we too must have when we lift the body of the sick poor.

It is seeing that made Father Damien the apostle of

the lepers, that made St. Vincent de Paul the father of the poor. . . . Such also was the case of St. Francis of Assisi who, when meeting a leper completely disfigured, drew back, but then overcame himself and kissed the terribly disfigured face. The result was that St. Francis was filled with an untold joy, and the leper walked away praising God for his cure. St. Peter Claver licked the wounds of his Negro slaves. St. Margaret Mary sucked the pus from a boil. Why did they all do these things if it was not because they wanted to draw nearer to the heart of God. . . .

Spiritual life. "I kept the Lord ever before my eyes because He is ever at my right hand that I may not slip."

The true inner life makes the active life burn forth and consume everything. It makes us find Jesus in the dark holes of the slums, in the most pitiful miseries of the poor, in the God-man naked on the cross, mournful, despised by all, the man of suffering, crushed like a worm by the scourging and the crucifixion.

What does the Society expect of its members? To be co-workers of Christ in the slums. Where will we fulfill that aim? Not in the houses of the rich, but in the slums. That is our kingdom. That is Christ's kingdom and ours, the field we have to work in. If a boy leaves his father's field and goes to work in another, he is no longer his father's co-worker. Those who share everything are partners giving love for love, suffering for suffering. Jesus, you hve given everything, life, blood, all. Now it is our turn. We should put everything into the field also.

. . . Our prayers should be burning words coming forth from the furnace of a heart filled with love.

. . . In our work we may often be caught in idle conversation or gossip. Let us be well on our guard for we may be caught while visiting families; we may talk about the private affairs of this or that one and so forget the real aim of our visit. We come to bring the peace of Christ but what if, instead, we are a cause of trouble? We must never allow people to speak against their neighbors. If we find that a family is in a bad mood and is sure to start their tale of uncharitableness, let us say a fervent prayer for them and say first a few things that may help them to think a little about God; then let us leave the place at once. We can do no good until their restless nerves are at peace. We must follow the same conduct with those who want to talk with the aim of wasting our precious time. If they are not in search of God, do not argue or answer their questions; leave them. Pray for them that they may see the light, but do not waste your time.

Hear Jesus your Co-Worker speak to you: "I want you to be my fire of love amongst the poor, the sick, the dying and the little children. The poor, I want you to bring them to me." Learn this sentence by heart and when you are wanting in generosity, repeat it. We can refuse Christ just as we refuse others.

"I will not give you my hands to work with, my eyes to see with, my feet to walk with, my mind to study with, my heart to love with. You knock at the door but I will not open. . . ." That is a broken Christ, a lame Christ, a crooked Christ deformed by you. If you give this to the people, it is all they will have. If you want them to love Him, they must know Him first. Therefore, give the whole Christ, first to the Sisters, then to the people in the slums, a Christ full of zeal, love, joy, and sunshine.

Am I a dark light? a false light? a bulb without the connection, having no current, therefore shedding no radiance? Put your heart into being a bright light.

Holy Communion. If we want to have life and have it more abundantly, we must live on the flesh of Our Lord.

This needs no explanation, for who could explain "the depth of the riches of the wisdom and knowledge of God"? "How incomprehensible are His judgments," cried St. Paul, and "how unsearchable His way, for who has known the mind of the Lord?"

. . . "O Lord God, give me grace this very day really and truly to begin, for what I have done till now is nothing. . . ." The easiest form of self-denial is control over our bodily senses . . . that we may truly say with St. Paul: "One thing I do, forgetting the things that are behind and stretching forth myself to these that are before, I press toward the mark. . . ."

The danger for us is to forget that we are sinners.

Humility. Humility is nothing but truth. "What have we got that we have not received?" asks St. Paul. If I have received everything what good have I of my own? If we are convinced of this we will never raise our heads in pride.

If you are humble, nothing will touch you, neither praise nor disgrace, because you know what you are.

... It is one thing for me to say I am sinner, but let someone else say that about me and then I feel it—I am up in arms.

If I am falsely accused, I may suffer, but deep down there is joy, because the correction is founded on reality, if even in the smallest way.

... Make it possible and even easy for your Superior to treat you and operate on you like the surgeon whose knife must cause pain in order to heal. When a sculptor carves a statue, what has he in his hand? A knife, and he cuts all the time.

Self-knowledge puts us on our knees, and it is very necessary for love. For knowledge of God gives love, and knowledge of self gives humility. St. Augustine says: "Fill yourselves first and then only will you be able to give to others." Self-knowledge is very necessary for confession. That is why the saints could say they were wicked criminals. They saw God and then saw themselves—and they saw the difference. Hence they were not surprised when anyone accused them, even falsely. . . . Each one of you has plenty of good as well as plenty of bad in her. Let none glory in her success but refer all to God.

We must never think any one of us is indispensable. God has ways and means. He may allow everything to go upside down in the hands of a very talented and capable Sister. God sees only her love. She may exhaust herself, even kill herself with work, but unless her work is interwoven with love it is useless. God does not need her work. God will not ask that Sister how many books she has read, how many miracles she has worked, but He will ask her if she has done her best, for the love of Him. . . .

If you are discouraged it is a sign of pride, because it shows you trust in your own powers. Never bother about people's opinions. Be humble and you will never be disturbed. Remember St. Aloysius, who said he would continue to play billiards even if he knew he was going to die. Do you play well? Sleep well? Eat well? These are duties. Nothing is small for God.

. . . We have grown so used to each other that some think they are free to say anything to anybody at any time. They expect the Sisters to bear with their unkindness. Why not try first to hold your tongue? You know what you can do, but you do not know how much the other can bear.

Prayer: The interest of friendship that unites us, that binds the young and old, is a chain of gold, a thousand times stronger than flesh and blood, because it permits the defects of the body and the vices of the soul to be seen, while charity covers all, hides all, to offer exclusively to admiration and love the work of the hands of God. . . . He it is who in your old age desires to decorate and adorn the fair beauty of your soul with toil and grief. . . . To all the ills that assail either heart or body hold up the shield of faith and patience. In your old age you will complete for the glory of God the tower of your soul that you began to build in the golden days of your youth. And when He comes, go forth to meet Him in the company of the wise virgins, your lamp filled with oil and a flame.

Recreation is a means to pray better. Relaxation sweeps away the cobwebs in the mind. . . .

In one of her apparitions to St. Catherine Labouré, Our Lady had rings on every finger, from some of which rays shone forth while from the other rings no rays came. Our Lady explained that the rays were blessings granted by her to those who had asked for them, while the rayless rings represented graces that had not yet been asked for and given.

. . . In our Home for the Dying we understand better the value of a soul. The very fact that God has placed a certain soul in your way is a sign that God wants you to do something for him or her. It is not chance; it has been planned by God. We are bound in conscience to help him or her. When visiting the families you will meet with very much misery. Sometimes you will find a little child holding the head of the dead mother. It is then that you must use all your energy to help that little child in his sorrow.

Once there were found two little children near the dead body of their father, who had died two days before. . . . God will use you to relieve this suffering . . .

To prove that Christ was divine. . . .

Suffering into Joy

Prepared and edited by
Eileen Egan and Kathleen Egan, OSB

Contents

❧

Do not be surprised, beloved, that a trial by fire is occurring in your midst. It is a test for you, but it should not catch you off guard. Rejoice instead, in the measure that you share Christ's sufferings. When his glory is revealed, you will rejoice exultantly.

1 Peter 4:12–13

1
The Face of Suffering in Today's World

ॐ

For I was hungry and you gave me food, I was thirsty and
you gave me drink. I was a stranger and you welcomed me,
naked and you clothed me. I was ill and you comforted me,
in prison and you came to visit me.' Then the just will ask
him: 'Lord, when did we see you hungry and feed you or
see you thirsty and give you drink? . . .' The King will
answer them, 'I assure you, as often as you did it for one of
my least brothers, you did it for me.
   Matthew 25:35–40

We picked our way among the masses of brown bodies
packed into the waiting room of the cavernous Sealdah
Railway Station: women in discoloured saris, men with
chests like birdcages and cloth *dhotis* wrapped around their
loins, children half or wholly naked. It was Calcutta in 1955,
and I* had just met a small vigorous woman in her mid-
forties who had been receiving American goods through
my agency, Catholic Relief Services. My stay could not be
long because I was booked to fly from Calcutta to Saigon
(now Ho Chi Minh City).

   This unknown woman, wearing a sari with its wrap-
around headpiece, introduced some young Indian women

*The use of the word 'I' throughout the text refers to Eileen Egan, who
travelled and served with Mother Teresa for over thirty years.

dressed in similar garb who were ladling out a sort of gruel from steaming vats. Then she spoke directly to me: 'They like the rice,' said Mother Teresa. I knew that we had supplied the rice, parboiled wheat and soy that was now being poured into all kinds of receptacles, including brass pots. 'There must be over a thousand people here in Sealdah – and another 10,000 in the area,' she added, referring to the latest refugees from across the border of nearby Pakistan. Over a million destitute refugees had already cascaded into Calcutta since the subcontinent had been partitioned into India and Pakistan in 1947.

Through the experience with Catholic Relief Services, the overseas aid arm of the American Catholic community, I had become intimately acquainted with the face of human suffering and massive human pain. I had seen Europeans digging out of huge heaps of war ruins, and mourning those who had perished in them. I had worked in a camp for Polish survivors of deportation into Siberia. I knew the camps of the 'displaced persons'. Eastern Europeans dragooned into forced labour to serve the dreadful war machine. I had talked with a special group of displaced persons, the survivors of the Holocaust, and I had listened to their stories of unspeakable suffering. Now, in Asia, the face of suffering was intrusively and excruciatingly evident.

'After Sealdah, we will go to Shishu Bhavan, and then Nirmal Hriday,' said Mother Teresa. Shishu Bhavan was the Children's Home, whose children were the city's throwaways. Mother Teresa explained that some children had been found in rubbish heaps; some had been brought in when their mothers had died. 'We do our best to nurse them back to life,' Mother Teresa explained, cradling a baby with a wizened little face and tiny limbs. 'There is life in him,' she added. 'The life of Jesus is in him.'

Nirmal Hriday means 'Pure or Immaculate Heart'. Mother Teresa told me that Nirmal Hriday, also referred to as 'Kalighat', had been opened in 1952, when the City Fathers of Calcutta gave her the use of the former pilgrims' hostel. Kalighat took its name from the nearby shrine to Kali, and from *ghat*, which refers to the broad steps leading to a nearby river bank where the dead were carried for cremation. I entered it fearfully. This Home of the Dying in the pilgrims' hall near the Kali temple was often the final refuge for those found breathing their last on the streets and in the gutters of the anguished city.

I watched Mother Teresa as she sat on the parapet next to the low pallets of men, patting their heads or stroking their stick-like arms, murmuring to each one. Sometimes only the eyes seemed alive in men whose skin was drawn so tightly that the skull seemed struggling to burst through. Some were even smiling, as though amazed to be alive. It was the same in the women's hall. Seeing me, they held out their wasted hands, searching for human consolation. I turned away in fear and shame. I wondered how she could face, day after day, caring for those who were brought in covered with the filth and spittle of the gutter.

Mother Teresa explained that her work and the work of the Sisters called for them to see Jesus in everyone, including the men and women dying in the gutter. She said:

They are Jesus. Everyone is Jesus in a distressing disguise.

This overpowering concept is what I carried away from my first of many visits to Calcutta and my first of many encounters and travels with Mother Teresa.

From Calcutta With Love

❧

In the earlier days of Mother Teresa's ministry there were those who had wondered about her calling to the streets of Calcutta, as they watched her don the garb of the poorest woman, living out her 'call within a call'.

> In the choice of work, there was neither planning nor preconceived ideas. We started our work as the suffering of the people called us. God showed us what to do.

Soon after the founding of the Society in 1950, young women began to fill the novitiate training centre at the Mother House in Calcutta. Teams of five or six were soon on their way all over India. Additional teams of Sisters founded slum schools, conducted Mother and Child clinics, and went by ambulance to clusters of leper patients in and around Calcutta. Eventually, sixty centres brought loving care to the mothers and children of every slum in Calcutta.

By 1965, the Missionaries of Charity were recognized as an international Society by the Church. Now they were a group that could go wherever Church authorities and local officials invited them. The only provision, according to the rule of the Society, was that the work should be 'right on the ground', and serve the 'poorest of the poor'. Soon, the Missionaries of Charity were in demand around the world. Mother Teresa responded by sending teams of Sisters to Harlem and the South Bronx in New York City; to poor areas of Rome; to cities in Africa, the Caribbean and Latin America; and to the aboriginal peoples of Australia.

The work of Mother Teresa and the Missionaries of Charity first became known to the public through the book *Something Beautiful for God* by Malcolm Muggeridge. It was published in 1971 and was translated into many languages. Later, a documentary film *Mother Teresa*, made by Ann and Jeanette Petrie, brought the drama of the works of mercy to countless people through television showings and videotapes.

Young women, fired by the blazing witness of the Missionaries of Charity, poured into the training centres that were set up in various parts of the world. In addition to the first novitiate in Calcutta, later novitiates were opened in the Philippines, in Europe, in Africa, and in the United States. As the work developed, over 500 small teams of Sisters brought works of mercy into some 105 countries and areas of the world.

In 1986 Pope John Paul II came to the Home for Dying in Calcutta, to comfort those whom Mother Teresa called 'her treasures'. She called that day 'the happiest day of my life'. The visit of the Holy Father to her most dramatic work of love validated her whole life's work of serving Jesus in 'his most distressing disguise'.

From 1988 onward, Mother Teresa took Sisters to Poland, Eastern Europe, and the former Soviet Union. In 1990 they began to work in Siberia, and in 1991 in Albania.

On 2 June 1993 Mother Teresa was made a Freeman of the city of Dublin. She was the first nun to receive the honour. Spiritual leaders of many denominations joined with Irish government officials for the ceremony. On that day, this capital city put aside its other business in order to honour the woman who had come there sixty-five years before to begin her life as a religious sister in the Mother House of the Sisters of Loreto. From Dublin she had gone out to form a new religious family that spanned the globe.

The Mystery of Suffering

If one were to ask what is the most enduring challenge of people of faith, many would answer in one word: suffering. Sometimes suffering, especially the suffering of the innocent and the just, is seen as an evil, presenting an unfathomable mystery. In the secret places of the heart, it is sometimes harder to bear the knowledge that God allows his own children to suffer such misery – without his direct intervention – than to endure physical pain. Where is God while his children destroy each other? Where is the justice of God when children suffer and die in the prime of life? Does God cause suffering?

Pope John Paul II, in his February 1984 Apostolic Letter, *The Christian Meaning of Human Suffering*, states: 'At one and the same time Christ has taught man to do good by his suffering and to do good to those who suffer. In this double aspect, he has completely revealed the meaning of suffering.' In a special way, Mother Teresa illustrates the living out of this double aspect. A symbol of hope in the midst of almost overpowering darkness and poverty, Mother Teresa teaches that suffering can be turned to good to produce true joy in the heart of a believer.

When Mother Teresa visited former President Ronald Reagan at the White House shortly after an assassin's bullet nearly ended his life, she pointed out to the President the good that could come even out of his brush with death:

> You have suffered the passion of the cross. There is a purpose in this. Because of your suffering and pain, you will now understand the suffering and pain of the world.

With these words Mother Teresa would encourage anyone, even the poorest among us, struck down by an unexpected attack or by an illness. Whereas suffering can embitter a person, hardening the heart against those who have inflicted the suffering, Mother Teresa reminds us that suffering can also serve to enlarge the heart of the afflicted one, enabling him or her to experience compassion for the sufferings of others.

Compassion, Mother Teresa's life tells us, always finds its fullest expression in deeds, in the works of mercy performed sacrificially. Indeed, her life is a profound witness to the manner in which suffering ultimately works for the good of the human family. For Mother Teresa, compassion is essential to any work done in the name of Jesus. Compassion opens the heart of persons to the pain of others and moves them to works of mercy. As she pointed out in the Home for the Dying, however, her motivation is deeper than natural compassion.

Again, in the words of Pope John Paul II: 'The world of human suffering unceasingly calls for, so to speak, another world, the world of human love, and in a certain sense man owes to human suffering that unselfish love which stirs in his heart and actions' (*The Christian Meaning of Human Suffering*). Mother Teresa and the Missionaries of Charity, face to face with hopelessness, misery and death, give breathtaking witness to the world of human love, and amazingly, they give it with joy. To her Sisters Mother Teresa wrote:

> In the slums we are the light of God's kindness to the poor. To the children, to all who suffer and are lonely, give always a happy smile. Give them not only your care but also your heart.

How is it possible to emerge from such human squalor with

such a message of joy? That is Mother Teresa's gift. To her, the pain and agony she relieves are that of the Saviour himself. Therefore each person she serves has an inviolable dignity and sacredness.

We read in the New Testament accounts of Jesus' sufferings. How many of us would long to have been present when Jesus was ill-treated and spat upon? Mother Teresa reminds us that we are not born too late to show our love to Jesus, to console him, to clothe him, to slake his thirst, to feed him in his hunger. This conviction, that meeting others' needs shows mercy to Jesus in his 'distressing disguise', can only be achieved by the inspiration of the Holy Spirit, which is nourished by prayer. By joining their poverty and privation with the sufferings of Jesus, Mother Teresa and the Sisters share in the joy of the redemption, the great drama of the saving of the world. Not only is their suffering turned into joy, but they bring joy into the lives of others.

To the Missionaries of Charity and to all who serve others, Mother Teresa says:

> Keep giving Jesus to your people not by words, but by your example, by your being in love with Jesus, by radiating his holiness and spreading his fragrance of love everywhere you go. Just keep the *joy* of Jesus as your strength. Be happy and at peace. Accept whatever he gives – and give whatever he takes with a big smile. You belong to him.

2
Doing the Work of Jesus:
The Missionaries of Charity

❧

> When a woman is in labour she is sad that her time has
> come. When she has borne her child, she no longer
> remembers her pain for joy that a man has been born into
> the world. In the same way, you are sad for a time, but I
> shall see you again; then your hearts will rejoice with a
> joy no one can take from you.
>   *John 16:21–2*

Mother Teresa recognizes the importance of the contribution of social workers to the welfare of society. Yet she
makes an important distinction between the role of the
Missionaries of Charity and that of other people attending
to the physical needs of the poor:

> Jesus wanted to help by sharing our life, our loneliness,
> our agony, our death. Only by being one with us has he
> redeemed us. We are allowed to do the same; all the
> desolation of the poor people, not only their material
> poverty, but their spiritual destitution, must be redeemed,
> and we must share it, for only by being one with them can
> we redeem them, that is, by bringing God into their lives
> and bringing them to God.

The Sisters are asked to follow joyfully a path that contra-
dicts the values of a culture that honours, even glorifies,

ease and pleasure. They are to accept willingly whatever difficulty or suffering that may come to them from their closeness to the poor. Only the conviction that Jesus is in every poor or afflicted person could make their way of life possible, as Mother Teresa asserts:

> Without our suffering, our work would be just social work – it would not be the work of Jesus Christ, not part of the redemption.

When the young women in blue-bordered white saris came to New York City in 1981 they were seen as social workers. Mother Teresa, on a morning television programme, was described simply as a 'humanitarian'; her motivation was not relevant to their interview. By then, the Missionaries of Charity had become an international community. The faces framed by the wrap-around headcovering were all different, representing just about every nation under heaven – yet all with the same spirit.

Public wonderment still greets the Sisters today. With their choice of serving 'the poorest of the poor' comes poverty, separation from all the goods of consumerism. With their choice comes the renunciation of marriage and children. With their choice comes a life of obedience and a rigid schedule that starts with rising at five o' clock in the morning.

When I asked a young Englishwoman working in the South Bronx how she had come to join Mother Teresa's Society, she replied, 'I had what a lot of young women would want. I had a fine job as a literary agent – interesting work, meeting a variety of people. I had my own flat, a car, yet my life lacked meaning. The deeper meaning I found when I came to know the Missionaries of Charity.' By alleviating human need in the name of the Lord, she had found joy and peace of mind, and a life of meaning.

The Fourth Vow

❧

As with other religious orders, the Missionaries of Charity make three promises or vows: vows of poverty, chastity and obedience. In addition, the Missionaries of Charity take a special fourth vow, that of 'whole-hearted and free service to the poorest of the poor'. They will never graduate from their place on the lowest rung with God's children. If the poor they serve rise out of poverty, the Sisters move down, finding poorer people to serve – those who have fallen through the cracks of whatever social support system exists. The Sisters seek out those who are shunned and abandoned, the 'throw-away people' of the societies in which they live and minister.

All Missionaries of Charity, already trained in the spirit of the work, carry with them a copy of their rule. Those of us who have seen young Sisters in Calcutta's Home for the Dying, cleaning the spittle and filth from men and women from the gutter, know how their rule is put into practice. In other parts of the world, the Sisters choose to live near the garbage dumps of great cities like Mexico City or Cairo, so as to serve the garbage pickers. Their motivation could only come from seeing service to these impoverished men, women and children as a response to the call of Christ.

Mother Teresa assigns the highest dignity to those who are deprived and feel themselves the least members of society. She writes in the Constitution of the Missionaries of Charity:

> We need to be pure of heart to see Jesus in the person of the poor. Therefore, the more repugnant the work, or the more disfigured or deformed the image of God in the person, the greater will be our faith and devotion in seeing

the face of Jesus, and lovingly minister to him in the distressing disguise.

The Constitution further guides the Sisters with words that bind them equally to the poorest of the poor and to each other:

> Our response to the call of Christ is our fourth vow by which we bind ourselves to give whole-hearted and free service to the poorest of the poor according to obedience and so to ceaselessly quench the thirst of Jesus.

Three words of this vow have special significance to the Sisters: *whole-hearted, free* and *service*.

Whole-hearted means:

- with hearts burning with zeal and love for souls
- with single-minded devotion, wholly rooted in our deep union with God in prayer and fraternal love
- we give them not only our hands to serve, but our hearts also, to love with kindness and humility
- entirely at the disposal of the poor
- hard labour without counting the cost.

Free means:

- joyfully and with eagerness
- fearlessly and openly
- freely giving what we have freely received
- without accepting any return in cash or kind
- without seeking any reward or gratitude.

Service means:

- an unceasing and whole-hearted labour in making ourselves available to Jesus so that he may live, in and through us, his life of infinitely tender, compassionate and merciful love for the spiritually and materially poorest of the poor

- immediate and effective service to the poorest of the poor, as long as they have no one to help them, by:
  - feeding the hungry; not only with food, but also with the Word of God
  - giving drink to the thirsty; not only for water, but for knowledge, peace, truth, justice and love
  - clothing the naked; not only with clothes, but also with human dignity
  - giving shelter to the homeless; not only a shelter made of bricks, but a heart that understands, that covers, that loves
  - nursing the sick and dying; not only of the body but also of mind and spirit.

The Brothers of Charity

❧

This same spirit of service is seen in the Missionary Brothers of Charity, founded in 1963, thirteen years after Mother Teresa's founding of the Missionaries of Charity. The Brothers followed the Sisters in taking the fourth vow of 'whole-hearted and free service to the poorest of the poor', and in going to society's 'throw-aways'. One of their works was to open a shelter for Calcutta's street boys.

The head of the Missionary Brothers of Charity is called the 'General Servant'. This first General Servant, Brother Andrew, who was released by the Society of Jesus for this task, describes the service of the Brothers: 'The joys of work with the suffering poor are many and deep. There is the joy of seeing people relieved of at least a little of their suffering, of the sick cured, of families finding employment for a bread-winner, of children of the streets finding a home . . . overcoming difficulties.'

Brother Andrew goes on to tell of a homeless five-year-old boy who was found on a railway station platform beside his dead mother and dying father. The boy and his father were taken to the shelter, where the man died a few days later. Instead of giving up after the deaths of his parents, recalls Brother Andrew, the boy, who had only one leg, seemed to come to life and began to laugh and play with his new little brothers at the shelter, who had been similarly touched with love.

'There is great joy in seeing a little one-legged boy from the railway station playing happily in the room with me,' smiles Brother Andrew. 'Now he finds a home, food and a little love. Such sights and experiences are a great encouragement and happiness. I think that the faith and love of those from afar who share in the work is much greater, for they do not have the consolation of seeing the light in young eyes, or hearing the laughter and singing.'

The Love of a Parent

❦

I was wondering how I could explain to myself the tenderness of the Sisters in their lowly work as I watched a Sister console a dying mother with AIDS in 'The Gift of Love', the AIDS hospice in Washington, DC. I was reminded of passages in the Book of John where Jesus compares the suffering of his followers with childbirth. A mother forgets her suffering with which that child entered the world, and simply loves her baby. She doesn't tally up the loss of sleep, the constant feeding and washing, and the special care the child may need when sickness strikes. Love for her child motivates everything she does.

A mother's love becomes even more remarkable in the most difficult situations. Because she is the mother, her love supersedes natural affection for the attractive. She works even harder to tenderly serve the child who is afflicted with the grossest deformities, the child who may never have the full use of arms, legs or mental faculties. Her love is inextinguishable.

Mother Teresa tells the story of this kind of love, in this case a father's love for a child adopted from the Children's Home, the Shishu Bhavan, in Calcutta. Mother Teresa recalls:

> One of the abandoned children we had in our Shishu Bhavan I gave to a very high-class and rich family. After a few months I heard that the child had become very sick and completely disabled. So I went to that family and said, 'Give me back the child and I will give you a healthy child.' The father looked at me and said, 'Take my life first, then take the child.' He loved the child from his heart.
>
> In Calcutta, every night we send word to all the clinics, to all the police stations, to all the hospitals, 'Please do not destroy any children; we will take them all.' So our house is always full of children. There is a joke in Calcutta: 'Mother Teresa is always talking about family planning and abortion, but every day she has more and more children.'

On another occasion, Mother Teresa spoke of the tenderness she found in God the Father, depicted in Isaiah:

> I have called you by name; you are mine.
> When you pass through the water,
> I will be with you;
> in the rivers you shall not drown.
> When you walk through fire,

you shall not be burned;
the flames shall not consume you.
Isaiah 43: 1–2

See, upon the palms of my hands I
have written your name.
Isaiah 49: 16

When Mother Teresa visited Cuba, Premier Castro treated
her and her companions with respect as they discussed the
work of the Missionaries of Charity around the world. But
when Mother Teresa offered to bring the Sisters to Cuba to
serve the poor, Premier Castro declined her offer with
thanks, explaining that, in Cuba, the Government provided
for the people, giving them what they needed. Mother
Teresa did not argue with the Head of State. She said
simply, 'But the Government cannot give love.'

As it turned out, not long afterwards several teams of
Sisters were in fact invited to come to the island nation.
Cuba's shaky economy had depended for many years on
financial support from the Soviet Union but this aid was
discontinued when the Cold War ended. Arriving in Cuba,
the Sisters found much suffering as a result of this massive
political shift. They were able to open two houses to care,
with the love of Jesus, for members of the poorest families
who were terminally ill.

Simplicity of Faith
❧

Wherever they are, the Missionaries of Charity start the
day's work with the same prayer from their community
prayer book. From Novosibirsk to Papua New Guinea; from
Bucharest to Hong Kong; from Madras to Bourke, Australia,

they ask for strength in lifting up the burden of suffering. This they consider their privilege. This is their joy.

> Dear Lord, the Great Healer, I kneel before you, since every perfect gift must come from you. I pray, give skill to my hands, clear vision to my mind, kindness and meekness to my heart. Give me singleness of purpose, strength to lift up a part of the burden of my suffering fellow men, and a realization of the privilege that is mine. Take from my heart all guile and worldliness, that with the simple faith of a child, I may rely on you. Amen.

In reciting the prayer, each Sister reiterates her total dependence on God the Father. Besides praying for a pure and eager heart and strong arms, the Sisters rely entirely on God's provision for the material needs of the day. The Missionaries of Charity in each house use their faith as a kind of heavenly currency to provide for the expenses of serving the poor.

Mother Teresa herself invariably stresses this dependence. I think back to the steaming vats of food in the courtyard and the families who were kept alive by our gifts of regular food. I recall her spirited sharing:

> We have to pull out the wonderful things that are happening in the world. Now we feed more than 9,000 people in Shishu Bhavan every day.

One day, Mother Teresa beckoned us to stand in front of the world map with its little markers all over India, Asia, Australia, the Middle East, Africa, Latin America and North America. 'All those houses,' she said. 'Two hundred and fifty-seven, I think. A hundred and twenty in India.' Mother Teresa traced the outline of China until her finger found Beijing. 'That is where we must go.' Continuing to gaze at the map, she said:

Look what God is doing with nothing. People must believe that it is all his, all his. We must allow God to use us, without adding or subtracting anything.

Her earlier statement came back to me:

I am more convinced of the work being his than I am convinced that I am really alive.

3
A Cheerful Heart:
Renouncing All for Christ

❦

As we have shared much in the suffering of Christ, so through Christ do we share abundantly in his consolation. If we are afflicted it is for your encouragement and salvation, and when we are consoled it is for your consolation, so that you may endure patiently the same suffering we endure. Our hope for you is firm because we know that just as you share in the sufferings, so you will share in the consolation.

2 Corinthians 1:5–7

In *Something Beautiful for God*, Malcolm Muggeridge remarked:

Spending a few days with you, I have been immensely struck by the joyfulness of these Sisters who do what an outsider might think to be almost impossibly difficult and painful tasks.

Mother Teresa explained: 'That's the spirit of our Society, that total surrender, loving trust and cheerfulness. We must be able to radiate the joy of Christ, express it in our actions. If our actions are just useful actions that give no joy to the people, our poor people would never be able to rise up to the call which we want them to hear, the call to come closer to God. We want to make them feel that they are loved. If we went to them with a sad face, we would only make them much more depressed.'

Return to the Home for the Dying

❧

In Calcutta, I myself saw how the Missionaries of Charity start the day with joy, coming as they do from Mass, from receiving the Communion of the Bread of Life and the Saving Cup.

This time when I went in the van to Kalighat, the Home for the Dying, I discovered I was no longer afraid; I had lost the trepidation I felt the first time I'd crossed the threshold. I was no longer a stranger here. In addition, I had taken the precautions my doctors had ordered, and my shameful memory of turning away from the dying on my earlier visit was lessened by my sense of personal contribution to the work in the Sisters' many outposts.

Catholic Relief Services had been making regular shipments of food and medicaments from Food for Peace stocks, and these had to be warehoused and marked for distribution to Mother Teresa's centres in Calcutta, in Krishnagar and other parts of Bengal, as well as Bihar and Orissa. We needed a fuller port staff and more administrative staff in Calcutta, and I had determined that finding these workers would be my special task. In time I had become acquainted with the port area where an incredible array of relief goods was unloaded. Before long the staff of Catholic Relief Services was increased in size, which in turn allowed the feeding programme and other relief programmes to expand. It was exciting to see the famished being fed and countless lives being saved.

Charubala was an older woman I came to know at the Home for the Dying. She was truly the least of all. She could not walk, but could sit up on her pallet to eat her meals. Her grey hair was cropped close to her head, a sign that she was a widow. She had been an object of pity and disdain in her village, relegated to a life of near-slavery by her widowhood. This was despite the fact that her marriage, arranged for her when she was a small child, had never been consummated: the man to whom she had been promised had died before she was old enough to marry.

In Hindu society a woman's status and protection both come from her husband. Therefore, the death of her husband is the worst fate that can befall a woman. The ancient custom of *suttee*, by which a woman threw herself on her husband's funeral pyre to be consumed with him, indicated the hopelessness of the Hindu widow's plight. The practice of *suttee* had been done away with by British rule, but this did not address the cultural attitude behind the custom. For this reason, Charubala's story was not unique. Widows were still among the most impoverished of that society, with no one to look after them. When she had become disabled, Charubala had been cast out into the street. But she had been found and transported by the Sisters to the Home for the Dying.

We regularly went from pallet to pallet. There were greetings and chats in Hindi and Bengali, and in English for the few Anglo-Indians. I saw how Charubala's great brown eyes shone as Mother Teresa or a Sister came near her. When they put a caressing hand on Charubula's shorn head, she responded with intense joy. It was overpowering. Sometimes, she even burst into a Bengali song. I found myself included in her grateful response. Over and over again, I marvelled at the contented peace of these men and women from whom everything had been taken. I marvelled much more at the joy that was returned by them to their caretakers.

As time went on, I began to look forward to going to Kalighat. I knew many of the men and women, and they knew me. They appreciated my few words of Bengali, and even in their pain and weakness would hold out almost fleshless hands for me to hold and caress.

We took special care of those newly brought in from the street, that they would not over-eat after having hungered for so long. The effort was to make them feel loved and cared for. One time, I was able to help carry an aged and famished woman into the Home for the Dying. Her eyes were at first fearful, then tranquil as I fed her, spoonful by spoonful, her first meal. As I cradled her head to support her and prevent her from choking, I realized that the woman needed this gesture of tenderness almost as much as the food itself.

The Gift of Love

❦

'This is perfect joy – to share in the sufferings of the world as Christ did,' said St Francis of Assisi. The people who listened to St Francis in his day found it hard to consent to this response to Jesus. So does our world today, when the words come from the mouth of Mother Teresa. And yet many people took the *poverello*, the 'little poor man', at his word and chose to follow St Francis in the vowed life. Countless men and women then and now find that his word and his life resonate in the deepest recesses of their hearts. St Francis and Mother Teresa strike a universal chord that asserts a mysterious affinity between suffering and joy.

Mother Teresa prays:

Lord, help us to see, in your crucifixion and resurrection, an example of how to endure and seemingly to die, in the agony and conflict of daily life, so that we may live more fully and more creatively. . . . Enable us to go through [trials] patiently and bravely, trusting that you will support us; for it is only by dying with you that we can rise with you. Amen.

After returning from her visit to prisoners with AIDS in a jail near New York City, Mother Teresa commented that she had learned something from the people who suffer from AIDS. She had learned in a new way the need for greater compassion, the need for a renewed work of the tender love we all have inside, whether we are sick or healthy. She said:

God is giving us something so that we can show that tender love, that concern. This sickness has come to teach us something, to open our eyes to the need of the tender love that we all have and that has been forgotten, been pushed out. I remember when those people with AIDS were in jail and we had to sit in that jail, one said, 'I don't want to die here, I don't want to die in jail.' And then, thank God, we prayed and prayed to Our Lady, and then we called the governor and the mayor. A big miracle, I believe, happened. Within a few hours the men were released from prison.

We call our home in Washington, DC, 'The Gift of Love'. One of the AIDS patients had to leave the home to go to the hospital. When I visited him, he said to me, 'Mother Teresa, you are my friend. I want to talk to you alone.'

What did he say after twenty-five years of being away from God? 'When I get the terrible pain in my head, I share it with Jesus and suffer as he did when he was crowned with thorns. When I get the terrible pain in my back, I share it with him when he was scourged at the pillar, and when I get the pain in my hands and feet, I share it with him when he was nailed to the cross. I ask you to take me home. I want to die with you.'

I got permission and took him to our home, The Gift of

Love, and took him into the chapel. I never heard anyone talk to Jesus like this man talked to him, so tenderly, so full of love. Three days later he died.

The Joy of Renunciation

❦

Besides the young women who specifically choose to be 'part of the redemption' as vowed Missionaries of Charity, there are people around the world of all faiths who respond to Mother Teresa's way of life. This way of life is an enigma to non-Christians and worldly Christians alike. Such teachings point to the true source of joy. Mother Teresa's life shows to us the surprising places where joy can be found. As she writes in the Constitution:

> Renunciation is one of these places. Our life of penance will have that twofold quality of renunciation and joy, since it is deeply rooted in the mystery of the cross and resurrection.
>
> Joy is indeed the fruit of the Holy Spirit and a characteristic mark of the Kingdom of God, for God is joy. Christ wanted to share his joy with his apostles ' . . . that my joy may be in you, and that your joy may be full' (John 15:11 RSV). Joy is prayer, the sign of our generosity, selflessness, and close and continual union with God. Joy is love – a joyful heart is the normal result of a heart burning with love.

She has said to her Sisters:

> Keep the joy of loving God, loving Jesus in your heart, and share that joy with all you meet.

More and more every day I realized the importance of Mother Teresa's insistence that the Missionaries of Charity renounce gloominess along with everything else of the world. She requires that the Sisters be persons of cheerful disposition in their work with people who lead deprived lives. 'A joyful Sister', she says, 'is like the sunshine of God's love.'

'Joy', affirms the guideline of the Society, 'is a net of love by which we catch souls. A Sister filled with joy preaches without preaching. Joy is a need and a power for us even physically, for it makes us always ready to go about doing good. "The joy of the Lord is your strength." (Nehemiah 8:10 RSV)'

When one of the Sisters, wearing a mournful expression on her face, was getting ready to visit the poor, Mother Teresa said, 'Don't go. Go back to bed. We cannot meet the poor with sad faces.'

Even in small things, Mother Teresa does not tolerate long faces. Sitting with a group of volunteers who were dispirited after working with the needy, she joked about a traveller whose car broke down at the edge of a lonely, barren region. The only refuge was a monastery and the only means of transportation the monks could offer the man was a donkey. The traveller insisted on continuing his journey, so the monks explained that to manage the animal the man must remember to say 'Amen, Amen' when he wanted it to stop, but 'Thank God, thank God' when he wanted it to go forward.

All went well until a precipice yawned before him, and the nervous man remembered just in time to shout 'Amen, Amen'. The donkey stopped at the very edge of the precipice. Then the man said fervently, 'Thank God' – and over he went!

No one laughed harder than Mother Teresa herself, who is known for saying 'Thank God' on any and every occasion.

Other times, she recounts humorous incidents from her

daily rounds. For example, she recalls trying to help a woman on a street in London. The woman, who was very drunk, turned to her saying, 'Mother Teresa, didn't Jesus turn the water into wine for us to enjoy it?'

As St Francis said to his many followers, recorded in Thomas Celano's *St Francis of Assisi:* 'For what else are servants of God, but minstrels, whose work it is to lift up people's hearts and move them to spiritual gladness?'

The Joy of Service

❧

While Mother Teresa daily sees intense suffering, she sees joy as the heart of the Good News. In the Constitution of the Missionaries of Charity she writes:

> In Bethlehem, 'Joy' said the angel; Christ wanted to share his joy with his Apostles – 'that my joy may be with you'. *Joy* was the password of the first Christians; St Paul often repeats, 'Rejoice in the Lord always; again I say to you, rejoice.' In return for the great grace of baptism, the priest tells the newly baptized, 'May you serve the Church joyfully.'

Mother Teresa teaches that true joy must come from God. Teaching Sisters, for example, can become easily discouraged to the point of becoming 'burned out', especially after serving year after year in deprived neighbourhoods. Some wonder if they will ever succeed in reaching those they are serving. For these people, Mother Teresa says simply:

> God has not called us to be successful. He has called us to be faithful.

When a group of American teachers visited the work in

Calcutta, they asked for some advice to take home to their families. 'Smile at your wives,' Mother Teresa told them. 'Smile at your husbands.'

This advice seemed surprising, coming from an unmarried person. One of them asked, 'Are you married?'

'Yes,' she answered. 'And I find it very hard sometimes to smile at Jesus. He can be very demanding.'

In a talk to the teaching Sisters of the diocese of Scranton, Pennsylvania, Mother Teresa reminded them of the password of the ancestors of all Christians living in the world, those early Christians who so often faced brutal persecution:

> We are all working together, to bring Christ to the university or high school or right down to the slums. We are doing it together. The work that you do is his gift to you. Today, talking about the poor is in fashion. Knowing, loving and serving the poor is quite another matter. The little St Thérèse said, 'In the heart of the Church, I will be love.' That is what we are, love in the heart of the Church. The password of the early Christians was joy. Serve the Lord with joy.

4

The Suffering of the Innocent

❧

> . . . but we do see Jesus crowned with glory and honour
> because he suffered death: Jesus, who was made for a little
> while lower than the angels, that through God's gracious
> will he might taste death for the sake of all men.
> *Hebrews 2:9*

At a Eucharistic Congress, timed with the celebration of the
United States' Bicentennial in 1976, Mother Teresa was the
centre of attention. In a stadium filled with 8,000 people she
was called upon to speak on the role of women in the
Church. People ran after her, tugged at her sari, begged for
advice, or simply asked for her prayers. Those days of the
Congress were among the most trying days of her life. But
nothing could stop Mother Teresa from responding to the
call of people who needed her – for encouragement, for
consolation, or merely for a smile.

One of those was a mother who brought her tiny baby to
Mother Teresa. The mother explained that her ten-week-old
daughter had Down's Syndrome. She knew that the child
would need complete care for the rest of her life. The infant
also needed a heart operation. The mother kept repeating,
through falling tears, 'I want my child to live. Pray, Mother
Teresa, that my Shannon will live.'

Mother Teresa put her hand gently on the little head,
noting the pallid face and limp hands. She spoke gently for

some time to the mother. I heard her say, 'God has given you this great gift of life. If God wants you to give the gift back to him, give it willingly, with love.'

Later, the mother wrote to Mother Teresa to tell her that Shannon had died when she was seven months old. Mother Teresa's words had given her courage throughout her grieving. There was no trace of bitterness in the mother as she faced the great mystery of the suffering and death of an innocent child.

The Bread of Life and Co-Redemption

During the Eucharistic Congress her face was drawn with tiredness, yet Mother Teresa continued to respond to invitations to speak at a number of evening events. One of these was a Mass for young people. Large numbers of young people, prior to the youth meeting, had started a programme called SIGN, which stood for 'Service in God's Name'. In the spirit of Mother Teresa, the youth movement focused on works of mercy for the sick, the needy and the lonely around them.

In her address to the young people, Mother Teresa spoke sombrely of the Passion of Christ and of the stations of the cross by which he made his way to the place of crucifixion. As usual, she spoke without notes, making an unobtrusive sign of the cross with her thumb on her lips:

> Today, in young people of the world, Jesus lives his Passion in the suffering, in the hungry, in the handicapped young people – in that child who eats a piece of bread crumb by crumb, because when that piece of bread is finished, there will be no more and hunger will come again.

That is a station of the cross.

Are you there with that child?

And those thousands who die not only for a piece of bread, but for a little bit of love, of recognition. That is a station of the cross.

Are you there?

And young people, when they fall, as Jesus fell again and again for us, are we there as Simon Cyrene to pick them up, to pick up the cross?

The people in the parks, the alcoholics, the homeless, they are looking at you. Do not be those who look and do not see.

Look and see.

We can begin the stations of the cross step by step with joy. Jesus made himself the bread of life for us.

We have Jesus in the bread of life to give us the strength.

When the evening service was over, the young people, many deeply moved, came to thank her. They were grateful that she had talked of suffering and the cross, they explained, because of Eileen Potts. Mother Teresa showed surprise. She had never heard of Eileen Potts. The young people explained that it was Eileen Potts who had been the inspirer and leader of SIGN. She had herself arranged the evening for youth.

However Eileen had been unable to attend the youth Mass. Instead, she was in hospital. Eileen, at twenty years of age, had been struck down by leukaemia. Her friends were still shocked by the news, and asked Mother Teresa how she had known what to say to them that night. 'I don't know what made me talk like that,' said Mother Teresa to the grieving young people. 'It just came to me.'

Learning that Eileen was in a hospital near Philadelphia, Mother Teresa promised to visit her. On her return trip to

New York, Mother Teresa stopped at the Cherry Hill Hospital to sit with the young woman. The beautiful young girl was overwhelmed with joy to have a quiet time with Mother Teresa in her hospital room.

A photographer who had followed Mother Teresa's trip to the hospital took a photograph of the meeting which was to become a treasured memento for Eileen's parents and her friends. During a remission of the disease, Eileen returned to the University of Scranton to finish her studies, but death took her a few years later. She was an only child.

In her talk to the young people, Mother Teresa, in vivid examples, had pictured the suffering of the innocent, had described the need for responding to that suffering, and had pointed to the source of strength for that response. Through Mother Teresa's deep understanding of the power of innocent suffering, countless ordinary people, weighed down by loss and suffering, see their plight in a new and hopeful light. Like Shannon's mother, they realize that they are part of life's greatest drama.

Mother Teresa addressed herself to the suffering of the innocent in response to a query, 'How can a merciful God allow such suffering – children dying of hunger, people killed in earthquakes in Guatemala?' Mother Teresa spoke softly and meditatively:

> All that suffering – where would the world be without it?
> Innocent suffering is the same as the suffering of Jesus. He
> suffered for us, and all the innocent suffering is joined to
> his in the redemption. It is co-redemption. That is helping
> to save the world from worse things.

Mother Teresa was also invited to join a group of 300 theologians and leaders of various religious groups who had gathered to discuss the Eucharistic meal. When it was her turn to speak, Mother Teresa simply asked them to pray with her the prayer of Cardinal Newman: 'Lord help me to spread thy fragrance everywhere I go. Flood my soul with thy spirit and life.'

An earnest young woman, who was challenged by Mother Teresa's call to joyful service, queried her, 'But isn't it next to impossible to be a Christian in our society?' Mother Teresa replied:

> Yes. It is hard. And we cannot do it without help, without prayer. We have the body of Christ that gives us the strength we need. Jesus comes to us in the form of bread to show us his love for us, and he makes himself the hungry one so that we can feed him. He is always there, the hungry one, the homeless one, and the naked one.

In a similar vein, one Lutheran theologian remarked: 'The Eucharist loved is the Eucharist lived.'

Job and the Suffering Servant

❧

In Hebrew scriptures, suffering is linked to punishment for sin, both personal sin and the communal sin of the children of Israel. All sin is related to the original sin of disobedience of our first parents, the evil from which suffering and death ensue. Sin is followed by retribution, as presented in the calamities visited on Israel.

In the powerful drama of Job, however, another view of suffering shows itself. Job, the wealthy and pious man of Uz, is visited by a succession of evils. He is deprived of his children and stripped of all his possessions. He is left a derelict, scratching the sores that cover his body.

Job is resolute in maintaining his innocence. This is despite the insistence of his friends that he confess to the wrongdoing that he must have committed, evidenced by the disasters which had been visited on him. When his wife cries for Job to curse God and die, Job's response rings down the ages:

> Naked I came forth from my mother's womb,
> and naked I shall go back again.
> The Lord gave and the Lord has taken away;
> blessed be the name of the Lord.
> *Job 1:21*

Job's trust was not shaken by all that he had endured, and his fidelity was rewarded by the return of his prosperity. Job's story lifts suffering away from any necessary tie to punishment for wrongdoing.

One has only to look at the teaching of Jesus to see that there is not always a direct cause-and-effect relationship between sin and suffering; to understand that the innocent sometimes *do* suffer. In dealing with the man born blind, Jesus corrected his disciples who wanted to place blame for the affliction on the man himself, or on his parents. The man's blindness, removed by the miracle of Jesus, occurred '. . . to let God's works show forth in him' (John 9:3).

In Isaiah 53 we see the prefiguring of the sufferings of Christ, of innocent suffering willingly borne:

> Yet it was our infirmities that he bore,
> our sufferings that he endured,
> While we thought of him as stricken,
> as one smitten by God and afflicted.
> But he was pierced for our offences,
> crushed for our sins;
> Upon him was the chastisement that makes us whole,
> by his stripes we were healed.
> We had all gone astray like sheep,

each following his own way;
But the Lord laid upon him
the guilt of us all.
Though he was harshly treated, he submitted
and opened not his mouth;
Like a lamb led to the slaughter
or a sheep before the shearers,
he was silent and opened not his mouth.
  Isaiah 53:4-7

Jesus, the long-desired Messiah, broke into history to incarnate the prophecy of the suffering servant.

Love Until It Hurts

❧

In *The Christian Meaning of Human Suffering* Pope John Paul II asserts: 'The world of human suffering calls for another world: . . . the world of human love.' This world of human love shines clearly in the life of Mother Teresa as she ministers to the needs of all those around her. Often I have watched her, palms together, fingers touching slightly, bowing in a gesture of respect to remind herself of the presence of Christ in each person she encounters. She and her helpers endeavour to ease the pain, loneliness, deprivation and confusion of the people around them, but the magnitude of such human suffering does not overwhelm the Sisters' human love, which is suffused with divine love.

By allowing God's Spirit to empower them, she told a group of lay-workers, they could go out to minister joyfully to those they met, following the example of Jesus himself:

As St Paul has said, '. . . the life I live now is not my own;
Christ is living in me' (Galatians 2:20). Christ prays in me,

Christ works in me . . . Christ looks through my eyes, Christ
speaks through my words, Christ works with my hands.
Christ walks with my feet, Christ loves with my heart. As St
Paul's prayer was, nothing will be able to separate us from
the love of God, that comes to us in Christ Jesus, our Lord.

Romans 8:35-9

When Christ lives in us, we can love as Christ loves: a sacri-
ficial love. Mother Teresa's simple way of driving it home is
to say, 'Love until it hurts'.

Although she has seldom spoken of these experiences,
Mother Teresa's life has been marked by times when she
was called upon to do just that – to continue the work of
love while accepting hurt and personal grief without
complaint.

Joyful call, painful departure The first such experiences
occurred when she was parted from her widowed mother,
Drana Bojaxhiu. Mother Teresa was named Agnes Gonxha
Bojaxhiu and she was only eighteen years old when she left
a loving home in Skopje, in the former Yugoslavia. In those
days, the decision of a young Catholic to be a missionary in
a foreign land was a great sacrifice – it meant never seeing
one's family again. Besides her mother, young Agnes left
behind an older sister, Age, and an older brother, Lazar.

Her imagination had been fired by the stories sent back
by priests from her area who had been stationed in Bengal,
India. She wanted to join a mission there. Her time in
Skopje, where Roman Catholics were a minority among a
population of Orthodox Christians and Muslims, helped to
prepare the young woman for her work in faraway Bengal,
with its own religiously-divided society.

To India Accepted by the Sisters of Loreto (Institute of the

Blessed Virgin Mary), she lived briefly at their Mother House in Dublin. Then, with another young candidate she boarded a ship for the long voyage to India, in obedience to the clear call to serve God as a missionary. On 6 January 1929 (the Feast of the Epiphany) she arrived in Calcutta, a sprawling port city of the province of Bengal where wealth and culture flourished not far from utter destitution.

The Loreto Sisters from Ireland had been running schools for girls for nearly a century in the teeming metropolis. The city was a meeting place for great currents of thought, for poets and philosophers like Nobel Prize winner Rabindranath Tagore. At the same time it was a focal point for all the problems of Asia. As they opened schools for girls from more comfortable families, the Loreto Sisters also opened schools for the poor, and institutions for orphans.

The young nun from Skopje, now known as Sister Teresa, was so effective as a teaching Sister that she was named the headmistress of a school run by the Indian branch of Loreto, the Daughters of St Ann.

Independence With the Second World War, famine came to northeastern India. Rural people flocked from the reaches of Bengal to Calcutta's soup kitchens. Many perished: their bodies were burned in the crematory *ghats* next to the nearby Hooghly River.

The movement for Indian freedom from British rule had been building up during the years of the Second World War. Mohandas K. Gandhi, the Mahatma ('great soul'), had gathered a mighty following of *satyagrahis*, non-violent fighters for freedom. They were mostly Hindus, but many Muslims and members of the Christian minority participated as well. Gandhi had hoped for an undivided subcontinent, where the water and other resources could be shared. But Muslim leadership called for a separate Muslim state, and they won their case. When India became free of British rule on 15 August 1947, three states were formed: the primarily Hindu state of India, and the primarily Muslim states of East and West Pakistan.

Caught in the middle of the upheaval, displaced Muslim and Hindu families fled to their respective new homelands. Trains were crowded; oxcarts filled the roads; countless men, women and children died by the roadside. Since Bengal had nearly equal numbers of Hindus and Muslims, the travail was even more intense in the newly-partitioned region than elsewhere. In the capital city of Calcutta, communal violence between the Hindu and Muslim communities had often darkened the streets with blood. By far the worst riot in Calcutta's history erupted on 16 August 1946, the 'Day of Great Killing', during which at least 5,000 people died.

'Call within a call' About a month after that riot, on 10 September 1946, Sister Teresa experienced a second call, a 'call within a call', to work on the recently blood-spattered streets that now thronged with the homeless. God's voice in her spirit seemed clearly audible above the noises of the train compartment in which she was travelling to Darjeeling.

> It was on that train that I heard the call to give up all and follow him into the slum – to serve him in the poorest of the poor.

Years later Mother Teresa explained to her Sisters:

> When there is a call within a call, there is only one thing to do, to say 'yes' to Jesus. That's all. If we belong to him, he must be able to use us without consulting us . . . I had only to say a simple 'yes'.

But to leave the community of Loreto was a difficult wrench

of Sister Teresa's heart, equal to the parting from her own family. Replacing the voluminous floor-length habit with the rough sari of the poor, she walked out into the streets on sandalled feet.

Sister Teresa knew she belonged there, but she did not know to what work God would lead her. She went first to the school-less, near-naked children in shanties around a black sump-water pond called *Moti Jihl*, 'Pearl Lake'. She gathered the children around her and taught them the alphabet by drawing the letters in the dust with a stick.

She took her food with her, wrapped in paper. At midday, she knocked at the door of a convent to ask for water to take with her meal. She was given water, but was told to go to the back of the building. There she sat on the back stairs and ate her food like a street beggar. She was tempted to return to her dear community of Loreto, she recalls, but knew she had to persist in her new calling.

In her journal, she wrote:

> God wants me to be a lonely nun, laden with the poverty of the cross. Today I learned a good lesson. The poverty of the poor is so hard. When I was going and going till my legs and arms were paining, I was thinking how the poor have to suffer to get shelter.

The cool reception she received from many Calcuttans was not surprising. A lone European nun making her way to the alleyways of the poor in the garb of the poor aroused incredulity. Why would a gifted teacher frequent places where sewage ran in rivulets near the shanties? Even the missionary priests found it hard to understand. One of them, who later became a strong supporter, candidly admitted, 'We thought she was cracked.'

A family reunion   The years went by. She was joined in her street work by some of her former students. Sister Teresa became Mother Teresa and her group of workers became the Missionaries of Charity. In time the rigid rules of missionary life began to change, and it would have been possible for Mother Teresa to visit her mother and sister had they not lived in Albania, which had become a closed country. (They had moved to Tirana after the Second World War.) When I accompanied Mother Teresa to Rome in 1960, after her first visit to the United States, she was reunited with her brother Lazar, who had married an Italian woman, and also met her only niece, Agi. On this visit Mother Teresa was able to request an official recognition from Rome of the Missionaries of Charity.

Drana Bojaxhiu wrote that her one wish in life was to see her daughter again. However, Mother Teresa's mother and sister were not permitted to join the rest of their family in Rome. The Albanian Government, sealed off from the rest of Europe, would issue no visas. Mother Teresa appealed to Albanian officials in Rome to allow her mother and sister to join her and her brother, who was ready to share his home with them, but the officials remained firm.

Mother Teresa suffered as she learned that her mother's health was failing. She, whose heart was open to the world and who helped all within her reach, was unable to help the one who had given her life. Mother Teresa's uncomplaining, silent grief over this deprivation allowed her to more deeply identify with the suffering of the innocent, especially those in exile around the world who are separated, often for ever, from their own loved ones. More years passed, a decade; but nothing could move the Albanian officials. Finally news came of her mother's death, and then that of her sister.

She had hoped against hope to enter the officially atheist country of Albania, home place of her ancestors, and would say, 'It will happen in God's time.' When at last Albania – along with the Soviet Union and Eastern Europe – threw open its doors to the outside world, Mother Teresa was finally a most welcome guest. Undoubtedly, she was the most famous person of Albanian origin in the world.

Her visit, however, was bittersweet. A photograph taken in a Tirana cemetery in 1990 shows Mother Teresa kneeling at the grave of her mother and sister. The long-sought reunion could only occur at their burial place. By that time, her brother Lazar had also already died. At eighty years old, she was the only one left of the original family of five. Poignantly, Mother Teresa observed:

> We will meet in heaven. When I go home to God, for death is nothing else than going home to God, the bond of love will be unbroken for all eternity.

On native soil Mother Teresa's personal grief was intensified by the knowledge of the deprivations of the Albanian people and of the persecution visited on believers in her native country. When she was permitted to re-enter Albania she witnessed abysmal spiritual as well as material poverty. During its isolation from the rest of Europe, Albanian authorities had persecuted all religions without mercy; during that time at least 160 Catholic priests had been killed. Many innocent citizens continued to suffer from the persecution.

Bringing in teams of Missionaries of Charity, Mother Teresa began to set up homes for orphans and abandoned children. One building, given to her by the authorities, had once been a mosque, she discovered. The Sisters cleaned it, made it habitable for the children and then turned it over to Muslim authorities, believing that God is the ultimate provider for the innocents of the world, whether here or in eternity.

5
Simplicity
The Joy of Material and Spiritual Poverty

❦

Be compassionate, as your Father is compassionate. Do not judge, and you will not be judged. Do not condemn, and you will not be condemned. Pardon, and you shall be pardoned. Give, and it shall be given to you. Good measure pressed down, shaken together, running over, they will pour into the fold of your garment. For the measure you measure with will be measured back to you.

Luke 6:36-8

In their first days in Harlem, the Missionaries of Charity began their work slowly and simply by getting to know the people and their needs. Mother Teresa recalls:

When the Sisters came to Harlem, they began to visit the old people, the shut-ins who often lived alone. They would do the simple things, clean the rooms, wash the clothes.

Once they came to a door and no one answered. The woman [who lived inside] had been dead for five days and no one knew – except for the odour in the hallway. So many people are known only by the number on their door.

The worst disease today is not leprosy; it is being unwanted, being left out, being forgotten. The greatest scourge is to forget the next person, to be so suffocated with things that we have no time for the lonely Jesus – even a person in our own family who needs us.

Maybe if I had not picked up that one person dying on the street, I would not have picked up the thousands. We must think, '*ek*' [Bengali for 'one']. I think, *ek, ek*. One, one. That is the way to begin.

One of the difficulties with the English language is the confusion which can occur between some words, for example the word 'joy' with the word 'happiness'. Americans are aware that their Constitution contains the phrase 'the pursuit of happiness', and sometimes mistakenly assume that happiness always can be found, if it is pursued. Followers of Jesus realize, on the other hand, that happiness is a by-product, often unsought, of activities which may also have onerous aspects. A further confusion arises from the fact that happiness is often associated with pleasure. Certainly happiness and pleasure can be achieved, but they are short-lived – perhaps a moment, a day, a limited time. 'The joy of Christ risen', so central to Mother Teresa's teaching, is something that persists. This is the true joy that becomes a habit of the heart and persists through pain, suffering and the trials of life that are part of the human condition.

For most people, the very word 'poverty' suggests suffering: going without enjoyable comforts, pleasurable activities – the renunciation of the good things that society offers. Poverty, as lived in the vowed life and by many lay followers of Jesus, is rather the stripping of life to its essentials. As Mother Teresa warned her first recruits, 'You will have to renounce yourself. Your life will require constant self-denial.' Rather than suffering, this poverty brings with it a certain carefree joy, a dependence on God, a willingness to enjoy simple things. Such poverty, however, is not to be confused with destitution. Poverty, in this context, denotes having enough to meet one's basic needs.

The call to simplicity does indeed involve giving up the worldly things that distract us from our true calling, but it is a renunciation which does not despise the world and all it offers. Instead, it relinquishes even good things for a greater good. In the rule of the Missionaries of Charity, Mother Teresa writes:

> Let us not look for substitutes which restore to us the wealth we have given up. Christ, who emptied himself to work out our redemption, calls us: to listen to the voice of the poor, especially in our times. This, in turn, urges us to make reparation for the selfishness and greed of man, craving for earthly riches and power to the point of injustice to others.
>
> Our poverty should be true Gospel poverty: gentle, tender, glad and open-hearted, always ready to give an expression of love. *Poverty is love before it is renunciation.*

Poverty is so often seen solely as the lack of material things, of food, of clothing, of shelter. But it means more than that. It represents a more fundamental need that is often forgotten. Even in the poorest communities and the poorest countries, it is never enough to meet only the need for rice, for a garment, for some sort of shelter. Mother Teresa sees the larger reality:

> Today our poor of the world are looking up at you. Do you look back at them with compassion? Do you have compassion for the people who are hungry? They are hungry not only for bread and for rice, they are hungry to be recognized as human beings. They are hungry for you to know that they have their dignity, that they want to be treated as you are treated. They are hungry for love.

A daily prayer in the prayer book of the Missionaries of Charity comes from Pope Paul VI: 'Make us worthy, Lord, to

serve our fellow men [and women] throughout the world
who live and die in poverty and hunger. Give them through
our hands, this day their daily bread; and by our understanding love, give peace and joy.' This attitude of praying
to be worthy to serve God's poor shines through the work
of the Sisters.

In 1976, when she spoke to the Habitat Conference in
Vancouver, Canada, Mother Teresa began with this prayer.
As she spoke she noticed that a young woman with flying
fingers translated the words into sign language for the deaf
people in the audience. The hall was filled, but in the front
rows were special guests: long benches of the deaf and
dumb; of wheelchair-bound people with elephantine,
useless legs, or with necks held in metal braces. Moved by
the sight of these special guests, she started by declaring
her unity with them:

> We are all handicapped in one way or another. Sometimes
> it can be seen on the outside; sometimes it is on the inside.
> You and I come together not to plan any big thing, but to
> give until it hurts. The poor and the needy enrich us.

Mother Teresa did not leave the hall until she had shaken
the hand of each person in a wheelchair and of each mute
person on the long benches. A crush of participants was
waiting, each wanting a word with her or just to shake her
hand. But first she insisted on honouring the least in that
hall. Her prayer was to be worthy to serve them and to
bring them joy. That joy I saw in the glistening eyes of many
of the disabled.

A Double Poverty

❦

A double poverty is contained in the special witness of Mother Teresa and the Missionaries of Charity – the poverty of the giver, as well as the poverty of the receiver.

The Sisters live with utmost simplicity. When the order first started, each Sister owned two saris – one to wear and one to wash. In time, they could own three – one to wear, one to wash, and a third to mend. Their careful mending and reweaving of the rough cotton allows them to use one cheap sari for years. The Constitution of the Missionaries of Charity states:

> Desiring to share Christ's own poverty and that of the poor, we should be poor both in fact and in spirit – as individuals, as a community, and as a society. We shall have great simplicity of life and freedom from all unnecessary and artificial needs, retaining at the same time the spirit of total liberty in the use of created things when necessary.

Because the Sisters are often called upon to move from highly-developed societies to less-developed parts of the world, the call to poverty has a practical element as well: promoting unity of spirit among all the Missionaries of Charity and enabling them to move freely from one house to the next, wherever they are called to serve. In the documentary film *Mother Teresa* the Sisters in a newly-opened house in the United States are shown removing the serviceable rugs that kind volunteers had installed in their convent and throwing them out of the window. They knew that such luxurious floor covering would not be theirs in a house in another country or continent. Meanwhile, the Sisters politely explained to the donors that a more fitting use could be found for the carpeting. While this might

strike some as an extreme case of ingratitude, for the Sisters
it is a sign of solidarity. How could the Sisters in a house in
New York or in San Francisco enjoy soft rugs on the floors,
for example, when their Sisters in Papua New Guinea have
only hard cement?

Even when boiling August heat envelopes New York, the
Sisters have no electric fans to cool the convent quarters.
They would not have such fans in New Guinea, in Israel, in
Jordan, in Ethiopia, or in Haiti. Indeed, neither do the
Sisters have fans to counter the murderous heat of Calcutta.

The Sisters 'live lightly upon the earth', faithful to a
lifestyle that many might call ecologically sound. At the
same time, the voluntary poverty of the Sisters helps them
to identify with the involuntary poverty of the poor around
them.

Mother Teresa goes to great lengths – some people think
absurd lengths – to preserve this poverty. She relates:

> I remember when we first came to New York, and Cardinal
> Cooke wanted to give every Sister $500 every month. And I
> looked at him, I said, 'Cardinal, do you think God is going
> to be bankrupt in New York?' He looked at me. I believe he
> thought, 'Maybe she's a little bit off.' He has brought it up
> again, again, and again, and each time I answered the same
> way.

In Paris there was a similar experience. Mother Teresa
recounts:

> When our Sisters went to Paris to begin the work, the
> Church leaders explained about health insurance. They
> were going to have all the Sisters insured and they had the
> forms ready.
>
>   I said, 'No, that is not for us.' Everybody was shocked
> and tried to make me change my mind. But I asked them,

'Do the poor that we work with have health insurance?'

That settled it. If we live with the poor, we must share their poverty and depend on the providence of Almighty God for his help. That is our faith.

Mother Teresa follows many holy people from the past, and numbers of vowed and lay Catholics today, in a rock-like dependence on the providence of God. She told a group of volunteers:

We do not accept any government grants. We do not accept Church maintenance. We have no salaries, receive nothing for the work that we do. So we fully depend on divine providence. We deal with thousands and thousands of people, and there never has been a day when we have to say to somebody, 'Sorry, we don't have.'

We cook for about 9,000 people every day in Calcutta. One day the Sister came to me and said, 'Mother, there's absolutely nothing. We don't have anything at all.' I couldn't answer her.

About nine o'clock in the morning a large truck full of bread came to the door. The schools were closed that day. They dropped thousands of loaves inside our walls, and the people had nice bread for two days. How he gives, how he brings things. That is how we are able to care for thousands upon thousands of lepers.

I was not surprised when I heard about the truckload of bread. I did feel gratitude that our Lord keeps showing his daily care for all his children, and especially for the poor. Occasionally God's providential kindness takes forms which intensify our gratitude and reduce our anxiety about our own resources.

On another occasion, Mother Teresa pointed out:

Our dependence on divine providence is a firm and lively

faith that God can and will help us. That he can is evident, because he is almighty; that he will is certain because he promised it in so many passages of Holy Scripture and because he is infinitely faithful to all his promises.

Christ encourages us to have this confidence in whatever we ask in prayer, to believe that we have received it (Matthew 18:19). The apostle St Peter also commands us to throw all cares upon the Lord, who provides for us (1 Peter 5:7). And why should God not care for us, since he sent us his Son, and with him, all?

The generosity of the poor themselves is always a source of delight for Mother Teresa. One of her favourite stories, and thereby one of her frequently repeated examples, concerns a family of poor Hindus. She loves to narrate:

I had the most extraordinary experience with a Hindu family who had eight children. A gentleman came to our house and said, 'Mother Teresa, there is a family with eight children; they have not eaten for so long; do something.' So I took some rice and I went there immediately. And I saw the children – their eyes shining with hunger. I don't know if you have ever seen hunger. But I seen it very often. And the mother took the rice, divided and she went out.

When she came back, I asked her, 'Where did you go? What did you do?' She answered simply, 'They, the neighbours, are hungry also.' What struck me most was that she knew – and who are they? a Muslim family. I didn't bring more rice that evening because I wanted them to enjoy the joy of sharing.

Mother Teresa always follows this narration urging us to enlarge our hearts with self-forgetting generosity and a joyful trust in a loving providence.

Suffering in God's Love

❧

It was near Christmas and in one of the many slums (*bustees*) of Calcutta lived a cluster of leper families whose ramshackle huts huddle beside a pipal tree. To this desolate community the ambulance of the Missionaries of Charity came regularly, bringing a doctor-specialist and Sisters trained in anti-leprosy work. I went to distribute food, since supplying medicine without extra food would accomplish nothing. Mother Teresa later told us of talking with the lepers:

> I was talking to our lepers and telling them that the leprosy is a gift from God, that God can trust them so much that he gives them this terrible suffering. And one man, who was completely disfigured, started pulling at my sari. 'Repeat that,' he said. 'Repeat that this is God's love. Those who are suffering understand you when you talk like this, Mother Teresa.'

Wherever they go in the world, the Sisters carry out the guiding spirit of their Constitution:

> In fulfilment of our special mission in the Church, following the lowliness of Christ, we shall remain right on the ground, by living Christ's concern for the poorest and lowliest.

When they arrived in Lima, Peru, the Sisters sought out the lowliest inhabitants and gathered them into a large, empty convent. It was arranged Spanish-style, around a large square patio. The convent was known as *Hogar de la Paz*, the Home of Peace. When I visited the Home of Peace, the abandoned of every age and affliction were being cared for. Sister Pauline showed us the home and was especially happy that a practical vegetable garden was growing in the patio, alongside peach and lemon trees.

On one side, next to the kitchens and washrooms, were the children; on another side, sick and elderly women; and on a third side, destitute and homeless men. Standing on the fourth side of the rectangle was a large chapel which had once served the large community of Sisters as well as the surrounding district. The convent of the Missionaries of Charity, along with a second, much smaller chapel, occupied rooms on the second floor of the spacious building.

Mother Teresa walked about the dusty, unused larger chapel, surveying the cracks in the wall. It needed structural repairs before it could serve as a sanctuary for the Missionaries of Charity and for the crowded *bárriada*. It could accommodate at least 400 people.

We talked with the residents, some very old, some nearly blind, some hardly able to move because of arthritis. Mother Teresa was particularly pleased that the doorkeeper for the Sisters' compound was named Jesús. One of the other residents bore the name of Messias. He was an articulate young man with classic features who had been a newspaperman and writer. A wasting disease had attacked his muscles so that he could only move about in a wheelchair. Messias told me that once he had had so many friends he could not number them, but when he could no longer earn his living and was confined to his room, he could not count on them. They did not want to see his affliction and left him alone. He still had hopes he would improve, and that some of his friends would rescue him.

He asked me for some books so that he could become proficient in English. I found an English grammar and Spanish-English dictionary in downtown Lima. When I presented them to Messias, his incapacitated neighbour, Theophane, told me that he, too, wanted to study English. Messias offered to help him. This was not merely a meaningless gesture of empty willingness. A letter from Sister Pauline informed me that Messias continued to practise so that he could speak English quite well, and he did help Theophane to learn the language, too. Both, she wrote, had caught the spirit of the *Hogar*.

The Sisters in Lima soon learned from a small group of priests that they were not wanted because their work was 'only a work of today', instead of a work that struck at the fundamental societal injustices that caused poverty. The critics felt that feeding the hungry and sheltering the helpless were a waste of time. But the Sisters persevered in their back-breaking work and were soon helped by residents of Lima, who came forward to volunteer with them. Mother Teresa's view was in keeping with the aim to 'remain right on the ground'. She explained:

> For us it's not a waste of time or life to spend that time just feeding the person today. The work of tomorrow? There are many people who can do that, who can remove the works of injustice and so on. But for us that person needs a shelter now. I think our part is fulfilled there. And by doing our part many people are getting concerned to do the second part – to improve and to help the people, to remove that poverty and that hunger and that nakedness.

The Community of the Poor

❧

Evidence is all around us that poverty brings suffering, especially to those who are helpless to change their lot. The living example of Mother Teresa and the Missionaries of Charity is a powerful one in dramatizing the fact that the involuntary poverty of the afflicted and deprived may be healed by those who move toward a measure of voluntary poverty. Their example speaks to millions in the world who possess more than enough to satisfy their needs.

Many already share their time, treasure and talents with generosity. Many could decide to share even more by giving, to use Mother Teresa's words, 'until it hurts'. The small suffering involved in such giving would lessen the vast suffering of a world in need.

Dependence on the providence of God, of course, must never be used as an excuse to escape from personal responsibility. Extreme interpretations of these principles of faith, for example, might tempt the head of a household to take a passive attitude toward supplying the needs of his family. Those people St Paul clearly cautions: 'If anyone does not provide for his own relatives, and especially members of his immediate family, he has denied the faith; he is worse than an unbeliever.' (1 Timothy 5:8)

God calls us to active and joyful service, wherever we may be, accomplishing the work he has given us today. To share the lot of the poorest ones is the particular daily task of the Missionaries of Charity. Mother Teresa's identification with the poor is instilled in the Sisters. May her spirit give us courage to follow her example.

My true community is the poor – their security is my security, their health is my health. My home is among the poor, and not only the poor, but the poorest of them: the people no one will go near because they are filthy and suffering from contagious diseases, full of germs and vermin-infested; the people who can't go to church because they can't go out naked; the people who can no longer eat because they haven't the strength; the people who lie down in the street, knowing they are going to die, while others look away and pass them by; the people who no longer cry because their tears have run dry!

The Lord wants me exactly where I am – he will provide the answers.

6
The Joy of Teaching by Example
Living in Love and Making Peace

❧

A man who listens to God's word but does not put it into practice is like a man who looks into a mirror at the face he was born with; he looks at himself, then goes off and promptly forgets what he looks like. There is, on the other hand, the man who peers into freedom's ideal law and abides by it. He is no forgetful listener, but one who carries out the law in practice. Blest will this man be in whatever he does.

James 1:23-5

Mother Teresa tells her Sisters:

Keep giving Jesus to your people, not by words, but by your example, by your being in love with Jesus, by radiating his holiness, and by spreading his fragrance of love, wherever you go. Just keep the joy of Jesus as your strength. Be happy and at peace. Accept whatever he gives you, and give him whatever he takes from you. True holiness consists in doing God's will with a big smile.

The life and work of Mother Teresa would have been instructive of the Gospel of Jesus even if she had never spoken a word in public or if no word of hers had appeared in print. Her example, along with that of the Missionaries of Charity, teaches us as powerfully as the spoken word.

The words of Mother Teresa become powerful simply

because they are so completely reflected by her actions. Deed and word are one, inextricably intertwined. The actions of the Sisters produce stunning and often unexpected effects on people. Mother Teresa relates:

> A Hindu gentleman stood, unnoticed, behind a young Sister who was washing a man just brought into the Home for the Dying. After a time, the man came to me and he said, 'I came into this home empty, full of bitterness and hatred, godless. I am going out full of God. I saw the living love of God through the hands of that Sister, the way she was touching and caring for that man.'

He did not say another word and he left.

Face to Face with Sin

❦

The light of Christ shines most brilliantly in the places of greatest darkness. Some years after the end of the Second World War Mother Teresa and I visited the Dachau concentration camp near Munich, preserved as a memorial of hate and destruction. Over 2,500 Catholic priests, many of them Polish, were among the tens of thousands of human beings that are known to have perished in Dachau.

As Mother Teresa prayed on those bloodstained acres, her face clouded over with intense grief. At the end of a row of blockhouses was a round tower constructed of rough stones. Above the tower was a jagged crown of thorns, made of shining copper. It was the Chapel of the Agony of Christ, a reminder of all innocent suffering, dedicated to all who had died in the concentration camp. Mother Teresa said softly:

Colosseum. This stands for the Colosseum of our day. Then it was the pagans who threw innocent people to their death. It was not idolaters of those pagan gods who threw these lives away – and how many millions of them. We are getting worse, not better.

As we walked slowly out of Dachau she said, 'How could some human beings do these things to other human beings?' We were face to face with the mystery of sin, face to face with the senseless destruction of life. We saw what the human will is capable of when it exerts its freedom by turning from the law of God. We can choose to reject grace, becoming unspeakably cruel, destroying the children of God. In such actions, the sacredness of human life is negated. This time, it was expressed in the construction of death camps and the Holocaust of a people.

In Dachau, Mother Teresa saw that which was diametrically opposite to her life's mission. Devoted to the showing forth of the deepest affinity between the human and divine, she starts with her own relationship to Jesus:

> By blood and origin, I am all Albanian. My citizenship is Indian. As to my heart, I belong entirely to the heart of Jesus.

Jesus Living in Us

❧

Mother Teresa's identity with Jesus gives her the clean heart necessary to see Jesus in those from whom the world turns away. It gives her the power to see each human being, even those rotting with disease, as repositories of the divine.

God's Spirit, freely communicated to the human soul

through grace, is most fully communicated through the gift of Jesus himself. Those who would emulate Mother Teresa's conviction of belonging entirely to Jesus might be moved to follow her in her openness to the grace of God. Belonging entirely to Jesus and living a life of grace is not simply for those committed to the vowed life: it should be the aim of all followers of Jesus. It provides a focus for daily life and for carrying out Jesus' command to 'Love as I have loved you'. This is the redemptive life that led Jesus to Calvary. In all likelihood, it may lead his followers to self-denial and hardship.

The willing acceptance of innocent suffering, as Mother Teresa points out, is co-redemptive: joined with that of Jesus, it relieves the weight of sin on a fallen world. The sufferings of all the just and innocent are joined in this great mystery. Can any suffering be meaningless or lost, even the sufferings of those who do not understand why it is visited upon them, but who, like Job, refuse to curse God? Mother Teresa points out:

> Today the Passion of Christ is being relived in the lives of those who suffer. Suffering is not a punishment. God does not punish.

The experiences of Mother Teresa and the Missionaries of Charity may illumine some facets of the great mystery of suffering, and may help us in our lowest moments. Mother Teresa's example has brought light, hope and joy to countless people worldwide. Her life can encourage us in our daily struggles, helping us as we too console the inconsolable and feed the famished.

While Mother Teresa's example is a source of tremendous inspiration, it is also important to remember her limitations; she, too, is human, prone to human limitations. People sometimes comment, when called upon for a particularly generous gesture of love or forgiveness, 'I am no Mother Teresa'. In response, Patrick Jordan, editor of *Commonweal* magazine, once commented: 'While we may not be Mother Teresa, Mother Teresa is one of us, ennobling our condition, drawing our deepest aspirations into focus, and helping us to recognize God's active presence in the world.'

A frequent reminder from Mother Teresa is:

> What you do, I cannot do. What I do, you cannot do. But together, we can do something beautiful for God.

Living Out the Words

❦

On 25 April 1983, Mother Teresa was one of the speakers at an inter-religious gathering in London on peace and the needs of humankind, along with the Dalai Lama and other world figures.

For many years, the Missionaries of Charity maintained shelters for the homeless in some of London's most dismal streets. Mother Teresa went with the Sisters and volunteers to see the plight of those who had no shelter at all. Many homeless men and women swathed themselves in quilts and blankets and lay like mummies on park benches. Others, after wrapping themselves as warmly as they could, spent the nights in coffin-like containers fashioned from cardboard boxes.

When it came time for Mother Teresa to address the gathering, she did not talk in abstractions of the sufferings in far-off Calcutta. She talked about the concrete example of what she had just experienced in London. She brought into the hall the very presence of human beings, not too many minutes away, whose best shelter might only be cardboard coffins. When Prime Minister Margaret Thatcher met with Mother Teresa, she was given a description of those who had been failed even by the night shelter programmes of a great city. With Mother Teresa, the deed precedes the word in pointing to human misery.

Thanksgiving
❦

Calcutta had been a crucible of violence between Hindus and Muslims at the time of the partition of the subcontinent in 1947. But by 1975 it was a city of comparative peace. This was the year of the Silver Jubilee of the Missionaries of Charity who had been founded as an order on 7 October 1950. In addition to operating the Home for the Dying, they were conducting schools, leper stations, and Mother and Child clinics in sixty centres. Mother Teresa and the Sisters intended to share their own deep joy at having been privileged for twenty-five years to serve the poorest of the poor in this city.

At Mother Teresa's invitation, the two major religious factions – the Hindus and Muslims – joined in thanksgiving with the Sisters. They were delighted when 5,000 Muslims met them in the great 'lung' of Calcutta – the green stretches of the *maidan* ('park') where Calcuttans can breathe fresh air – to make their gratitude known. It was during Ramadan (the month of fasting for Muslims) and, respectful of Muslim custom, the Sisters met at a distance from the sea of white-garbed men.

The birthday of the 'Father of our country', as Mother Teresa calls Mahatma Gandhi, was also remembered during that week of thanksgiving. On 2 October, the Leprosy Rehabilitation Centre was dedicated as the *Gandhiji Prem Nivas Centre*, The Gandhi Centre of Love. Because the

Missionary Brothers of Charity had grown in numbers, the Centre was turned over to their care.

The example of Gandhi meant much to Mother Teresa and to large numbers of Indian Christians. He had urged Christians to *live* by the Sermon on the Mount, rather than only to *talk* about it. Gandhi's movement of 'truth-force' depended on the persuasive power of innocent suffering to cause self-rule to replace colonial shackles. He described the movement as 'the argument of suffering'. Mother Teresa and Gandhi agreed that the eventual achievement of peace – personal, communal and national peace – would be 'the certain result of suffering voluntarily undergone'.

At the celebration, the Jewish community of Calcutta expressed their joy through the rabbi of the synagogue, who prayed:

Almighty God, it is with a heart full of joy that we have assembled here to express our great joy and render thanksgiving on the occasion of the Silver Jubilee of the Society of the Missionaries of Charity, for their humanitarian and selfless work, and through them for the poor of the world.

'This is the day that the Lord hath made, we will be glad and rejoice therein.' And now the day Mother Teresa has hoped for has come . . . . We, the Jews of Calcutta, join in thanksgiving unto the Lord and pray that the Heavenly Father in his mercy preserves Mother Teresa and her band of workers, guard and deliver them from all trouble and sorrow. Hasten the days when the children of men understand that they have one Father, that one God created us all. Then shall the light of universal justice flood the world, and the knowledge of God cover the earth, as the waters cover the sea. Amen.

A Fragile Peace

❦

The peace did not last. In 1992 the long-simmering rivalry between the Muslim and Hindu communities in Calcutta erupted in violence when a Muslim mosque, built upon the birthplace of the Hindu god Rama, was destroyed by a group of Hindus. Calcutta exploded in waves of looting, burning and murder – not unlike the chain of events in 1947 that induced Gandhi to fast until the violence between the two communities subsided. One Sister wrote from Calcutta:

> Thousands lost their lives. Only army trucks helped calm the riots. We had to walk with raised hands for several days.
> Mother Teresa, as usual, braved everything and went by ambulance to all the hot spots where people needed rice, oil and bulgur wheat. She was asked by many groups to come and pray with them for peace.

At the same time, violence was rending apart her birthplace, the former Yugoslavia. Her family had been part of the Albanian community in the city of Skopje. Mother Teresa asked her sisters to pray incessantly for peace in India and in the world.

She stopped her work and concentrated on a letter to the press – an appeal for peace, asking all opponents to 'bring the joy of loving through the joy of sharing', and reminding them 'not to use religion to divide us'. Mother Teresa's peace message has meaning – not only for India, but for countless places in the world where violence destroys peoples' lives and livelihoods, and where religion and ethnic division are used to inflame the passions of destruction.

> My Brothers and Sisters in India and all over the world, we are all God's children, and we have been created for greater

things: to love and to be loved. God loves each one of us with an everlasting love – we are precious to him. Therefore, nothing should separate us. Religion is a gift of God and is meant to help us to be one heart full of love. God is our Father, and we are all his children – we are all brothers and sisters. Let there be no distinctions of race or colour or creed.

Let us not use religion to divide us. In all the holy books, we see how God calls us to love. Whatever we do to each other – we do to him because he has said, 'Whatever you do to the least of my brothers you do it for me.'

Works of love are works of peace – to love we must know one another. Today, if we have no peace, it is because we have forgotten that we are all God's children. That man, that woman, that child is my brother, my sister. If everyone could see the image of God in his neighbour, do you think we would still have such destruction and suffering?

Religion is meant to be a work of love. Therefore, it should not divide us. It should not destroy peace and unity. Let us use religion to become one heart full of love in the heart of God. For this we need to pray that we may fulfil God's purpose for us: to love and to be loved.

My brothers and sisters, let us ask God to fill us with the peace that only he can give. Peace to men of good will – who want peace, and are ready to sacrifice themselves to do good, to perform works of peace and love.

So please, please, I beg you in the name of God, stop bringing violence, destruction and death to each other, and especially in the poor who are always the first victims.

Let us remember that the FRUIT OF RELIGION is to bring the JOY OF LOVING through the JOY OF SHARING.

God bless you,
Mother Teresa, MC

In July 1992, Mother Teresa's peacemaking efforts were recognized by a United Nations agency. The Peace Education Prize of UNESCO (the United Nations Education, Scientific and Cultural Organization) was awarded to her. The citation said: 'The prize crowns a life entirely consecrated to the promotion of peace and to combating injustice.' With the prize went an award of $60,000 toward the continuance of her work.

Nobel Recognition

❦

The UNESCO prize was not the first time that Mother Teresa's empathy for the poor had received public recognition. Her awareness of the suffering of the poor, and the love that could relieve that suffering, were also central to Mother Teresa's address upon receiving the 1979 Nobel Peace Prize.

Her white cotton sari shone under the spotlight as her slightly stooped figure stood on the stage of the Aula Magna of the University of Oslo. Before she began her address, she asked everyone in the hall to join her in the prayer of St Francis, the poor man of Assisi (copies had been distributed before the ceremony).

Lord, make me an instrument of your peace;
Where there is hatred, let me sow love;
Where there is injury, pardon;
Where there is despair, hope . . .

intoned over 800 voices. Among the lifted voices were those of a king, a crown prince and his princess – as well as academics, diplomats, politicians, members of the armed forces in full uniform, and a large press corps.

Oh Divine Master, grant that I might seek
Not so much to be consoled, as to console;
To be understood, as to understand;
Not so much to be loved, as to love another.

For it is in giving, that we receive;
It is in pardoning, that we are pardoned;
It is in dying, that we are born to eternal life.

Of all the holy people in history, it is to Francis of Assisi that Mother Teresa is most often compared. His poverty, his compassion, and his dependence on the providence of God are hers. Her Franciscan gesture of refusing the customary Nobel Award banquet so that the money saved could go to the poor resulted in an additional gift of $6,000, to be added to the Nobel Prize fund.

Undoubtedly, Mother Teresa's address was the simplest of all those ever delivered at a Nobel Award ceremony:

The poor are wonderful people. One evening we went out and picked up four people from the street. One of them was in a most terrible condition. I told the Sisters: 'You take care of the other three. I will take care of this one that looks worse.' So I did for her all that my love can do. I put her in bed, and there was such a beautiful smile on her face. She took hold of my hand, as she said one word only, 'Thank You', and she died.

I could not help but examine my conscience before her, and I asked, 'What would I say if I was in her place?' And my answer was very simple. I would have tried to draw a little attention to myself. I would have said, 'I am hungry; I am dying; I am cold; I am in pain,' or something. She gave me much more – she gave me her grateful love. And she died with a smile on her face.

Like the man whom we picked up from the drain, half-eaten with worms; we brought him to the Home. 'I have lived like an animal in the street, but I am going to die like an angel, loved and cared for.'

And it was so wonderful to see the greatness of a man who could speak like that, who could die like that, without blaming anybody, without cursing anybody, without comparing anything. Like an angel – that is the greatness of our people.

And that is why we believe what Jesus has said, 'I was hungry, I was naked, I was homeless, I was unwanted, unloved, uncared for, and you did it to me.'

Mother Teresa often spoke of the abortions occurring around the world and she did so again on this occasion. She reminded her hearers of the sacredness of the child in the womb with the simple New Testament story: When Mary, awaiting the birth of Jesus, visited Elizabeth, who was to become the mother of John the Baptist, the unborn child in Elizabeth's womb leapt for joy.

He recognized the Prince of Peace, he recognized that Christ had come to bring the Good News for you and for me. And as if that was not enough – it was not enough to become man – Jesus died on the cross to show that greater love.

He died for you and for me, and for that leper, and for that person dying of hunger, and for that person lying in the street, not only of Calcutta, but of Africa and New York and London and Oslo. And he insisted that we love one another as he loves each of us. And we read in the gospel very clearly: 'Love as I have loved you' (John 13:34). We too must give to each other, until it hurts.

It is not enough to say 'I love God but I do not love my neighbour.' St John says that you are a liar if you say you love God and you don't love your neighbour. *How can you*

love God whom you do not see, if you do not love your
neighbour whom you do see, whom you touch, with whom
you live? And so, this is very important for us to realize that
love, to be true, has to hurt.

This is something that you and I can do – it is a gift of
God to be able to share our love with others . . . . Let us
keep that joy of loving Jesus in our hearts, and share that
joy with all we come in touch with. That radiating joy is
real, for we have no reason not to be happy, because we
have Christ with us. Christ in our hearts, Christ in the poor
that we meet, Christ in the smile that we give, and the smile
that we receive.

Choose the Way of Peace

❦

In July 1991, Mother Teresa was invited by a Community of
Reconciliation to Corymeela ('Hill of Harmony' in Gaelic) in
Northern Ireland. The Peace People community was
founded in 1981 in Belfast as an attempt to heal the tragic
wounds between the two major religious communities.
Mairaed Corrigan and Betty Williams received the Nobel
Peace Prize for their efforts to make peace an attainable
goal there. The work continues in Northern Ireland as the
Community of Peace People.

Mother Teresa found herself in a landscape of a special
kind of suffering – a suffering caused by ancient enmities.
This was the same kind of suffering she knew and experienced in Calcutta, with its repeated riots and acts of
violence committed by Hindus, Muslims and even British
soldiers. The hatred and distrust in both countries seemed
to be self-perpetuating. It was as if a great infected wound,

caused by events which happened before living memory, festered and caused new grief each year.

Mother Teresa's talk was held in a large tent overlooking the sea, fifty miles north of Belfast. There Mother Teresa came into contact with people from both sides of the conflict in Northern Ireland. She found herself in the midst of people who were mourning the men, women and children who had been cut down in the years of sporadic violence. Some had family members in prison. She talked in Gospel terms of love and forgiveness.

After Mother Teresa's talk, Mairaed Corrigan noted the importance of aligning word and deed. She commented: 'Mother Teresa said nothing I had not heard before or read from the gospels, but she brings the whole thing to life. I think what makes Mother Teresa's words so effective is that she is living out her words in her life.'

Ciaran McKeown, who had framed the Declaration of the Peace People, was also at Mother Teresa's talk, and later wrote that he had come in thanksgiving to Mother Teresa 'for her unknown help to me in some of the darker moments of the Peace People experience'. He offered an example of how Mother Teresa's tirelessness in the face of daunting schedules could provide enormous inspiration. 'Many's the late and lonely night', wrote McKeown, 'when exhaustion threatened to induce hopelessness in the struggle to suggest non-violence for Northern Ireland. The thought of Mother Teresa's tireless exercise of love, in vastly more intimidating circumstances, provided energy and strength.'

Mother Teresa told the people, McKeown continued, to be mindful of the suffering of Mary at the crucifixion of her son, and how 'entitled to be bitter, Mary was'. A woman who could see her only son subjected to a cruel death, and not respond with bitterness, might move some hearts to set aside their centuries-old bitterness.

Mother Teresa has spoken out for peace wherever she saw it threatened. Her appeal, coming as a cry from the heart of peace, could apply to any countries that are on the brink of war.

Early in January 1991, Mother Teresa wrote to two faraway Heads of State, begging them not to inflict the suffering of war on human beings. President George Bush and President Saddam Hussein received her impassioned appeal just before the unleashing of the Gulf War. Mother Teresa wanted to bring home to the two men the need for compassion, for recognizing the preciousness of life, and the unity of humanity under the Creator. In her appeal to the two presidents, Mother Teresa begged 'for the innocent ones', the ones who would continue to suffer months and years after the weapons were stilled.

> I come to you with tears in my eyes and God's love in my heart to plead to you for the poor – and those who will become poor if the war that we all dread and fear happens. I beg you with my whole heart to work for, to labour for God's peace, and to be reconciled with one another . . . .
>
> You have the power and the strength to destroy God's presence and image, his men, his women and his children. Please listen to the will of God. God has created us to be loved by his love and not to be destroyed by our hatred.
>
> In the short term there may be winners and losers in this war that we all dread, but that never can, and never will, justify the suffering, pain and loss of life which your weapons will cause.
>
> I come to you in the name of God, the God that we all love and share, to beg for the innocent ones, our poor of the world, and those who will become poor because of war. They are the ones who will suffer most because they have no means of escape. I plead on bended knee for

them. They will suffer and when they do, we will be the ones who are guilty for not having done all in our power to protect and love them.

I plead to you for those who will be left orphaned, widowed and left alone, because their parents, husbands, brothers and children have been killed. I beg you please to save them.

I plead for those who will be left with disability and disfigurement. They are God's children. I plead for those who will be left with no home, no food and no love. Please think of them as being your children.

Finally, I plead for those who will have the most precious thing that God can give us, life, taken away from them. I beg you to save our brothers and sisters, yours and ours, because they are given to us by God to love and to cherish. It is not for us to destroy what God has given to us. Please, please let your mind and your will become the mind and will of God.

You have the power to bring war into the world, or to build peace. *Please choose the way of peace.*

I appeal to you – to your love, your love of God and your fellow man. In the name of God and in the name of those you will make poor, do not destroy life and peace. Let the love and peace triumph, and let your names be remembered for the good you have done, the joy you have spread, and the love you have shared.

Mother Teresa's attempt to stave off the war failed. The people of Iraq, especially the children, suffered the brunt of the hostilities, and many died. The Iraqi government now had enormous health problems to solve. Lack of full food rations and medical supplies (both due to an embargo) hurt not the élite, but children and the poorest families. The Iraqis struggled to reconstruct a bomb-shattered water-purification plant and a partially destroyed sewage disposal plant.

When the bombing stopped, Mother Teresa went to Baghdad to relieve some of the suffering of child war victims. Behind the Church of St Raphael, a church of the Chaldeans, two teams of Sisters laboured to help disabled and orphaned children, the most vulnerable and threatened members of the Iraqi population. However, what the Sisters, along with voluntary and even United Nations relief agencies, were able to do for the people of Iraq seemed to be all but negated by the embargo which prevented Iraq from meeting its own needs.

Watching Mother Teresa's efforts in spite of everything, I was reminded of something she had said to a group of Franciscan friars years before: 'Let us keep the joy of loving Jesus in our hearts, and share this joy with all we meet and so become carriers of God's peace.'

7
Count It Pure Joy...
The Secret of Prayerful Perseverance

❧

> My brothers, count it pure joy when you are involved in
> every sort of trial. Realize that when your faith is tested this
> makes for endurance. Let endurance come to its perfection
> so that you may be fully mature and lacking in nothing.
>> *James 1:2-4*

With her gift for the concrete, Mother Teresa illustrated a
mysterious and transcendant concept, that of the co-
redemptive power of innocent suffering, in her reply to the
halting question of a woman totally disabled with cerebral
palsy. It was in the setting of a church meeting. The
woman's words were difficult to understand due to the
incessant twitches of her head and body: 'What . . . can . . .
people like me . . . do?' As spasms contorted the woman's
face, Mother Teresa replied simply:

> You can do the most. You are the one who lives with Jesus
> on the cross every day. You pray for the work, and help
> and give us the strength to *do* the work.

Her answer is meant for any of the house-bound, the para-
lysed, the wheelchair-bound, the helpless sufferers
throughout the world whose agony seems to be useless to
themselves, useless to society and useless to the world at
large.

Here grace enters in, the grace to accept the suffering and

to unite it with the 'Lamb of God who takes away the sin of the world'. Christ's death, while it seemed the greatest evil, is, in reality, the greatest good. Jesus on the cross is a co-sufferer with every suffering human being. In him, we see the suffering of God with, and in, his suffering people. In him, we see the risen King and the empty tomb beyond suffering. In the words of Mother Teresa:

> Never let anything so fill you with pain or sorrow, so as to make you forget the joy of Christ risen.

Though it may be supremely difficult, she asks us to see 'suffering as a gift'.

> Like all gifts, it depends on how we receive it. And that is why we need a pure heart to see the hand of God, to feel the hand of God, to recognize the gift of God in our suffering. He allows us to share in his suffering and to make up for the sins of the world.

Some suffering is relatively minor but besets us every day in the form of vexations. We become tired and lose our joy because of the accumulated problems we need to conquer. One day in 1976, I had filled a conversation with a litany of problems, some seemingly insoluble. Mother Teresa remarked, 'Everything is a *problem*, Eileen. Isn't there another word?' I had no synonym to offer. She suggested, 'Why not use the word *gift*?'

Our vocabulary changed. The first time I used the new terminology was on our return from the Habitat Conference in Canada. Mother Teresa was extremely anxious to have time with her Sisters in New York. I had just learned that our flight had to be broken en route with a four-hour delay in Toronto. As I was about to explain the 'problem', I paused . . . 'Mother, I have to tell you about a *gift*. We have to wait four hours here and you won't arrive at the convent until very late.' Mother Teresa responded with a rueful smile.

Perhaps the most insidious suffering, and one that is often locked into the most secret compartment of the heart, is the fear of dying. Mother Teresa, in the Home for the Dying, faces dying men and women every day of the year. Numbers of them are young people, cut off from living before they have tasted life's joys or achievements. She relates how so many of them, loved and cared for in their last hours, pass into eternity with a look of peace on their faces, and a word of thanks on their lips. 'These are our treasures,' she says, mindful of their gift to the world. 'They die', she keeps reminding us, 'without blaming anybody, without cursing anybody.'

Mother Teresa reflects the love of God in reaching out to the afflicted. She tells us that dying is simply going home to the source of all love, God. Jean Vanier, author of spiritual books and founder of a movement to care for the retarded and mentally afflicted, made a remark in the course of a 1971 joint interview with Mother Teresa. He said he hoped that Mother Teresa would be holding his hand when he was dying. Mother Teresa, by her consoling, loving hand in the Home for the Dying, only points to the hand of God – consoling, loving, ever-present. 'No one dies alone,' she seems to be reminding us. The Creator, source of all life, is close to all his children. As earthly life ebbs, we are simply going home to the source of all love, the Creator of us all.

But what is the right response to the suffering we have brought on ourselves? This applies to all, since no one is without sin. St Paul reminds us, 'Where sin increased, grace abounded all the more' (Romans 5:20 RSV). Forgiveness, like grace, is there for the asking – in the firmament, as it were – ready for all who call. As the poet Christopher Marlowe reminds us in the play *Dr Faustus*:

See, see where Christ's blood streams in the firmament!
One drop would save my soul – half a drop: ah my Christ!

No Slums in Heaven

❦

Heart problems have brought Mother Teresa close to the
gates of heaven on more than one occasion. The first time
was in June 1983 during a visit to Rome, when Mother
Teresa fell out of bed and later complained of a pain in her
side. Hospital tests revealed that she was suffering from
heart failure. Cheerful as always, Mother Teresa related:

> The doctor joked with me, 'I cannot say that Mother Teresa
> has a bad heart.'
>   They told me that if the fall had not made me come to the
> hospital, I would have had a heart attack. See the
> wonderful ways of God. St Peter must have said, 'Hold her
> back there. There are no slums in heaven.'

During her seven weeks of enforced rest in hospital, her
many visitors included the King and Queen of Belgium.
Messages came from around the world, including one from
Jyoti Basu, the communist Chief Minister of West Bengal,
telling her that the people were concerned about her.

Mother Teresa's daily regimen now included regular
heart medication and she was warned not to climb stairs.
However, she did not defer to her health, but responded
with joy at new openings for the work. After leaving
hospital, she flew to Warsaw and, within a year, opened a
novitiate there for candidates for the Missionaries of
Charity.

Eventually Mother Teresa's failing heart needed a pacemaker. In 1991, on a visit to the Sisters in Tijuana, Mexico, she collapsed again. Brought to San Diego, California, through the efforts of lay Co-Workers, she was cared for in Scripps Medical Center. For a time she lay between life and death. Again she rallied, and again resumed her travels, moving between India, Eastern Europe, Latin America, Africa and the United States. Then in August 1993, in Delhi, India, Mother Teresa's heart failed once more. Even the action of the pacemaker was not sufficient to stimulate heart action. Doctors at the All-India Institute of Medical Sciences issued guarded bulletins about her condition.

Her eighty-third birthday was approaching when a birthday gift came for which Mother Teresa and the Sisters had long been praying: to bring the work to China. Mother Teresa had long wished to take the Sisters into the vast expanse of the Peoples' Republic of China. Already many young women of Chinese origin were counted among the Missionaries of Charity and were members of the teams active in Hong Kong.

Missionaries of Charity bring tender mercy to those from whom the world turns away, especially the innocent. Each time selfless love overcomes self-concern; each time we transcend our own needs to meet the needs of another, the world of redemptive love comes into being. The 'not yet' of the reign of God breaks into existence in 'the already'. And into this reign, joy enters.

During a short visit to China in 1985 Mother Teresa had met with Deng Pufang, the head of the Chinese Federation for the Disabled. Mother Teresa had offered to provide help for China's disabled and impoverished citizens. Deng, the son of the Chinese leader Deng Xiaopeng, was himself disabled, wheelchair-bound as a result of injuries he received when thrown out of a window by the Red Guards in the Cultural Revolution of the 1960s. Yet he said no. In turning down Mother Teresa's offer of help for all the country's poor, Deng made it clear that China could meet its own needs.

Mother Teresa, who yearned to relieve the pain of China's disabled and other victims of China's communist regime, had to accept the verdict of 'not yet'. She recognized that God would allow the Missionaries of Charity to enter China in his time – just as he had allowed them to go into Albania in 1990. But it se ed that God's time came more quickly than anyone h expected. In time for her eighty-third birthday on 26 August 1993, and still in the All-India Institute after her collapse from heart failure, Mother Teresa received a visa to pay another visit to China.

Upon her return to Calcutta from the Institute, Mother Teresa's condition worsened and a painful operation for the unblocking of arteries was necessary. Mother Teresa told the Sisters that she had offered up the pain for China and the work of the Sisters there. She had been advised to rest for three months but instead she began to make plans to leave for China in October, less than three months later.

Time Breaks All Walls Asunder

❧

Just before she was to leave for Beijing, on 16 October 1993, a visitor from Germany presented Mother Teresa with a replica of the Berlin Peace Clock. The creator of the eight-foot-high Berlin Peace Clock, a famous jeweller by the name of Jens D. Lorenz, made the presentation in the court-yard of Shishu Bhavan, the Children's Home.

The original Berlin Peace Clock had been displayed for the first time on 9 November 1989. That evening, one of the most dramatic events of the century occurred: the Berlin

Wall was torn down. In his presentation, Lorenz explained that the inscription on the Peace Clock and its replicas was: Time Breaks All Walls Asunder. Four replicas had been made and three of them had been given to Ronald Reagan, Mikhail Gorbachev and Helmut Kohl. The first replica, however, had been reserved for Mother Teresa.

Present for the ceremony were representatives of Calcutta's many religious communities, including monks from the Ramakrishna Mission, Sikhs and various Christian denominations. The children of Shishu Bhavan, many rescued from the streets, drains and dustbins of the city, danced around the Peace Clock before it was installed in the chapel of the Mother House of the Sisters.

Jens Lorenz, in his talk, put into context the significance of Mother Teresa's contribution to humankind:

The walls between rich and poor, the walls which set apart religiously or politically fanaticized minds have not been dismantled: disease-like they progress on their invasive course, destroying communities which had once lived in peace.

Through the sheer force of her faith, Mother Teresa has been helping to overcome such walls for over sixty years. In her devoted caring for others, she has never paid any heed to race, creed, nationality or ideology, always speaking the language of God's love.

Mother Teresa herself has had to overcome many walls, including those of the order, for the Missionaries of Charity work outside the convent walls, living and working in poverty among the poorest of the poor. They help where help is needed, bringing comfort to the sick and suffering, feeding the hungry, restoring strength to the frail and praying for those who mankind has no power to help.

The active compassion shown by Mother Teresa and the

Missionaries of Charity reveals a path to deliverance from the web of hatred and violence which continues to convulse entire regions of the world. This living humanity demonstrates every day, every hour, every minute, that the hope for a world without walls, a world of peace, tolerance and brotherhood is not a vain hope – and this hope will grow every minute, every hour and every day that people, wherever they may be, follow in their own way the selfless example of the Missionaries of Charity.

Finally, 'Borne aloft on the wings of zeal', as a bishop remarked, Mother Teresa took off for China on 19 October 1993. On her return to Calcutta, Mother Teresa told of her trip in a Christmas 1993 letter to her Co-Workers. This Christmas letter also came to be Mother Teresa's farewell to the Co-Workers, particularly to those not working directly with the Missionaries of Charity. (See Appendix 1).

Thank God I am back home. Thank you for praying with such faith and love for my intentions. Your prayers must have helped me, for Jesus took great care of me all along. I am sure you are all anxious to know how God, in his loving providence, directed everything during our visit to China and Vietnam.

In China, we first went to Shanghai and met the Archbishop of Shanghai. The next day we went to Beijing to meet Mr Deng Pufang, the head of the organization for the care of the handicapped. He himself is in a wheelchair as a result of an accident. He received us very kindly and said he looked forward to the day China could have the Missionaries of Charity reaching out tender love and care to the poor in that beautiful country. While in China we were able to visit the Cathedral of Our Lady of Sheshan who is patroness of China. It was beautiful to see the love and devotion that the Chinese people have to Our Lady. Let us continue praying that Our Lady may take this foundation under her special protection and make it a reality soon.

I was also able to go to Vietnam where I met the Archbishop who is very anxious to have a community of our Sisters there. There are many beautiful young Vietnamese girls wanting to become Missionaries of Charity.

My prayer for you this Christmas is that you too may experience the joy that comes from seeing Jesus in all the distressing disguises in which he comes, through circumstances and people in your home, your neighbourhood, your parish, your city.

Regrettably, no additional invitations or visas were extended to Mother Teresa or the Missionaries of Charity after her visit, despite Deng Pufang's kind words. But Mother Teresa was patient as always, remembering what had happened in Albania, in Cuba, and in many other countries.

All-Surrounding Love

❦

Mother Teresa's view of innocent suffering is that of Martin Luther King, Jr, who called it 'unearned suffering'. She also joins Mahatma Gandhi, who, like King, taught that love for opponents is shown by accepting abuse rather than inflicting retaliatory pain. This is the path to an eventual change of heart for one's enemies. Like Mother Teresa, both leaders taught that love does not seek vengeance, but instead is willing to walk through the dark valley of trouble for the sake of peace and reconciliation.

In a world anguished by suffering, it is the active compassion, taught and lived by Mother Teresa, that is animating many to look beyond their immediate circumstances to meet the needs of others. The insistence on continuing the works of mercy in the midst of conflicts, rather than assenting to engage in war, brings a more fundamental peace to the world than the mere temporary cessation of hostility. Mother Teresa was overjoyed when her works of active compassion and works of mercy for the human community, expressed by the Missionaries of Charity, were recognized by the Nobel Award as being authentic works of peace.

Mother Teresa asks us as the followers of Jesus to cling to him as the centre of our lives, and to receive as providence the role he provides for us to play. She encourages each one of us to become a true and faithful branch on the vine, Jesus, by accepting him in our lives as it pleases him to come:

as the Truth . . . to be told;
as the Life . . . to be lived;
as the Light . . . to be lighted;
as the Love . . . to be loved;
as the Way . . . to be walked;
as the Joy . . . to be given;
as the Peace . . . to be spread;
as the Sacrifice . . . to be offered in our families, and with our close neighbours, as well as our faraway neighbours.

Appendix 1
Do the Small Things with Great Love:
The Co-Workers of Mother Teresa

❧

The History of the Co-Workers

❧

Mother Teresa had shown from the early days of her work with the poor a rare genius for inspiring others to take part in the work. The Co-Workers, as the lay family of the Missionaries of Charity, grew out of the desire of ordinary men and women to volunteer their time and talents to Mother Teresa.

It was the simplest of organizations. All officers were called 'links' – local, regional, national and international. There were no dues – Mother Teresa had to curb the enthusiasm of early Co-Workers by forbidding any collecting of funds. Meetings were held as needed. In the case of national meetings in countries such as Italy, France or the United States, they were timed so that Mother Teresa could be present. Co-Workers with greater means paid for the fare and expenses of those without means. One of the meetings of the Co-Workers of the United States was held in a Cistercian monastery in a desert-like expanse in Utah. At the meeting/retreat, Mother Teresa stressed, 'If we really love Jesus in the poor, then our first connection must be with him. Only after that can we really see him in the poor.' Communication was maintained through reports, often simply copied, shared locally, nationally and internationally.

The Co-Workers started in Calcutta, where Mrs Ann Blaikie, an English woman living there, began to help in feeding and changing the children in the Children's Home, cradling in her arms tiny infants close to death. Soon other volunteers joined in the work, putting themselves at the disposal of Mother Teresa and the Missionaries of Charity. Men also volunteered at the Home for the Dying. Some men, like Rama Coomaraswamy, would help by clipping the fingernails and toenails of the patients. (Rama was moved to study medicine by his experience, and later became a medical doctor and psychiatrist in the United States.)

The Co-Workers took on many roles and offered much helpful support. Frank Collins, who was in the American consular service, devoted his free time to transporting Mother Teresa and the Sisters to slum clinics and leprosy stations. Women who knew English volunteered to teach it to the young women entering the Missionaries of Charity from every part of India. (Mother Teresa had decided that in view of India's many languages and dialects, English would be the standard language of communication.)

Eventually, simple guidelines for the Co-Workers were formulated by Mother Teresa and Ann Blaikie. They were translated into numerous languages as the Co-Workers were planted in various countries. On 23 March 1969 a simple Constitution was blessed by Pope Paul VI, and Ann Blaikie became the first international link of the International Association of Co-Workers of Mother Teresa.

An International Effort

❦

While Catholics formed the core of the Association, people of many spiritual paths, moved by the example of Mother Teresa and the Missionaries of Charity, joined with the Co-Workers. They shared the vision of the work. A Co-Worker of Mother Teresa is one who sees the presence of God in every human being and chooses to fully share in the real service of the poor, using hands to serve and hearts to love.

In the United States, the work of the Co-Workers was begun by Dr Warren and Mrs Patricia Kump of Minneapolis. Along with local young doctors and their wives, they reached out to ill and troubled individuals, and to those in nursing homes. The Kumps also prepared and mailed the Co-Workers' International Newsletter which contained examples of Co-Worker action around the world and up-to-date information concerning the growth of the Missionaries of Charity. Here are some examples of the loving service which Co-Workers do around the world:

In Australia, aboriginal children are invited to leave the 'reserve' to have meals and spend holidays with local families. Birthday parties and Christmas festivities bridge the gap between Australia's first people and other Australians.

In Mexico City, Co-Workers found that if they presented themselves regularly at the airline companies, they would be given the meals unused in-flight. They give this food to the Missionaries of Charity who serve it to the men, women and children living at the edge of the city searching among the rubbish tips for saleable items. These people appreciate the change from their basic food rations.

In the United States, the Sisters who run five AIDS hospices (in New York, Baltimore, Washington, Atlanta and

San Francisco) needed men who would give one night or more a week to care for the patients. Co-Workers came forward in each city. In a Mid-Western town, a group of Co-Workers came to the aid of a young mother struggling with four small children. She and her husband could barely meet their basic needs and the young mother had almost reached the breaking point. In a practical offer of support, one of the Co-Workers would cook the evening meal each evening and prepare the children for bed.

In Zimbabwe, one Co-Worker, a poor woman, sold a sewing machine, part of her livelihood, so that two hungry families in her neighbourhood could lay in stocks of food.

In South Africa, teams of Co-Workers volunteer seven nights a week at a night shelter. The shelter, at Usindiso (The Saving Place), provides hot meals and a place to wash for over a hundred people.

In Indonesia, young Co-Workers decided to volunteer regularly at a state home for disabled children. A young woman wrote, 'I sit with a child whose head is very big. He can't leave his bed, but he looks for me. I learn to love this poor little Jesus.'

Co-Workers Disbanded

❧

On 30 August 1993 Mother Teresa sent a letter in her own hand to leaders of the Co-Workers of Mother Teresa around the world. Her message was that the Co-Workers of Mother Teresa was to be disbanded as an international association. Some of the recipients were surprised, while others understood the change. They realized that Mother Teresa herself was in a period of frail health when she wrote to them. She could no longer give the attention to the Co-Workers that she had previously been able to give for twenty-five years.

The word was received and shared throughout the network of Co-Workers that the organization was to be dismantled. Mother Teresa explained, however, that the Co-Workers would continue to exist in a decentralized form. Only those who worked directly with the Missionaries of Charity, with the Sisters and Brothers, would be called Co-Workers. Others, who had performed their works of mercy under the name of Mother Teresa, would now carry on in the same spirit but without the binding link of the name. This applied to thousands of groups, from Japan to Indonesia, from Zimbabwe to South Africa.

Many remembered that Mother Teresa had often said, 'Never forget you are Co-Workers of *Jesus* in this work.' Now, more than before, each voluntary group would need to find its strength in prayer and its inspiration in seeing the face of God in the poor.

The Final Guidelines

❧

Mother Teresa's advice had been and will be repeated in towns and villages around the world: 'Do the small things with great love.'

Co-Workers in all walks of life will continue to recite the prayer inaugurated by Mother Teresa in St James's Church, Piccadilly, London. (She had been chosen by an ecumenical group as the person to unite large numbers of the human family.)

Lead me from death to life,
    from falsehood to truth.
Lead me from despair to hope,

from fear to trust.
Lead me from hate to love,
   from war to peace.
Let peace fill our hearts, our world,
   our universe.
Peace. Peace. Peace.

The fullness of compassion Mother Teresa finds in Jesus; and through Jesus, the compassion of God. Others will continue to join her in doing the works of peace and love in accordance with their own vision.

The final guidelines of the Co-Workers began with a favourite reminder of Mother Teresa's:

> Love to pray – feel often during the day the need for prayer and take the trouble to pray. Prayer enlarges the heart until it is capable of containing God's gift of himself. Ask and seek, and your heart will grow big enough to receive him and keep him as your own.
>
> *God bless you,*
> *Mother Teresa, MC*

Appendix 2
National Prayer Breakfast
Washington, DC

❧

On 3 February 1994 the Annual National Prayer Breakfast was held at the Hilton Hotel in Washington, DC. Over 4,000 people filled the hall to hear Mother Teresa. She was flanked by President and Mrs Clinton, Vice-President and Mrs Gore, and the leaders of Congress. In the audience were many congressional members and their families.

On this occasion, Mother Teresa departed from her custom by reading from a prepared text. Even in her Nobel Peace Prize acceptance speech, Mother Teresa had had no prepared text. I had watched her in Oslo as she followed her custom of making an almost imperceptible sign of the cross on her lips with her thumb. Then she began to speak without referring to a single note. In Washington, the newspapers reported rapt silence in the hall as Mother Teresa spoke and an acclamation as she finished. What follows are excerpts from that speech:

> On the last day, Jesus will say to those on his right hand, 'Come, enter the kingdom. For I was hungry and you gave me food, I was thirsty and you gave me drink, I was sick and you visited me.' Then Jesus will turn to those on his left hand and say, 'Depart from me because I was hungry and you did not feed me, I was thirsty and you did not give me to drink, I was sick and you did not visit me.' These will ask him, 'When did we see you hungry, or thirsty or sick and

did not come to your help?' And Jesus will answer them, 'Whatever you neglected to do unto one of the least of these, you neglected to do unto me!'

As we have gathered here to pray together, I think it will be beautiful if we begin with a prayer that expresses very well what Jesus wants us to do for the least. St Francis of Assisi understood very well these words of Jesus and his life is very well expressed by a prayer. And this prayer, which we say every day after Holy Communion, always surprises me very much, because it is very fitting for each one of us.

I always wonder whether 800 years ago, when St Francis lived, they had the same difficulties that we have today. I think that some of you already have this prayer of peace – so we will pray it together . . . .

Let us thank God for the opportunity he has given us today to have come here to pray together. We have come here especially to pray for peace, joy and love. We are reminded that Jesus came to bring the good news to the poor. He had told us what is that good news when he said, 'Peace I leave with you; my peace I give unto you' (John 14:27). He came not to give the peace of the world which is only that we don't bother each other. He came to give the peace of heart which comes from loving – from doing good to others.

God loved the world so much that he gave his Son – it was a giving. God gave his Son to the Virgin Mary, and what did she do with him? As soon as Jesus came into Mary's life, immediately she went in haste to give that good news. And as she came into the house of her cousin, Elizabeth, Scripture tells us that the unborn child – the child in the womb of Elizabeth – leapt with joy. While still in the womb of Mary – Jesus brought peace to John the Baptist, who leapt for joy in the womb of Elizabeth.

And as if that were not enough, as if it were not enough

that God the Son should become one of us and bring peace and joy while still in the womb of Mary, Jesus also died on the cross to show that greater love. He died for you and for me, and for that leper and for that man dying of hunger and that naked person lying in the street, not only of Calcutta, but of Africa, and everywhere.

Our Sisters serve those poor people in 105 countries throughout the world. Jesus insisted that we love one another as he loves each one of us. Jesus gave his life to love us and he tells us that we also have to give whatever it takes to do good to one another. And in the Gospel Jesus says very clearly, 'Love as I have loved you.'

Jesus died on the cross because that is what it took for him to do good to us – to save us from our selfishness in sin. He gave up everything to do the Father's will – to show us that we too must be willing to give up everything to do God's will – to love one another as he loves each of us. If we are not willing to give whatever it takes to do good to one another, sin is still in us. That is why we too must give to each other until it hurts.

It is not enough for us to say 'I love God', but I also have to love my neighbour. St John says that you are a liar if you say you love God and you don't love your neighbour. How can you love God whom you do not see, if you do not love your neighbour whom you see, whom you touch, with whom you live?

And so it is very important for us to realize that love, to be true, has to hurt. I must be willing to give whatever it takes not to harm other people and, in fact, to do good to them. This requires that I be willing to give until it hurts. Otherwise, there is no true love in me and I bring injustice, not peace, to those around me.

It hurt Jesus to love us. We have been created in his image for greater things, to love and to be loved. We must put on Christ, as Scripture tells us. And so, we have been created to love as he loves us. Jesus makes himself the hungry one, the naked one, the homeless one, the unwanted one, and he says, 'You did it to me.'

On the last day he will say to those on his right, 'Whatever you did to the least of these, you did to me.' And he will also say to those on his left, 'Whatever you neglected to do for the least of these, you neglected to do it for me.'

When he was dying on the cross, Jesus said, 'I thirst.' Jesus is thirsting for our love, and this is the thirst of everyone, poor and rich alike. We all thirst for the love of others, that they go out of their way to avoid harming us and to do good to us. This is the meaning of true love, to give until it hurts.

I can never forget the experience I had in visiting a home where they kept all these old parents of sons and daughters who had just put them into an institution and forgotten them – maybe. I saw that in that home these old people had everything – good food, a comfortable place, television, everything, but everyone was looking toward the door. And I did not see a single one with a smile on their face. I turned to Sister and I asked, 'Why do these people who have every comfort here, why are they all looking toward the door? Why are they not smiling?' I am so used to seeing the smiles on our people, even the dying ones smile.

And Sister said, 'This is the way it is nearly every day. They are expecting, they are hoping that a son or daughter will come to visit them. They are hurt because they are forgotten.' And see, this neglect to love brings spiritual poverty. Maybe in our own family we have somebody who is feeling lonely, who is feeling sick, who is feeling worried. Are we there? Are we willing to give until it hurts in order to be with our families, or do we put our own interests first?

These are the questions we must ask ourselves, especially as we begin this Year of the Family. We must remember that love begins at home and we must also remember that 'the future of humanity passes through the family'.

I was surprised in the West to see so many young boys and girls given to drugs. And I tried to find out why. Why is it like that, when those in the West have so many more things than those in the East? And the answer was: 'Because there is no one in the family to receive them.' Our children depend on us for everything – their health, their nutrition, their security, their coming to know and love God. For all of this, they look to us with trust, hope and expectation. But often father and mother are so busy they have no time for their children, or perhaps they are not even married or have given up on their marriage. So the children go to the streets and get involved in drugs or other things. We are talking of love of the child, which is where love and peace must begin. These are the things that break peace.

But I feel that the greatest destroyer of peace today is abortion, because it is a war against the child, a direct killing of the innocent child, murder by the mother herself. And if we accept that a mother can kill even her own child, how can we tell other people not to kill one another? How do we persuade a woman not to have an abortion? As always, we must persuade her with love, and we remind ourselves that love means to be willing to give until it hurts. Jesus gave even his life to love us.

So, the mother who is thinking of abortion, should be helped to love; that is, to give until it hurts her plans, or her free time; to respect the life of her child. The father of that child, whoever he is, must also give until it hurts. By abortion, the mother does not learn to love, but kills even her own child to solve her problems. And, by abortion, the father is told that he does not have to take any responsibility at all for the child he has brought into the world. That father is likely to put other women into the same trouble. So abortion just leads to more abortion. Any country that accepts abortion is not teaching its people to love, but to use any violence to get what they want. This is why the greatest destroyer of love and peace is abortion.

Many people are very, very concerned with the children of India, with the children of Africa where quite a few die of hunger, and so on. Many people are also concerned about all the violence in this great country of the United States. These concerns are very good. But often these same people are not concerned with the millions who are being killed by the deliberate decision of their own mothers. And this is what is the greatest destroyer of peace today – abortion, which brings people to such blindness.

And for this I appeal in India and I appeal everywhere: 'Let us bring the child back.' The child is God's gift to the family. Each child is created in the special image and likeness of God for greater things – to love and to be loved. In this Year of the Family we must bring the child back to the centre of our care and concern. This is the only way that our world can survive because our children are the only hope for the future. As older people are called to God, only their children can take their places.

But what does God say to us? He says, 'Even if a mother could forget her child, I will not forget you. I have carved you in the palm of my hand.' We are carved in the palm of his hand; that unborn child has been carved in the hand of God from conception and is called by God to love and to be loved, not only now in this life, but for ever. God can never forget us.

I will tell you something beautiful. We are fighting abortion by adoption – by care of the mother and adoption for her baby. We have saved thousands of lives. We have sent word to the clinics, to the hospitals and police stations: 'Please don't destroy the child; we will take the child.' So we always have someone tell the mothers in trouble: 'Come, we will take care of you, we will get a home for your child.' And we have a tremendous demand from couples who cannot have a child – but I never give a child to a couple who have done something not to have a child. Jesus said, 'Anyone who receives a child in my name, receives me.' By adopting a child, these couples receive Jesus, but by aborting a child, a couple refuses to receive Jesus.

Please don't kill the child. I want the child. Please give me the child. I am willing to accept any child who would be aborted and to give that child to a married couple who will love the child and be loved by the child. From our Children's Home in Calcutta alone, we have saved over 3,000 children from abortion. These children have brought such love and joy to their adopting parents and have grown up so full of love and joy.

I know that couples have to plan their family, and for that there is natural family planning. The way to plan the family is natural family planning, not contraception. In destroying the power of giving life, through contraception, a husband or wife is doing something to self. This turns the attention to self and so destroys the gift of love in him or her. In loving, the husband and wife must turn the attention to each other as happens in natural family planning, and not to self, as happens in contraception. Once that living love is destroyed by contraception, abortion follows very easily.

I also know that there are great problems in the world, that many spouses do not love each other enough to practise natural family planning. We cannot solve all the problems in the world, but let us never bring in the worst problem of all, and that is to destroy love. And this is what happens when we tell people to practise contraception and abortion.

The poor have very great people. They can teach us so many beautiful things. Once one of them came to thank us for teaching her natural family planning and said, 'You people who have practised chastity, you are the best people to teach us natural family planning because it is nothing more than self-control out of love for each other.' And what this poor person said is very true. These poor people maybe having nothing to eat, maybe they have not a home to live in, but they can still be great people when they are spiritually rich.

When I pick up a person from the street, hungry, I give him a plate of rice, a piece of bread. But a person who is shut out, who feels unwanted, unloved, terrified, the person who has been thrown out of society – that spiritual poverty is much harder to overcome. And abortion, which often follows from contraception, brings a people to be spiritually poor, and that is the worst poverty and the most difficult to overcome . . . .

We are not social workers. We may be doing social work in the eyes of some people, but we must be contemplatives in the heart of the world. For we must bring that presence of God into your family, for the family that prays together, stays together. There is so much hatred, so much misery, and we with our prayer, with our sacrifice, are beginning at home. Love begins at home, and it is not how much we do, but how much love we put into what we do.

If we are contemplatives in the heart of the world with all its problems, these problems can never discourage us. We must always remember what God tells us in Scripture: 'Even if a mother could forget the child in her womb' – something impossible, but even if she could forget – 'I will never forget you.' . . .

God will never forget us and there is something you and I can always do. We can keep the joy of loving Jesus in our hearts, and share that joy with all we come in contact with. Let us make that one point – that no child will be unwanted, unloved, uncared for, or killed and thrown away. And give until it hurts – with a smile . . . .

One of the most demanding things for me is travelling everywhere – and with publicity. I have said to Jesus that if I don't go to heaven for anything else, I will be going to heaven for all the travelling with all the publicity, because it has purified me and sacrificed me and made me really ready for heaven.

If we remember that God loves us, and that we can love others as he loves us, then America can become a sign of peace for the world. From here, a sign of care for the weakest of the weak – the unborn child – must go out to the world. If you become a burning light of justice and peace in the world, then really you will be true to what the founders of this country stood for. God bless you!

Why would thousands of people turn out to be in the presence of a small, bent woman of eighty-three whom they could see behind the podium only by craning their necks? While many present that morning did not agree with her view on the protection of the unborn child, they came for something else – to see a person who had 'put on Christ', a person who in the twentieth century lived as Christ lived. President Clinton did not respond directly to Mother Teresa's statements on abortion, but he thanked her for 'her life of commitment', a commitment, he stated, that she had 'truly lived'.

When I met with Mother Teresa a few days later in the Harlem house of the Missionaries of Charity, she handed me the four-page copy of her talk. 'Wasn't this the first time you ever read a talk?' She agreed.

Mother Teresa recounted that after the Prayer Breakfast, President and Mrs Clinton had talked with her. She told them of the work in Calcutta, of the Shishu Bhavan where rescued children are cared for. 'Then I asked Mrs Clinton', said Mother Teresa, 'if we could have a house for children in Washington. I would be ready to send our Sisters to take care of it. Mrs Clinton said nothing for a while. She was thinking about it. Then she said, "Yes, I will help you to get a house." '

Mother Teresa talked of other plans. She hoped to open two houses in Vietnam: one in Hanoi, and the other in 'that other city', referring to the city of Ho Chi Minh. 'I still have hope for China,' she said.

Many people were grateful for her defence of life, including not only her objection to abortion, but to the killing of war and capital punishment as well. 'Not long ago,' she told me, 'a judge in the United States telephoned me in Calcutta. He asked my advice about a man who could be sentenced to death. All I said was, "Do what Jesus would do in your place." '

We talked about personal suffering: 'When someone does something that hurts you, let it pass through.' She pointed with her index finger to her left ear, and then to her right ear, as though the hurt were leaving, not remaining. 'Never let it stay here,' she said, placing her hand over her heart. 'When you do that, you can go on happily. You do not lose joy.' She continued:

> The important thing, is not to waste suffering. Join it to the suffering of Christ; offer it up with his suffering. Don't waste suffering.

Mother Teresa wants all people to see innocent suffering as part of the greatest drama of the world, the redemption of the human family.

Contemplative in the
Heart of the World

Introduced by
Brother Angelo Devananda

To Mary, the Mother of Jesus and our Mother, in the bimillenial year of her birth as first carrier of the Word.

And to Mother Teresa of Calcutta, mother figure of compassion in the world today, on her seventy-fifth birthday.

Her children, the Universal Brothers of the Word, with devoted heart and soul.

Jay-Jayanthi!
(Happy Birthday!)

Contents

Preface

BEFORE COMMITTING MYSELF to this book, I have pondered, prayed, and hesitated about my involvement; Mother Teresa has always encouraged me to avoid publicity regarding her life and the work of the Sisters and Brothers. She is concerned lest time be taken from our service and unnecessary distractions endanger the essence of our life. "We are to remain right on the ground by serving Christ in the poorest of the poor."

The Missionary of Charity Sisters have specified in their constitutions: "We shall proclaim the word of God through our personal presence and not by writing books or articles." Yet I was faced with a dilemma: we, the Universal Brothers of the Word, are specifically founded to spread the word of God to the spiritually hungry. Mother Teresa herself has said that the United States is now ripe for a contemplative message. The spiritually poor of the world urgently need to be evangelized. "Jesus is both the life to be lived and the word to be spoken." My role as priest and servant leader of our brotherhood faced me with the choice of how to spread the word most effectively. I recalled the words of St. Bernard to one of his abbots: *"Pasce vita; pasce doctrina; pasce exemplo"* or "Feed with your life; feed with your doctrine; feed with your example."

What better food could I choose than the life and example of one who had inspired me so greatly to follow in the footsteps of Jesus? The rule of life for our brotherhood explains it this way: "We believe that we have been called by the Father in the likeness of the first Christians to be a community of Brothers in Jesus, the Lord; to follow him through the inspiration, teachings, and example of Mother Teresa of Calcutta; to be of one heart and mind in a community of goods; to humbly submit to one another and to our servant leaders; to remain single for the Lord; to persevere daily in prayer, adoration, and the breaking of the bread; to be available as carriers of God's word to the spiritually poorest of the poor, in season and out of season, to the ends of the earth." With this in mind and with the encouragement of my Brothers, I decided to take the responsibility and the risk of reaching toward a better understanding of the spiritual vision and teaching of Mother Teresa, and that is how this book came to birth.

Mother Teresa: Contemplative in the Heart of the World is presented as a gift of filial love to Mother Teresa on her seventy-fifth birthday. To quote St. Augustine, *"Panem iste quaerit famem."* It is my hope that this very special kind of bread will meet a very special kind of hunger in the countless disciples all over the world who draw inspiration and courage from the example of Mother Teresa.

BROTHER ANGELO DEVANANDA

Acknowledgments

I would like to thank two people who really are at the root of this book. Bert Ghezzi, editorial director of Servant Books, first proposed the idea for this book. Ann Spangler helped me bring the idea to birth through her editing skill, perseverance, and hard work. I consider each a real brother and sister in the Word.

Note to the Reader

Part One of this book has been written to introduce the reader to the life and spiritual vision of Mother Teresa. Part Two contains selections which have been extracted from the writings and teachings of Mother Teresa, taken from the following sources: The Constitution of the Missionary of Charity Sisters; The Explanation of the Original Constitution, edited by Sister Nirmala and based on the words of Mother Teresa; Mother's Instructions to the Sisters; Mother Teresa's Instructions to Superiors, Tertians, and Novices; and Mother's General Letters to the Sisters. Selections from the Constitution appear in italics. The song, "Something Beautiful for God," reprinted at the beginning of Part Two, was written by one of the Missionaries of Charity and is taken from the Missionary of Charity Songbook. The prayer at the beginning of Part One is taken from a meditation Mother Teresa made on June 19, 1983, while in the hospital in Rome.

These extracts remain the right and property of Mother Teresa.

It should be noted that the essential aspects of Mother Teresa's spiritual vision and way of life have been settled from the time she left the convent of the Loreto nuns to live on the second floor of Michael and Agnes Gomez's home in Creek Lane. And it is also true that the constitution contains the essence of her teaching. Everything else flows from it and points back to it. As Mother has said: "The simplicity and humility that prevails in the M.C. constitutions is very clear and its spirit may be used as so many have done and are doing. Not to us, O Lord, not to us but to your name be glory!" Now its spirit is being made more broadly available to the many disciples of Mother Teresa throughout the world.

Part One

To me—
Jesus is my God.
Jesus is my Spouse.
Jesus is my Life.
Jesus is my only Love.
Jesus is my All in All.
Jesus is my Everything.

—Mother Teresa.

ONE

Mother Teresa
and Beyond

THIS YEAR MARKS the seventy-fifth birthday of the woman known throughout the world as Mother Teresa of Calcutta. Members of nearly every faith and nationality, from east to west, claim kinship with her simply by calling her "Mother." A diminutive figure, she has come to wield an influence of gigantic proportion in the world today. Her work is a humble one of begetting, defending, and nurturing life in the midst of an increasingly hostile and uncaring society.

Over the years, she and the Missionaries of Charity have rescued thousands of dying outcasts from the squalor of a lonely death on the streets of Calcutta and indeed throughout the world. They have salvaged abandoned infants and aborted babies from garbage heaps where they were thoughtlessly discarded and callously left to die.

From its early beginnings in Calcutta, the Missionaries of Charity have spread rapidly throughout the world. The Sisters and Brothers who follow in the footsteps of Mother Teresa proclaim the love of God by dedicating themselves to the service of the poorest of the poor—to dying destitutes, lepers, orphans, and alcoholics. Wherever the work is most desperate, wherever the need is greatest, there you will find the Missionary of Charity. "Christ calls each of us to be his co-worker by allowing

Him to radiate and live his life in us and through us in the world of today, so that the poor, seeing us, may be drawn to Christ and invite Him to enter their homes and their lives; the sick and the suffering may find in us real angels of comfort and consolation; the little ones of the street may cling to us because we remind them of Him, the friend of the little ones" (The Constitution).

Perhaps more than any figure of modern times, Mother Teresa represents a sign of contradiction. Her life of radical poverty and humble service challenges our materialism, selfishness, and unquenchable thirst for power. Her example of wholehearted service to God and neighbor convinces us of the foolishness and complacency of our lives. Even so, she succeeds in adding hope and inspiration to our vision of life. She speaks the truth about us, yet so lovingly that we find her words and example irresistible.

People who know Mother Teresa cannot resist asking her, "What will happen to your society, Mother, when you die?" With characteristic simplicity, Mother replies mischievously, "Let me die first, and then you shall see."

But the question is an important one, and we cannot afford to wait for Mother Teresa to pass from the scene in order to consider it. One oriental proverb advises the seeker after truth: "If you find the Buddha, kill the Buddha." In other words, destroy the myth and you will discover the reality behind it, something which is far more beautiful and enduring. The same is true about Mother Teresa. She has become a legendary figure in her own day. But we make a tragic mistake if we settle for the legend or the magic of Mother Teresa rather than delving deeper to the source of her spiritual life. Our task is to look beyond the messenger in order to discover the message itself. Mother Teresa is, herself, the first to point out that she is simply a "pencil in the hand of God." Hers is a message of love which comes to us from the mind and heart of Jesus.

From time to time, God especially reveals himself in a particular person, in a specific time and place, in order to more powerfully convey the unchanging message of his love. Mother

Teresa communicates this good news in our own day.

In this capacity she points, lovingly but relentlessly, to a missing dimension in our lives: Jesus disguised in the distress of the poor. In turn, the poor point us to Him, who being rich became poor for our sake. They confront us with areas of our lives that are distasteful and painful—our own hidden material and spiritual poverty. They cry out for the love of God just as we cry out for his love and saving power in our own lives.

Mother Teresa first came to public attention in an article on the first page of the *Statesman*, the leading newspaper in Calcutta. Dr. B.C. Roy, former chief minister of West Bengal, a physician to Gandhi and Nehru, was asked by a journalist how he felt on the occasion of his eightieth birthday. Instead of speaking of his years with Gandhi or his intimate relationship with Nehru and the long years of their struggle together for an independent India, Dr. Roy chose to reflect on the work of an insignificant nun, active in the streets of Calcutta. "As I climbed the steps of the building leading to my office," he said, "I was thinking of Mother Teresa, who devotes her life to the service of the poor." This tribute was the open door by which the work of Mother Teresa began to be more widely known.

One Jesuit living in the Calcutta province at that time wrote: "Truly no bishop, no priest, no Catholic institution has made a greater impression on Indians and been more representative of the Christian spirit than this nun who dresses in a white sari with a blue border bearing a small metal crucifix pinned to the left shoulder on the side of the heart. Mother Teresa stands for what Indians admire most in Christianity."

Part of Mother Teresa's extraordinary success in Calcutta comes first from the fact that she offers solutions to problems that government and town officials have considered beyond solution; like no one else, she has been able to meet impossible needs.

The Calcutta police commissioner was one of the first to offer Mother his help. She had established a home for the dying on the sacred grounds of the Temple of Kali. To the Hindu priests who lived in the temple, the presence of Mother Teresa represented a terrible profanation. She was a Christian, a nun, and worse yet, she brought dying people onto holy ground. To Hindus, nothing is considered more polluted than a corpse.

The priests pressed their case with the police commissioner. Surely he would evict her and her Sisters. When the commissioner visited Mother at the home for the dying, he observed the Missionaries of Charity as they went about their work feeding the hungry, washing their wounds, and tenderly alleviating their suffering. After his visit, he said to the priests: "I promised I would get that woman out of here, and I shall. But, listen to me, I shall not get her out of this place before you get your mothers and sisters to do the work these nuns are doing. In the temple you have a Goddess in stone; here you have a living Goddess." (Edward Le Joly, *Servant of Love*, [New York: Harper & Row, 1977], p. 58) His words put a speedy end to their opposition. From then on, Mother Teresa was free to continue her work.

In the years that followed, her efforts to serve the poor became more widely known. Her photo appeared in *Time* Magazine, donations poured in from western women's organizations, and she received the Padma Sri Award from India and the Magsaysay ward from the Philippines. In 1964, Pope Paul VI gave her the white Lincoln Continental in which he rode through Bombay on the occasion of the Eucharistic Congress. She promptly sold it and used the money to feed the poor.

If all the medals from the prizes, awards, recognitions, and degrees were pinned on Mother Teresa, there would be no room for them on her sari. In 1979, the Nobel Peace Prize catapulted her into a measure of worldwide fame that she neither expected nor desired. Since then, she has belonged not simply to the Missionaries of Charity but to the world at large. Those of us who follow in her footsteps have had no choice but to share her with millions of others, eager to imitate her example and grasp her spiritual vision. She truly lives what she has written in the constitution, "Let the people eat you up."

My own contact with Mother Teresa stems from my first

glimpse of her in Calcutta in 1976. I will never forget it. For the very first time in my life, I had a real grasp of what Mary must have been like in the flesh. I told myself: "How good it is to be good. I would pay any price and would go to any length to be good as she is good." Little did I realize that a year later Mother would ask me to help her establish a brotherhood composed of men who were to be "contemplatives in the heart of the world."

At the time, I believed that Mother could provide answers to many of the questions that characterized my own spiritual journey. Instead, I learned that her invitation simply led to more questions, until finally I reached the ultimate ones. I had to face the agony of losing and finding myself in total surrender to the One who knows why we must be buried in the death of his Son before we can rise to a newness of life. I began to realize that no one can effectively serve God's poor without first breaking out of the prison of his own ego. Mother told me that it takes a lot of humiliation to produce just a little bit of humility. The genesis and the wandering of the Universal Brothers of the Word through their exodus stage is, however, reserved for another chapter.

It is worth noting that Mother Teresa repeatedly stresses that she is intent on one thing—giving saints to the church. She tells her Sisters, "I will not be satisfied if you are just good religious. I want to be able to offer God a perfect sacrifice. 'To resolve to be a saint' means I will despoil myself of all that is not God." Her aim for herself and those in her care is perfection, not the kind that comes from self-striving, but the true holiness of life that comes from total dedication to Jesus and abandonment to his purposes. "Total surrender to God, loving trust in each other, and cheerfulness to everyone" is her recipe for sainthood. Unlike most of the world, she cares nothing about numbers, but is only interested in gathering disciples who want to follow Jesus wholeheartedly. "I don't need numbers," she says. "I need Sisters and Brothers full of love, full of zeal." Convinced that holiness is possible for everyone who is serious about following Jesus, she scolds those who attempt to put her on a pedestal, thereby implying that her life is extraordinary and impossible for others to live.

Mother Teresa represents to me what Mary must have been like in her old age. Like Mary, she can say, "My soul magnifies the Lord and my spirit exults in God, my Savior." Both Mother Teresa and Mary attract us because they lead us to Jesus and show us what he is like. When the time comes for Mother to leave us, much more than the mystique of Mother Teresa will live on. It will be the real heart and spiritual vision of her life that will endure and shine brightly as a light in the midst of the uncertainty of our world. Mother is like the true teacher, whose desire it is to point beyond and then to disappear.

TWO

A Further Call
within a Call

EXCELLENT BOOKS have been written about Mother Teresa and
her spiritual journey. Let me just rapidly review some of
the details of her life. She was born Agnes Gonxha Bojaxhiu, on
August 26, 1910, in Skopje, Albania, in present-day Yugoslavia.
Her older sister, Age, was born in 1904, and her brother, Lazar,
followed in 1907. Her mother, Dranafile Bernai, was familiarly
called "Nana Loke," literally "Mother Soul." Her father, Nikola
Bojaxhiu, died at the age of forty-five, victim of a political plot, a
consequence of his zeal for the national unity of his beloved
country.

I met Lazar in Rome in 1978, on the occasion of the national
gathering of the Italian co-workers of the Missionaries of
Charity. Mother Teresa introduced Lazar and his Italian wife, as
well as our little group of Brothers, to Pope Paul VI at a special
audience. Among other things, I can remember the Holy Father
saying to Mother Teresa: "I am your humble disciple in the
school of charity."

Signor Lazzaro Bojaxhiu, as they called him in Italy, was a tall,
handsome man with a certain military air about him, the result
of his commission as a lieutenant in the service of the Albanian
monarchy in 1928. In many ways he reminded me of one of my
uncles, who had also been active in the military. His perfect

Italian accent made me feel an even closer kinship.

Strangely enough, I was visiting Mother in Catia La Mar, Venezuela, discussing the needs of our foundation in Haiti, when a phone call came from Palermo, Sicily, with the news that Lazar had peacefully passed away after being hospitalized in Rome with cancer.

Mother received the news calmly and showed no sign of emotion. She called the Sisters to the chapel, and there I said the first requiem mass. The gospel reading moved me deeply because it was about Lazarus' resurrection.

The next day, Mother wrote: "Yesterday I got the news that my brother went home to God to join my family. My mother will be so happy to see her only son after so many human years."

Mother always had a deep love for each member of her family, although she never saw her mother or her sister again after leaving Albania to become a missionary sister in Calcutta. The promise of Jesus to the ones who have forsaken father and mother, brothers and sisters, children and land for his sake and for the sake of the gospel, must have special meaning to her.

But let me return to Mother Teresa's first call to the religious life. As a young girl, she belonged to a society dedicated to Mary. A branch of this Sodality, as it was called, had been established in her parish by a group of very zealous Croatian Jesuits, and it was through their influence that the young Gonxha Bojaxhiu decided to join the missionary sisters of Loreto in Bengal. When I was introduced to one of these Jesuits, Father Michael Gabric, in Calcutta, I had the feeling that I had met a true soul brother of Mother Teresa, in whose heart were still many well-kept secrets of Mother's first call.

After a short stop in Rathfarnham, Ireland, at the motherhouse of the Sisters of Loreto, Gonxha arrived in Calcutta, on January 6, 1929.

For nearly twenty years, she taught history and geography in the high school for Bengali girls at Loreto Entally, on the east side of Calcutta. Those years, uneventful and ordinary as they seemed, were to be the preparation for her second call, what Mother has always described as a "call within a call."

She was on a train bound for Darjeeling when she heard the message: "I was to leave the convent and help the poor while living among them. It was an order. I knew where I belonged, but I did not know how to get there." The Sisters now celebrate this day, September 10, as "inspiration day."

From the start, her clearcut aim was to share the lot of the slum people of Moti Jhil and the other slums of Calcutta, visiting them, teaching them, praying with them, and serving them as though she were serving Jesus himself.

Since then, her original vision has deepened and matured to a degree that it could be said that she has received yet "a further call within a call." This call involves the development of the contemplative aspect of the Missionaries of Charity. This is how the present constitution describes it: "A further special development of our society has been our contemplative branch which came into being on the feast of the Sacred Heart, June 26, 1976, in New York with the full permission of the Holy See. . . . This gift fulfills further needs in the Church and in the world today, and is the fruit of God's special love for us and our gradual growth in love for Him."

At first, Mother's vision of the aim of the Missionaries of Charity was primarily an active one: the Sisters were to spend themselves on service to the poorest of the poor. While this basic vision has not changed, its expression has grown to include a more contemplative quality and aspect. For instance, the constitution of 1954 provided for only one hour each week for the exposition of the blessed sacrament. Later, it increased to fifteen minutes a day. The revised constitution of 1973, on the other hand, specifies: "our one hour of daily adoration before the blessed sacrament is an expression of our faith, gratitude, love and reparation to Christ." Currently, contemplatives spend at least two hours a day in adoration of Jesus in the blessed sacrament. Every Friday the sacrament is exposed for the whole day. Likewise, we, the Universal Brothers of the Word, are faithful to our sunrise and sunset daily adoration and to the midnight vigil on Saturday night, which frequently turns out to be a rich time of intercession.

It seems to me that the essential charism of Mother Teresa consists of a spontaneous response, under the impulse of God's grace, to a precise need: the foundation of the Missionaries of Charity came as a response to the slums of Calcutta; the foundation of the active Brothers came as a response to a special need she had for men to become involved with the particular tasks of her work with destitute and dying men. The foundation of contemplatives also came as a response to something: it really began with an accident Mother had—a fall from bed!

Shortly before leaving for Australia, in September of 1969, Mother was in Rome preparing for her trip; she fell out of bed and dislocated her left arm and shoulder. Instead of postponing her trip, she left in that condition and then had to remain immobilized for a while. It was precisely on her feast day, that of "The Little Saint Teresa of Lisieux," that she was praying before the blessed sacrament. She began to consider the inevitability of sickness and old age, when she and the Sisters would no longer be able to physically express their service to the poor.

This incident, along with the influence of Sister Nirmala, a Nepalese convert from Hinduism who had a deep charism of contemplation, opened the door to her response. I have been told that she was also significantly affected by the writings of Brother Charles de Foucauld. Together, these influences slowly made their way into Mother's spiritual life until, after many inner struggles and setbacks, she decided, as the Missionary of Charity's silver jubilee celebration approached, that the specific call of Sister Nirmala would become an official part of the life of the Missionary of Charity Sisters.

As a result, Mother decided to send Sister Nirmala to spend some time with Father Bede Griffith at his ashram in Tamil Nadu, South India. Father Bede is a well-known scholar and a very wise man; he was a friend and student of C.S. Lewis and a writer on Hindu-Christian dialogue. He lives in Shantivanam, a Benedictine ashram founded by Father Jules Monchanin and Father Henry Lesoux, O.S.B., pioneers of the monastic and liturgical renewal in India.

While Sister Nirmala was with Father Bede, Mother left for New York to attend the Spiritual Summit Conference called by the Temple of Understanding in connection with the thirtieth anniversary of the United Nations. It was held on October 24, 1975.

Sister Nirmala and Mother had agreed that they would open a contemplative house at the foot of the Himalayas as soon as Mother came back from New York. But when she returned in December, she surprised everyone by announcing, with characteristic spontaneity, that the first contemplative house would be established not in India but in New York.

June 26, the feast of the Sacred Heart, was chosen as the foundation day, and Cardinal Cooke officially opened the old St. Anthony Convent in Union Street as the first contemplative community, to be called the "Sisters of the Word." Sister Nirmala was in charge and there were just a few candidates.

Later, when asked why she had started the contemplative branch in the United States rather than India, Mother simply replied, "In the United States they are ready for it."

In fact, what Mother Teresa had discovered in America was the neo-poverty of the developed world—the spiritual poverty of the rich, the devastating poverty of loneliness. To be "poor" in America was to be in desperate need of the sound of a human voice, the warmth of a human hand. It was to be shut-in, isolated from the rest of the world. It was the loneliness and confusion that bred drug addiction, alcoholism, perversion, and the fragmentation of family life. It was the material poverty of life in the slums of New York and Detroit. It was the tension between black and white.

This new poverty required a new method for dealing with it. That is why Mother Teresa changed her mind about locating the contemplative house at the foot of the Himalayas and, instead, chose the slums of New York, in the midst of the infamous South Bronx. Since then, she has established contemplative houses in Brooklyn, Chicago, and Washington, D.C., as well.

This insight into the importance of contemplative prayer as a spiritual weapon in combating poverty gradually penetrated the active branch of the Missionaries of Charity also. Mother continually stressed that she and her followers were not social workers but contemplatives in the heart of the world. "We are the servants of the poor. We give wholehearted free service to the poor. In the world the people are paid for their work. We are paid by God." As one Hindu official put it, "We do it for something, and you do it for someone."

A broad spectrum of people are interested in Mother Teresa's methods. One time, young activists in the communist party came to ask her how she succeeded in fighting poverty where they seemed to fail.

Wondering at her influence on the people and the success of her ventures, government officers from Delhi wrote to Mother Teresa asking her to train some of their social workers, to teach them her methods. What was her secret of success? They thought she had discovered a new social work technique, something that might add a further chapter to textbooks of sociology.

It was difficult to explain to these well-meaning people that they would find no new method, no new principle of sociology. The seeker would merely find the love of Jesus expressing itself through understanding hearts and dedicated hands, ready to perform any humble work of mercy. They would witness the gospel message entering into daily life.

This new approach to blending the contemplative and active lifestyles is reminiscent of St. Vincent de Paul's revolutionary act of establishing the Daughters of Charity. Their cloister was to be the streets of Paris, their convent a rented room, and their grill would be the fear of God. Through their work, the first hospital was established. Such a concept represented a remarkable breakthrough in an age in which consecrated women were not seen on the streets. It is the same with Mother Teresa's "contemplatives in the heart of the world." They represent a new way of blending prayer and service in today's world.

To Mother Teresa, there can be no charity without being united to love itself. Eucharistic adoration is central to her understanding of the spiritual life. The broken Jesus of the Eucharist satisfies the hunger of broken men and women. She says: "Jesus feeds us with his love; he becomes our spiritual nourishment in the Eucharist, and we feed Him with compassion in the disguise of the distress of the poor—the broken personality, the broken body and spirit of the street people, the alcoholic, the drug addict, the mental patient, the criminal."

The Explanation of the Original Constitution further elaborates: "The challenge and the call is to give those who are broken to Jesus, who hungers and thirsts for men and women to know him. 'I thirst,' Jesus said on the cross when He was deprived of every consolation, dying in absolute poverty, left alone, despised and broken in body and soul. He spoke of his thirst—not for water but for love, for sacrifice.

"Jesus is God: therefore, this love, this thirst is infinite. Our aim is to quench this infinite thirst of a God made Man. Just like the adoring angels in heaven ceaselessly sing the praises of God, so chastity, obedience, and charity towards the poor, ceaselessly quench the thirsting God by their love and by the love of the souls they bring to Him."

"I thirst" are the words that are written over the crucifix at the Mother House and in each house of the Missionaries of Charity. This phrase holds the key to Mother Teresa's spiritual vision.

THREE

In the Sandals of Mother Teresa

THE NAME OF the new contemplative branch, "Sisters of the Word," lasted just one year. The Sisters soon realized, for very practical reasons, that it would be better not to venture on a new name, especially now that the entire Missionary of Charity family had arrived at a fuller understanding of what it meant to be contemplatives in the heart of the world—"to be in Jesus, with Jesus, and to be motivated by Him twenty-four hours a day," as Mother Teresa puts it.

Yet the name didn't perish; it was reserved for a contemplative brotherhood.

The Eucharistic Congress held in Philadelphia in August 1976, after the foundation of the contemplative sisterhood, had a far greater impact on Mother Teresa than anyone ever expected. Perhaps it was partly through the influence of so many great Catholic speakers at the congress like Dorothy Day, Father Pedro Arrupe, Archbishop Helder Camara, and Archbishop Fulton Sheen, that Mother came to the new awareness that deep contemplation leads to evangelization. In the words of St. Dominic: "Contemplation must be given to others."

With this in her mind and heart she returned to Rome and met with a group of men working with the Sisters at the shelter located at the Rome Central Station. Mother shared her vision with them of a brotherhood in which the adoration of Jesus in the blessed sacrament and the evangelization of the spiritually poorest of the poor would go hand in hand. She also took time to consult church authority on the matter and received warm encouragement to found a male branch of contemplatives, to be called "Brothers of the Word."

Brother Andrew, the servant general of the Missionary of Charity Brothers, didn't think that his society was ready for this new development. It could, in fact, prove a distraction for them, so he decided that it was better not to become involved.

Mother began to pray fervently for a priest with contemplative experience to help her with the project.

My association with Mother Teresa began when I was in my mid-thirties, at a critical moment in my own life. A Benedictine monk since the age of seventeen, I had been trying to find a way of blending contemplation and missionary service. Let me briefly outline the story of my spiritual journey.

My intellect and spirit began to awaken with the shock of the last World War. I had witnessed the enormous moral and material destruction of my native city, Bari, in the region of Puglie, Italy, and the consequent effects on those closest to me. At a very early age, war had made me aware of the terrible struggle between good and evil in the human soul.

My grandmother, in her sorrow over the effect of the war on her family, had turned for consolation and guidance to a fascinating Capuchin friar, now known to the world as Padre Pio. Padre Pio was known throughout Italy for his extraordinary spiritual perception. Since Bari was in the same region as his friary, San Giovanni Rotondo, my grandmother would sometimes take me with her to see him. I would serve mass for him, and he would hear my confession.

My experience with Padre Pio sparked my search for a religious order and for an ideal for which I have always hungered: to be a monk and a missionary at the same time. After exploring various possibilities, I entered Camaldoli monastery a few days short of my seventeenth birthday. Later, for health reasons, I had to transfer to Monte Oliveto Congregation and was sent to France to finish my monastic formation under the care of a holy monk, Prior Dom Fulgence M. Lagrace. I was ordained a priest in December of 1965, the same month that the Second Vatican Council closed. A year later, Dom Fulgence died and I was left on my own. The next ten years were spent in Mexico, the United States, and India.

These were critical years for me. As a result of structural changes after the Second Vatican Council, many religious were questioning their vocation. Many times I felt my commitment to the service of the Lord challenged and was not quite sure of my own values, choices, and direction. Repeated times of retreat at Shantivanam Ashram in South India with Father Bede Griffith helped me to settle down to a life of basic simplicity and increased my desire to live a radical life in service to those who were lowest on the social scale.

In 1975 I returned to the U.S. and was assigned to be a member of a new monastic house paired with a middle-class parish in Northern Louisiana. But the impression that India had made on my character seemed to clash with the aims and purpose of my proposed new ministry, and I declined the assignment.

It was Christmas 1975. Someone gave me Malcolm Muggeridge's book about Mother Teresa, *Something Beautiful for God*. A door seemed to open. I was intrigued by the Missionaries of Charity. Would I finally be able to be both a monk and a missionary? I made a quick trip to Los Angeles, to visit the novitiate of the Missionary Brothers, and I felt increasingly drawn to them. Shortly after, my superiors accepted my proposal that I join the Missionaries of Charity. They knew of my spiritual search and thought it would be good for me to settle down to something definite.

From Los Angeles I wrote to Brother Andrew in Hong Kong in February 1977. "As you know," I told him, "I would like to join the family as I am convinced at this point in my life that contemplation of God requires a good share of service to the poor to be really fulfilled. This is a great need in me now!" The reply I received was a beautiful one, from a leader from whom much good could be expected. He offered me three possibilities: I could stay in Los Angeles, where, he explained, I was less needed; I could join a new foundation in South Korea; or I could join a novitiate in Calcutta, where life would be very difficult but where my services as a priest would be in great demand.

I decided on Calcutta. My decision was prompted by the fact that, along with Brother Andrew's letter, I had received an entrance visa for India in the mail that day. I had applied long ago, but there were political restrictions, and I hadn't expected to receive a visa just yet.

Shortly after, I left for Hong Kong. From there, Brother Andrew and I made our way to Calcutta through Bangkok. The same evening we arrived, May 10, 1977, Brother Andrew took me to the motherhouse to see Mother Teresa. After a few words of greeting, she asked me why I did not have the M.C. crucifix pinned on my shirt. Since, strictly speaking, I was not yet a novice, I had no right to be wearing it. Yet I felt compelled to answer: "Please give it to me, and I will be most pleased." Mother left me for a moment and returned with a lovely little crucifix: I knelt down in front of Brother Andrew, and Mother pinned the cross on my shirt, over my heart, and said this little prayer: "My dear Brother, receive the symbol of your crucified Lord. Follow his footsteps in search of souls. Carry him and his light into the homes of the poor, especially to the ones most in need. Spread the charity of his heart wherever you go and so satiate his thirst for souls." Something very special happened that evening between Mother and myself; I felt we had made a kind of unspoken covenant.

That same month, after the mass in which the Sisters made their perpetual vows, Mother came up to me and said that she was giving me a new name: Brother Lamba-Chul, which in Bengali means "Brother Long Hair." During my time at Shantivanam, I had grown my hair long, in the Indian style. I wore it knotted at the back.

After that, Mother telephoned and asked me to visit her. She said she had something she wanted to tell me before she left on a trip to Rome. I was a little afraid that she wanted to talk about my long hair. For moral support, I asked the novice master to accompany me. When we arrived, Mother gave me a brief talk about "love in action being service, and love in prayer being contemplation." She told me that she wanted to start a brotherhood in Rome that would be composed of contemplatives. She needed a priest with contemplative experience to help her. Would I join her in this endeavor?

"You are an answer to my prayers," she concluded confidently.

Her confidence that God had led me to her precisely for that purpose shook me completely. I was astounded to think that I could be an answer to anyone's prayer, let alone to the prayer of Mother Teresa. Even so, without fully understanding, I agreed to her request. I knew that I had found that something which Padre Pio had spoken to me about during my visits to him as a youth. My search for blending contemplation and action in the service of God had come to an end. The rest of my life would be dedicated to that goal.

Mother Teresa wasted no time once she arrived in Rome. She assisted Cardinal Poletti as he pinned the cross on six men aspiring to be "Brothers of the Word." It was, coincidentally, my thirty-sixth birthday. Later, she wrote to the Missionary of Charity Brothers in India:

My Dearest Brothers,

Happy birthday to our Holy Father in your house. As you know, on the 3rd of June, 1977, Cardinal Poletti offered Holy Mass and gave the crosses to six men who would form a pious association called the "Brothers of the Word." A contemplative group like the one I started in New York last year, they will both have the same constitution, the same life. But in time this group will become a completely new congregation known as the Brothers of the Word. They will in no way be connected with you, nor be a branch of yours. I ask you to pray much for them and for me, that we may together fulfill the will of God. Father Angelo is a real gift of God. He will be able to train the Brothers to be real contemplatives from his own experience. His stay with you has been very fruitful. I have one piece of advice to give you, my Brothers. Deepen your love for Jesus through adoration of the Eucharist and live your love for our Lady through fidelity to your daily rosary.

When she came back and it was my turn to leave for Rome, Mother gave me as a gift a Bible that had been presented to her by Cardinal Krol at the Eucharistic Congress in Philadelphia. I asked her to write something in it that would serve as the ideal of the Brothers of the Word. On the spur of the moment she wrote what I consider the proto-rule of the brotherhood:

Dear Brothers,

Know the word of God
Love the word of God
Live the word of God
Give the word of God
And the word of God will make you holy.

Mother also gave me $200 for expenses and a few pieces of cloth so that I could choose a distinctive style of dress for myself and my Brothers as a sign that we belonged fully to Jesus. At the last minute, she decided that others had more need of the money than I did. Smiling to me, she issued a challenge, saying, "Go with no money and trust God, and if you starve and die, let me know." Then she added with a slightly malicious smile, "But that will never happen."

That's how my uncharted journey with Mother Teresa began. What would it be like to follow in the sandals of this remarkable woman, so confident of God's care that she delighted to do the very things that seemed most foolish in the eyes of the world?

As it turned out, my time in Rome was anything but easy. I was no longer a Missionary of Charity Brother and had no specific formation in the kind of life that Mother Teresa and her Sisters lived. My own training had been Benedictine. How was I to establish the Brothers of the Word? Instead of answers to my questions, I was suddenly confronted with a host of new questions.

In Rome we lived in two rooms in the basement of San Gregorio-al-Celio Monastery, where the sisters had their shelter for the homeless. Our rooms were very crowded, and we depended on the shelter for our food. As yet, we were a brotherhood without a home.

I soon discovered that the aspirants in Rome had different expectations of what the brotherhood should be and different ideas of our apostolate and the contemplative life. Each had his own particular vision, and I began to realize that nothing was likely to develop there.

In fact, the longer I stayed in Rome the more convinced I became that I had nothing to give. If God wanted a contemplative brotherhood, he would have to establish it himself.

FOUR

The Word to the World

ROME WAS MY DARK NIGHT. At my lowest point, I knew that I had to find someone needier than myself to help. If I could forget about my own problems and focus my attention on giving to others, then I would progressively find my true self once again.

Providential circumstances took me to the spot most in need in the western hemisphere, the tiny republic of Haiti in the Caribbean Sea. With six million nominal Catholics, it had very few clergy. Material and moral conditions were so poor that it seemed a sister city to Calcutta. I realized that Haiti was the perfect ground for Mother's spirituality to take root and to bloom.

In August of 1980, with the help and encouragement of Mother Teresa, I rented two rooms in the slums of Saint Martin sans Fil. One room was the chapel and the other served as an all-purpose area with a portable charcoal stove in the corner. The door of the little house was practically always open. Small children would gather on the porch during the hour or two each day when water was available at the public faucet, and they would play endlessly outside in the dust and dirt of the road.

At the end of six months, several young men just simply walked into the house to live with me. They were all from Port au Prince. Three came at different times from the states, but they didn't last more than a few weeks. Life was very challenging in the months that followed. It was hard to pray because there was little privacy. To make matters worse, people played their beat music fullblast during the day and the voodoo drums continued their incessant beating far into the night.

In a moment of discouragement, I asked the Lord to give me a sign to sustain me. Would he provide for me, somewhere in this slum, a little parcel of land where I could plant some flowers? If I could watch plants growing, my hope would be sustained.

It happened exactly as I had asked.

A family of Syrian extraction, devoted to Padre Pio, had already given the Missionary of Charity Sisters a piece of land for their children's home. The family still owned a plot of land on a hill in the slum overlooking the bay. Until then the land had been used as a garbage dump. They generously offered to build three rooms for my growing community: one for the Lord, one for the brothers, and one for guests. There would also be plenty of room for a garden. Clearly, the Lord had answered my prayer.

Almost four years passed, and I struggled to educate my Brothers and to see that we survived amid the hardships of life in Haiti. It seemed right that we should work enough to be self-sufficient, as Mother had suggested. As a monk, I had received a certain amount of training in the arts. Fortunately, Haitians are the most creative people I have ever known. With the young men who had joined me, I began to design small statues out of tropical oak and acacia wood and to develop primitive paintings. Of course there would be no question of marketing them among the people of Haiti. But there were good possibilities in the United States. This factor, combined with the need to educate my unschooled postulants, prompted me to secure permission from the proper authorities for a house in the United States.

New Orleans with its French creole tradition and considerable black population first attracted my attention; so we opened a house there for a time. But events took me back to Haiti, and it was good once again to be close to the poorest of the poor.

Since then, with the permission of the archdioceses of Miami, we have also opened a house in a building which used to be the rectory of St. Mary's Cathedral in Miami, where a dedicated little group of priests and brothers live. Apart from the hours of community prayer, private prayer, and studies, the brothers spend the mornings serving the poor at a drug rehabilitation center and visiting the elderly, the sick, and the shut-ins, especially among the immigrant Haitian community in the neighborhood.

Finally, our rule of life and constitution was completed this year (1985) in Calcutta, with much strenuous work. The first part of it is printed at the end of the book.

Presenting it to the brothers, Mother repeated the message she had given us earlier: "My dear Brothers, I am sure it will give you great joy to know that we have worked at the constitution with great love. I hope and pray that this constitution will help you grow to be humble like Mary and holy like Jesus. Be faithful to know, love, and live the word of God, and only then will you be able to give that word of God to each other and to the poor you serve. Be only and all for Jesus, through Mary and a deep life of prayer."

To conclude the first part of this book, I should point out that it is just barely eight years since the Brothers of the Word were established. The brotherhood is still very much a seed, an embryo. Publicity, as Mother warns us, can be harmful. Yet, after winning the Nobel Peace Prize, she is less and less available to us. Currently, she is establishing new foundations of Missionary of Charity Sisters at the rate of twenty-five to thirty per year, over two each month.

All this makes the need for Mother's writings more apparent. Those associated with her and those who are co-workers will appreciate greater access to her writings. Clearly Mother Teresa now belongs to everyone, not just to the Missionary of Charity family. Her message, her grace, belongs to the universality of the Catholic Church, and I am convinced that the best way for her children to hold on to her message is to give it away.

Last October, after making my lifelong commitment to the Universal Brothers of the Word, I spent a while talking to Mother Teresa. We spoke about the future, about our constitutions, and about the fact that she would be turning 75 in the coming year.

I will never forget her words to me. "Claim Mother. Just claim me," she said. Implicit in her words was the realization that she simply could not take on more work or added responsibility. She would be no more physically available to me now than she had been during the early period of my association with her. But her spiritual vision would be there to guide me and to guide my Brothers along the way of wholehearted service to Jesus, disguised in the spiritually poorest of the poor. Our part was to simply claim that vision as our own.

In fact, Mother Teresa is there for all of us to claim. The poor and the rich, parents, single people, lay and religious, Christians and non-Christians, believers and non-believers. Anyone who wants to can claim for themselves a share in the spiritual vision of Mother Teresa of Calcutta. It takes only a willing heart and a spirit eager for the service of God.

The pages that follow contain selections from the writings of Mother Teresa and the Constitution of the Missionaries of Charity Sisters. They convey the true heart and core of her spiritual life and vision. It is my hope that the reader will meditate on these selections and so partake more fully in the legacy of Mother Teresa of Calcutta, the little nun who has decided to "take whatever God gives and to give whatever He takes with a big smile," and "to let Him use her without first consulting her."

Part Two

Something Beautiful for God

Come with me into a world of poverty,
Into a land where men are dying endlessly,
Into a world of inhumanity.
Can't you see they're starving where's your
* charity.*
They laugh and cry they're people just like you
* and me,*
They need help and not just sympathy.

Chorus:
Show each one something beautiful for God above,
Something beautiful to show your love,
Something beautiful for God above,
Something beautiful to show your love.

A day goes by, the night is long for everyone,
A child is crying, perhaps he'll live to see the sun,
And yet he knows the morning may not come.
Throughout the world our brothers live in poverty,
They're everywhere if only we have eyes to see,
So look around and find your sanity.

Show to men the love that He has shown to you,
And feed his lambs as He has fed each one of you,
He loves them as much as He loves you.

FIVE

Our Call

You have not chosen Me, but I have chosen you (Jn 15:16).

Let us make our society something beautiful for God.

*

He has chosen us; we have not first chosen Him. But we must respond by making our society something beautiful for God—something very beautiful. For this we must give all—our utmost We must cling to Jesus, grasp Him, have a grip on Him, and never let go for anything. We must fall in love with Jesus.

*

Our particular mission is to labor at the salvation and sanctification of the poorest of the poor not only in the slums but all over the world, wherever they may be, by:

—living the love of God in prayer and action in a life marked by the simplicity and humility of the gospel,

—loving Jesus under the appearance of Bread,

—serving Him in the distressing disguise of the poorest of the poor, both materially and spiritually, recognizing in them and restoring to them the image and likeness of God.

As members of the active branch by:

—nursing the sick and the dying destitutes,

—gathering and teaching little street children,

—visiting and caring for beggars, leprosy patients, and their children,

—giving shelter to the abandoned and homeless,

—*caring for the unwanted, the unloved, and the lonely,*

—*going out to the spiritually poorest of the poor to proclaim the Word of God by our presence and spiritual works of mercy, and by,*

—*adoration of Jesus in the blessed sacrament.*

We are called the "Missionaries of Charity."

A missionary is one sent with a mission—a message to deliver. Just as Jesus was sent by his Father, we too are sent by Him and filled with his Spirit to be witnesses of his gospel of love and compassion, first in our communities and then in our apostolate among the poorest of the poor all over the world.

As missionaries we must be:

—*carriers of God's love, ready to go in haste, like Mary—in search of souls,*

—*burning lights that give light to all men,*

—*the salt of the earth,*

—*souls consumed with one desire: Jesus. We must keep his interests continually in our hearts and minds, carrying our Lord to places where He has not walked before.*

—*fearless in doing the things He did, courageously going through danger and death with Him and for Him,*

—*ready to accept joyously the need to die daily if we want to bring souls to God, to pay the price He paid for souls,*

—*ever ready to go to any part of the world and to respect and appreciate unfamiliar customs of other peoples, their living conditions and language, willing to adapt ourselves if and when necessary,*

—*happy to undertake any labor and toil, and glad to make any sacrifice involved in our missionary life.*

"I Thirst"

"I thirst" Jesus said on the cross when He was deprived of every consolation and left alone, despised and broken in body and soul.

As Missionaries of Charity we are called to quench this infinite thirst of a God made Man, who suffered, died, yet rose again and is now at the right hand of his Father making intercession for us:

—*by living the life of fervent charity in the practice of the four vows of chastity, poverty, obedience, and wholehearted free service to the poorest of the poor,*

—*by a deep life of prayer, contemplation, and penance,*

—*by accepting all suffering, renunciations, and even death,*

—*by being spouses of Jesus Crucified,*

*

Hungry for love He looks at you
Thirsty for kindness He begs from you
Naked for loyalty He hopes in you
Sick and imprisoned for friendship He wants from you
Homeless for shelter in your heart He asks of you.
Will you be that one to Him?

*

Each time anyone comes in contact with us, they must become different and better people because of having met us. We must radiate God's love.

*

"To quench the thirst of Jesus," for souls, means for love—for love of me and for love of others. When Jesus was dying on the cross, He cried, "I thirst." We have these words in every chapel of the M.C.s to remind us that an M.C. is here to quench the thirst of Jesus for souls, for love, for kindness, for compassion. When Jesus was in pain on the cross, the soldier, in order to help Jesus forget his pains, prepared the bitter drink of vinegar and gave it to Him to drink. To avoid hurting the soldier, Jesus took it, but He only tasted it. He did not drink it because He did not want to forget the pain and the suffering. No . . . He loved me and He died for me . . . He suffered for me. Very often, we offer bitter drink to Jesus. This bitterness comes from the depth of our hearts and wells up in our words and our attitudes toward one another: "Whatever you do to the least of my brothers, you do it to me."

We have to quench the thirst of Jesus for others and for us. We do this by:

—nursing the sick and dying. By each action done to them I quench the thirst of Jesus for love of that person—by giving God's love in me to that particular person. How often we do not do that well!

—gathering and teaching little street children. I must give God's love to each of them and thus quench the thirst of Jesus.

—visiting and caring for beggars.

—giving shelter to the abandoned.

—caring for the unwanted, the unloved, the lonely—all the poor people.

This is how I quench the thirst of Jesus for others, by giving his love in action to them.

The Bread of Life

As Missionaries of Charity we are especially called upon to see Christ in the appearance of bread and to touch Him in the broken bodies of the poor.

Christ when He took bread said: "Take and eat, this is my Body delivered for you." By giving Himself, He invites us to grow in the power of His love to do what He has done.

Christ's love for us will give us strength and urge us to spend ourselves for Him. "Let the Sisters and the people eat you up." We have no right to refuse our life to others in whom we contact Christ.

*

Like Mary, let us be full of zeal to go in haste to give Jesus to others. She was full of grace when, at the Annunciation, she received Jesus. Like her, we too become full of grace every time we receive Holy Communion. It is the same Jesus whom she received and whom we receive at Mass. As soon as she received Him she went with haste to give Him to John. For us also, as soon as we receive Jesus in Holy Communion, let us go in haste to give Him to our Sisters, to our poor, to the sick, to the dying, to the lepers, to the unwanted and the unloved. By this we make Jesus present in the world today.

We cannot separate our lives from the Eucharist; the moment we do, something breaks. People ask, "Where do the Sisters get the joy and energy to do what they are doing?'' The Eucharist involves more than just receiving; it also involves satisfying the hunger of Christ. He says, "Come to Me.'' He is hungry for souls. Nowhere does the gospel say: "Go away,'' but always "come to Me.''

Our lives must be woven around the Eucharist. Ask Jesus to be with you, to work with you that you may be able to pray the work. You must really be sure that you have received Jesus. After that, you cannot give your tongue, your thoughts, or your heart to bitterness.

Put your sins in the chalice for the precious blood to wash away. One drop is capable of washing away all the sins of the world.

The Eucharist is connected with the Passion. If Jesus had not established the Eucharist we would have forgotten the crucifixion. It would have faded into the past and we would have forgotten that Jesus loved us. There is a saying that to be far away from the eyes is to be far away from the heart. To make sure that we do not forget, Jesus gave us the Eucharist as a memorial of his love. To make sure that we keep on loving Him, He gives us his hunger (to satisfy our hunger for Him)—He gives us the poorest of the poor.

We must be faithful to that smallness of the Eucharist, that simple piece of bread which even a child can take in, that giving of a bath, that smile. . . . We have so much that we don't care about the small things. If we do not care, we will lose our grip on the Eucharist—on our lives. The Eucharist is so small.

I was giving Communion this morning. My two fingers were holding Jesus. Try to realize that Jesus allows Himself to be broken. Make yourselves feel the need of each other. The Passion and the Eucharist should open our eyes to that smallness: "This is my body; take and eat''—the small piece of bread. Today let us realize our own littleness in comparison with the Bread of Life.

*

For us, we must never separate the Eucharist and the poor—or the poor and the Eucharist. You will really be a true M.C. when you go to the poor and take Jesus with you. He satisfied my hunger for Him and now I go to satisfy his hunger for souls, for love.

*

That is why Jesus made Himself bread, to satisfy our hunger for God. See the humility of God. He also made Himself the hungry one to satisfy our hunger for God through our love, our service. Let us pray that none of us will be unfaithful. Let us pray for our poor people. They are also hungry for God.

*

Many years ago an angel came to bring the good news to Mary. The Prince of Peace was anxious to come to earth and an angel was used to bring the good news that the Creator would become a little child. The Prince of Peace was attracted to a young girl, who was a nobody in the eyes of the world. Even the angel could not understand why he was sent to a creature like that. But she was so beautiful that the King of Kings wanted to become flesh in her. She was so full of grace, so pure, so full of God. She looked at the angel—she must have been surprised for she had never seen an angel—and asked, how? What are you saying? I don't understand what you are saying; it makes no sense to me. And the angel said simply that by the power of the Holy Spirit, Christ would be formed within her. And Mary answered with just one word: "Behold the handmaid of the Lord."

In heaven everything was beautiful—yet, what attracted Jesus to the earth? The Son of God wanted to feel what it meant to be a human being; to be locked up for nine months, so dependent on a mother. That is why we say, "He, being rich, became poor"—so helpless!

When we recite the Creed we say "God from God, Light from Light." And there was the little body, so small. We find it so difficult to become small, and Jesus says to us: "Unless you become like little children you cannot enter the kingdom of God." And Mary knew and replied, "Yes, behold the handmaid of the Lord."

On the way to Addis Ababa, August 21, 1977

Now, more than ever we need to live out the teaching of Jesus: "Love one another, as the Father has loved Me." We have to love as the Father loves his Son Jesus, with the same mercy and compassion, joy and peace. Try to find out how the Father loves his Son, and then try to love one another in the same way. Find out in all humility how much you are loved by Jesus. From the time you realize that you are loved by Jesus, love as He loves you.

In each of our lives Jesus comes as the Bread of Life—to be eaten, to be consumed by us. That is how He loves us. He also comes as the Hungry One, hoping to be fed with the bread of our life, with our hearts that love and our hands that serve. In so doing, we prove that we have been created in the image and likeness of God, for God is love. When we love we are like God. This is what Jesus meant when He said: "Be perfect as your heavenly Father is perfect."

Jesus has chosen us for Himself. We belong to Him. Let us be so convinced of this "belonging" that we allow nothing, however small, to separate us from his love.

*

Motherhouse, September 29, 1980

That you may know each other at the breaking of the bread, love each other in the eating of the Bread of Life, and serve each other and him in his poor by giving your wholehearted service.

When communicating with Christ in your heart—the partaking of Living Bread—remember what Our Lady must have felt when the Spirit overpowered her and she, who was full of grace, became full with the body of Jesus. The Spirit in her was so strong that she immediately rose in haste to go and serve.

Each Holy Communion, each breaking of the Bread of Life, each sharing should produce in us the same, for it is the same Jesus who came to Mary and was made flesh. We, too, should be in haste to give this life of Jesus to our Sisters and the poor.

We Are Chosen

"I will betroth you to Me forever in steadfast love, in mercy. I will betroth you to me in faithfulness" (Hos 19:20).

Thank God from the depths of your heart that He has chosen you for Himself and for life.

*

What is our vocation? What do we call vocation? Our vocation is Jesus. We have it in the scripture very clearly: "I have called you by name, you are precious to me . . . I have called you my friend. Water will not drown you." (Water symbolizes all the temptations of evil.) "I will give nations for you; you are precious." "How could a mother forget her child? Or a woman the child within her womb? But even if a mother could forget, I will never forget you. You are precious to me; you are carved in the palm of my hand."

Why are we here? We must have heard Jesus calling us by name. We are like St. Paul. Once he realized the love of Christ, he cared about nothing else. He did not care whether he was scourged or put into prison. For him, only one thing was important: Jesus Christ.

*

God loves me. I'm not here just to fill a place, just to be a number. He has chosen me for a purpose. I know it. He will fulfill it if I don't put an obstacle in his way. He will not force me. God could have forced Our Lady. Jesus could have come just like that. The Holy Spirit could have come. But God wanted Mary to say yes. It is the same with us. God doesn't force us, but he wants us to say yes.

God doesn't want one more congregation in the world—just 3,000 nuns more. We have been created and chosen to proclaim his love so that people may see the wonderful works of God. I will never forget a man in Kalighat who observed a Sister as she was taking care of a patient. The Sister did not know she was being watched. Afterwards the man came to me and said:

"Mother, I came here godless. Today I found God in that Sister—the way she was looking at the sick person and taking care of him." This is what we have been created for—to proclaim Christ's love, to proclaim his presence.

Called to Be Saints

"I am the Vine and my Father is the Vinedresser. Every branch that bears fruit He prunes that it may bear more fruit" (Jn 15:1-2).

I will give saints to Mother Church!

*

Let us live the life of union with God. All our little actions may be offered through the precious blood—through Jesus. We have learned that. Let us never be satisfied. Jesus poured out every drop of blood, not just some of it. Let us do the same. We have to learn to become virtuous. We must be full of holy ambition to be the holiest Sister.

*

God said to one of our sisters: "I have so many Sisters like you—ordinary, good Sisters; I can pave the streets with them. I want fervent ones: saints. 'I looked for one to comfort me and I found none.'"

There is so much unhappiness, so much misery everywhere. Our human nature stays with us from beginning to end. We must work hard every day to conquer ourselves. We must learn to be meek and humble of heart. Let us try to give everything to Jesus: every word, every moment. Jesus, use my eyes, my ears, my feet! My resolution must be firm: to become a saint.

Jesus said, "Learn of me." In our meditations we should always say, "Jesus, make me a saint according to your own heart, meek and humble." We must respond in the spirit in which Jesus meant us to respond. We know Him better now, through meditations and the study of the gospel, but have we really understood Him in his humility? Does this humility appeal to us, attract us? Humility is nothing but truth. What have we got that we have not received? asks St. Paul. If I have not received anything, what good have I on my own?

*

If you are humble, nothing will touch you, neither praise nor disgrace, because you know what you are. If you are blamed, you won't be discouraged; if anyone calls you a saint, you won't put yourself on a pedestal. If you are a saint, thank God; if you are a sinner, don't remain one. Christ tells us to aim very high, not to be like Abraham or David or any of the saints, but to be like our heavenly Father.

*

The more repugnant the work the greater should be our faith and cheerful devotion. That we feel repugnance is but natural, but when we overcome it for love of Jesus we may become heroic. Very often it has happened in the lives of the saints that a heroic overcoming of repugnance has been what has lifted them to sanctity.

This was the case with St. Francis of Assisi, who, when meeting a completely disfigured leper, drew back. But then, overcoming himself, he kissed the terrible, disfigured face. The result was that Francis was filled with an untold joy. He became the complete master of himself, and the leper walked away praising God for his cure.

*

Self-knowledge puts us on our knees and it is very necessary for love. For knowledge of God produces love, and knowledge of self produces humility. Self-knowledge is a very important thing in our lives. As St. Augustine says, "Fill yourselves first, and then only will you be able to give to others." Self-knowledge is also a safeguard against pride, especially when one is tempted in later life. The greatest mistake is to think one is too strong to fall into temptation. Put your finger in the fire and it will burn. Don't play with temptation.

Holiness is not the luxury of the few. It is a simple duty for each one of us, especially for us who have been chosen. We have been chosen to belong to Christ.

Nothing can make me holy except the presence of God and to me the presence of God is fidelity to small things. Fidelity to small things will lead you to Christ. Infidelity to small things will lead you to sin.

*

First Friday in October 1960

The first step "to becoming" is to will it. St. Thomas says that "sanctity consists in nothing else than a firm resolution, the heroic act of a soul abandoning herself to God." By an upright will we love God, we run towards God, we reach Him, we possess Him.

"O good, good will which transforms me into the image of God and makes me like to Him," so St. Augustine says. My progress in holiness depends on God and myself: on God's grace and my will.

We must have a real, living resolution to reach holiness. St. Teresa says that Satan is terribly afraid of resolute souls. Everything depends on these two or three words: "I will" or "I will not." I must put all my energy into this "will." St. John Berchmans, St. Stanislaus, St. Margaret Mary said "I will," and they did become saints. What is a saint but simply a resolute soul, a soul that uses power plus action? Wasn't this what St. Paul meant when he said: "I can do all things in Him who strengthens me?" My Sisters, I will not be satisfied if you are just good religious. I want to be able to offer God a perfect sacrifice. Only holiness perfects the gift.

"To resolve to be a saint" means I will despoil myself of all that is not God: I will strip my heart and empty it of all created things: I will live in poverty and detachment. I will renounce my will, my inclinations, my whims and fancies and offer myself as a willing slave to the will of God. Yes, my children, this is what I pray for daily, for each one, that you may become a slave to the will of God.

Rome, October 8, 1980

Holiness is the main reason for the existence of our society. For us, holiness should not be difficult—for in giving wholehearted free service to the poorest of the poor, we are with Jesus twenty-four hours. And, since every M.C. is the poorest of the poor, we live and observe the fourth vow even when we do small things for each other.

SIX

Our Response

Father, into your hands I commend my spirit (Lk 23:46).

An M.C. must be an M.C. of joy. By this sign the world will know you are M.C.s.

*

The spirit of our Society is one of total surrender, loving trust and cheerfulness, as lived by Jesus and Mary in the gospel.

Total Surrender

Our total surrender to God means to be entirely at the disposal of the Father as Jesus and Mary were. In giving ourselves completely to God, because God has given Himself to us, we are entirely at his disposal,
—to be possessed by Him so that we may possess Him,
—to take whatever He gives and to give whatever He takes with a big smile,
—to be used by Him as it pleases Him without being consulted,
—to offer Him our free will, our reason, our whole life in pure faith, so that He may think his thoughts in our minds, do his work through our hands, and love with our hearts.

*

Total surrender consists in giving ourselves completely to God. Why must we give ourselves fully to God? Because God has given Himself to us. If God, who owes nothing to us, is ready to impart to us no less than Himself, shall we answer with just a fraction of ourselves? To give ourselves fully to God is a means of receiving God Himself. I live for God and give up my own self and in this way induce God to live for me. Therefore, to possess God, we must allow Him to possess our souls. How poor we would be if God had not given us the power of giving ourselves to Him! How rich we are now! How easy it is to conquer God! We give ourselves to God; then God is ours and there can be nothing more ours than God. The money with which God repays our surrender is Himself.

*

Our total surrender will come today by surrendering even our sins so that we will be poor. "Unless you become a child you cannot come to me." You are too big, too heavy; you cannot be lifted up. We need humility to acknowledge our sin. The knowledge of our sin helps us to rise. I will get up and go to my Father.

*

It must have been so hard to have been scourged, to have been spat upon. "Take it away," Jesus prayed during his agony. His Father didn't come to him directly and say, "This is my beloved Son," but He consoled Him through a creature. Let us pray that we will fill our hearts with Jesus' surrender, that we will understand total surrender.

We should not be concerned with the instrument God uses to speak to us, whether the pencil writes in blue ink or green, but with what God is saying to us. Let us pray to understand what it means to be at his disposal.

*

God's tender love for us is great. We receive so much. People give to us so abundantly. Our answer to God for his tremendous love is total surrender. . . . He can do with us whatever He wants. Once the Cardinal of St. Louis asked me to write something for him in his breviary. I wrote, "Let Jesus use you without consulting you." He wrote back, "You don't know what you have done to me. I examine my conscience every day and ask, 'Did I allow Jesus to use me without consulting me?'"

Our vocation is the conviction that "I belong to Him." Because I belong to Him, He must be free to use me. I must surrender completely. When we look at his cross, we understand his love. His head is bent down to kiss us. His hands are extended to embrace us. His heart is wide open to receive us. This is what we have to be in the world today. We, too, must have our head bent down to our people—to the school where we are teaching or to the sick and dying destitute that we are helping. This is Jesus in his distressing disguise. Whether in the school or in the slum, it is the same Jesus. He said very clearly, "You did it to me. I was hungry . . . I was naked . . . I was homeless." Let us not make the mistake of thinking that the hunger is only for a piece of bread. The hunger of today is much greater; it is a hunger for love, to be wanted, to be cared for, to be somebody.

*

There is such a beautiful thing in India—the red dot on the forehead. The meaning for the Hindu is that his whole thought and attention, everything must be concentrated on God. For the married woman it is the same. The red marking along the part in her hair means that all her thoughts are for her husband. We, too, must be fully for Jesus, giving him that undivided love.

Loving Trust

One thing Jesus asks of me: that I lean on Him; that in Him and only in Him I put complete trust; that I surrender myself to Him unreservedly. Even when all goes wrong and I feel as if I am a ship without a compass, I must give myself completely to Him. I must not attempt to control God's action; I must not count the stages in the journey He would have me make. I must not desire a clear perception of my advance upon the road, must not know precisely where I am upon the way of holiness. I ask Him to make a saint of me, yet I must leave to Him the choice of the saintliness itself and still more the means which lead to it.

We need to trust our poor people. The greatest injustice done to our poor is that we fail to trust them, to respect them, to love them. How often we just push and pull.

*

Total surrender involves loving trust. You cannot surrender totally unless you trust lovingly and totally. Jesus trusted his Father because He knew Him, He knew of his love. "My Father and I are one." "The Father is in me and I am in the Father." "I am not alone, the Father is with me." "Father, into your hands I commend my Spirit." Read St. John's Gospel and see how many times Jesus used the word "Father." Jesus came to reveal the Father. In the time of the Old Testament, God was known as the God of fear, punishment, and anger. The coming of Jesus reverses this picture completely. God in the New Testament is the God of love, compassion, and mercy. That is why we can trust Him fully—there is no more fear. This loving trust implies that we know the love of God and that we proclaim this love, compassion, and mercy everywhere we are sent. Today we reveal Him.

*

God will never, never, never let us down if we have faith and put our trust Him. For the very first time one week we had no rice to give the people. We were feeding four thousand people each day and these were people who simply would not eat unless the Sisters fed them. But we had nothing. Then, about 9:00 A.M. on Friday, two truckloads full of bread arrived. It was more bread than these people had ever seen in their lives.

The schools had been closed unexpectedly and the bread that would have been used in the schools that day was sent to the Sisters. So, you see, God is thoughtful. He will never let us down if we trust Him, even if He has to play a trick on people and close down the schools. He will always look after us. So we must cleave to Jesus. Our whole life must simply be woven into Jesus. Jesus in the Mass, Jesus in my Sisters, in the poor, at adoration. It is the same Jesus. Just as the wine and the grape are one; just as the branch fits so tightly into the vine—so we must be completely one with Jesus.

Cheerfulness

Joy is indeed the fruit of the Holy Spirit and a characteristic mark of the Kingdom of God, for God is Joy.

Christ wanted to share his joy with his apostles "That my joy may be in you, and that your joy may be full" (Jn 15:11).

Joy is prayer,

—the sign of our generosity, selflessness and close and continual union with God.

Joy is love,

—a joyful heart is the normal result of a heart burning with love, for she gives most who gives with joy, and God loves a cheerful giver.

Joy is a net of love by which we can catch souls,

—a Sister filled with joy preaches without preaching. Joy is a need and a power for us even physically, for it makes us always ready to go about doing good.

The joy of the Lord is our strength.

*

Persuaded of our nothingness and with the blessing of obedience we attempt all things, doubting nothing, for with God all things are possible. We will allow the good God to make plans for the future, for yesterday has gone, tomorrow has not yet come, and we have only today to make Him known, loved, and served. Grateful for the thousands of opportunities Jesus gives us to bring hope into a multitude of lives by our concern for the individual sufferer, we will help our troubled world at the brink of despair to discover a new reason to live or to die with a smile of contentment on its lips.

*

We do not allow ourselves to be disheartened by any failure as long as we have done our best, neither do we glory in our success but refer all to God in deepest thankfulness.

With Jesus our Savior, "the Lamb led to the slaughter," and with our poor, we will accept cheerfully and in the spirit of faith all the opportunities He makes especially for us—those of misunderstanding, of being looked down on, of failure, disgrace, blame, lack of virtue, and correction.

*

Like Jesus, who submitted Himself to the common law of labor and the common lot of the poor, we will
—not seek any special privileges or treatment for ourselves, but be happy to be treated as one of the poor, ready to be insulted, ill-treated, refused, blamed falsely, or put to all kinds of inconveniences. We shall not seek to defend ourselves, but leave our defense to the Lord.
—we will not worry about tomorrow but will live the present moment intensely, with complete trust in God.

*

Free means: Joyfully and with eagerness, fearlessly and openly, giving freely what we have freely received, without accepting any return in cash or kind, reward or gratitude.

*

Cheerfulness should be one of the main points of our religious life. A cheerful giver is a great giver. Cheerfulness is a sign of a generous and mortified person, who, forgetting all things, even herself, tries to please God in all she does for souls. Cheerfulness is often a cloak which hides a life of sacrifice, continual union with God, fervor and generosity.

*

Joy is one of the most essential things in our Society. An M.C. must be an M.C. of joy. She must radiate that joy to everyone. By this sign the world will know you are M.C.s. Everyone in the world sees you and remarks and speaks out about the M.C.s, not because of what they do but because they are happy to do the work they do and live the life they live. "That My joy may be in you," says Jesus. What is this joy of Jesus? It is the result of his continual union with God, doing the will of the Father. This joy is the fruit of union with God, of being in the presence of God. Living in the presence of God fills us with joy. God is joy. To bring joy to us, Jesus became man. Mary was the first one to receive Jesus: "My spirit rejoices in God my Savior." The child in Elizabeth's womb leapt with joy because Mary carried Jesus to him.

In Bethlehem, joy filled everyone: the shepherds, the angels, the Kings, Joseph, and Mary. Joy was also the characteristic mark of the first Christians. During the persecution, people used to look for those who had this joy radiating on their faces. By that joy, they knew who the Christians were and thus they persecuted them. St. Paul, whom we are trying to imitate in our zeal, was an apostle of joy. He urged the early Christians to rejoice in the Lord always. Paul's whole life can be summed up in one sentence, "I belong to Christ." Nothing can separate me from the Love of Christ, neither suffering nor persecution nor anything. "I live, now it is no longer I who live but it is Christ who lives in me." That is why St. Paul was so full of joy.

Joy is love, the normal result of a heart burning with love. Our lamp will be burning with sacrifices made out of love if we have joy. Then the Bridegroom will say, "Come and possess the Kingdom prepared for you." It is a joyful Sister who gives most. Everyone loves the one who gives with joy and so does God. Don't we always turn to someone who will give happily and without grumbling? "Joy is a net of love by which we catch souls." Because we are full of joy, everyone wants to be with us and to receive the light of Christ that we possess. A Sister filled with joy preaches without preaching. Daily, we pray, "Help me to spread your fragrance," yours, Lord, not mine. Do we realize its meaning? Do we realize our mission of spreading this joy, of radiating this joy daily as we go about our lives?

*

April 1964

Joy is not simply a matter of temperament. In the service of God and souls, it is always hard to be joyful—all the more reason why we should try to acquire it and make it grow in our hearts.

Joy is prayer; joy is strength; joy is love; joy is a net of love by which we catch souls. God loves a cheerful giver. She gives most who gives with joy. If in the work you have difficulties and you accept them with joy, with a big smile—in this like in any other thing—they will see your good works and glorify the Father. The best way to show your gratitude is to accept everything with joy. A joyful heart is the normal result of a heart burning with love.

Joy is a need and a power for us, even physically. A Sister who has cultivated a spirit of joy feels less tired and is always ready to go on doing good. Joy is one of the best safeguards against temptations. The devil is a carrier of dust and dirt—he uses every chance to throw what he has at us. A joyful heart knows how to protect itself from such dirt: Jesus can take full possession of our soul only if it surrenders itself joyfully. St. Teresa was worried about her Sisters only when she saw any of them lose their joy. God is joy. He is love. A Sister filled with joy preaches without preaching. A joyful Sister is like the sunshine of God's love, the hope of eternal happiness, the flame of burning love.

In our society, a cheerful disposition is one of the main virtues required for a Missionary of Charity. The spirit of our society is total surrender, loving trust, and cheerfulness. That is why the society expects us to accept humiliations readily and with joy; to live the life of poverty with cheerful trust; to imitate the chastity of Mary, the cause of our joy; to offer cheerful obedience from inward joy; to minister to Christ in his distressing disguise with cheerful devotion.

Missionaries of Love

We must not be ashamed to love Christ with our emotions. A woman loves her husband with her whole heart. In her autobiography, the Little Flower tells about a relative who came to see her. This woman was always talking about her husband, about his long hair, his beautiful eyes, and so on. She expressed her love for him so beautifully. The Little Flower listened to her and then wrote these words in her diary: "I will never allow a woman to love her husband more than I love you, O Jesus Christ."

Jesus was everything to her. She was so attached to Christ. Is it the same for you? Do you love Christ like that? We must love Christ with our emotions. We are all women. Let us all make use of our ability to love.

*

Be one with Him, joined to Him and united to Him so that nothing, absolutely nothing, can separate you from the love of Christ. He belongs to you and you belong to Him. It's as simple as that. Accept whatever He gives and give whatever He takes with a big smile.

Yet, we forget. We can love the leper, the one with the broken and disfigured face, but we forget to love our Sister when she is proud or impatient. We forget that it is only a distressing disguise, that the person is really Jesus. We do not have undivided love for Christ but, instead, we let the devil trick us with the distressing disguise. We must be holy. We must be able to see Jesus in our Sisters and in the poor.

*

When the Little Flower was canonized, no great things were uncovered for her canonization. She was canonized for one thing only. As Pius X said, "She did ordinary things with extraordinary love"—small things with great love. This is what you and I gave when we gave our word to Jesus. This is our vow.

*

"A Missionary of Charity *must be a missionary of love.*" A missionary is one who is sent. God sent his Son. Today God sends us. Each one of us is sent by God. Why are we sent? We are sent to be his love among men, to bring his love and compassion to the poorest of the poor. We must not be afraid to love. An M.C. *must* be a missionary of love. Notice the words *"must be."* It is not that she should simply try to be. No, she *must be* a missionary of love. She is sent to *be* God's love.

Even Almighty God cannot fill what is already full. We must be empty if we want God to fill us with his fulness. Our Lady had to be empty before she could be full of grace. She had to declare that she was the handmaid of the Lord before God could fill her. So also we must be empty of all pride, all jealousy, of all selfishness before God can fill us with his love.

We must be able to give ourselves so completely to God that He must be able to possess us. We must "Give whatever He takes and take whatever He gives."

How unlike Him we are. How little love, how little compassion, how little forgiveness, how little kindness we have. We are not worthy to be so close to Him—to enter his heart. For his heart is still open to embrace us. His head is still crowned with thorns, his hands nailed to the cross today. Let us find out: "Are the nails mine? That sputum on his face, is it mine? What part of his body, of his mind has suffered because of me?" We should ask, not with anxiety or fear, but with a meek and humble heart. Let us find out what part of his body has wounds inflicted by our sin. Let us not go alone but put our hands in his. He is there to forgive seventy times seven. Our Father loves us. He has called us in a special way, given us a name. We belong to Him with all our misery, our sin, our weakness, our goodness. We are his.

*

Let us not be like the rich young man in the gospel. Jesus saw him and loved him and wanted him, but he had given his heart to something else—to his riches. He was rich, young, and strong. Jesus could not fill him. Instead, be like Zacchaeus. He was a little man—a small man—and he knew his smallness. He recognized his smallness and made a very simple decision in order to see Jesus. He climbed a tree because he knew he was small. If he hadn't opened his heart and responded to Jesus in that simple way, Jesus could not have shown his love, he could not have said, "Come down, Zacchaeus! Come down!" This is the foundation of everything: "Learn of me, that I am meek and humble of heart." Be small.

If my love for my Sisters is okay, then my love for Jesus will be okay. There are not two loves. The deeper my love for Jesus, the deeper that love for my Sisters, the greater the zeal to go to the poor.

SEVEN

Our Way of Life

I am the Way, the Truth, and the Life (Jn 14:16).

*Just as the seed is meant to be a tree—we are
meant to grow into Jesus.*

*

Each of us will accept:
—to live the life of poverty in cheerful trust
—to imitate the chastity of Mary, the cause of our joy
—to offer cheerful obedience from inward joy

Poverty

*"The foxes have holes and the birds of the air have nests but the Son of
Man has nowhere to lay his head" (Lk 9:5-7).*

Our poverty is our dowry.

*With regard to God, our poverty is our humble recognition and
acceptance of our sinfulness, helplessness and utter nothingness, and the
acknowledgement of our neediness before Him, which expresses itself as
hope in Him, as an openness to receive all things from Him as from our
Father.*

*Our poverty should be true gospel poverty—gentle, tender, glad and
openhearted, always ready to give an expression of love. Poverty is love
before it is renunciation. To love, it is necessary to give. To give, it is
necessary to be free from selfishness.*

Desirous to share Christ's own poverty and that of our poor:

—*We acccept to have everything in common and to share with one another in the Society.*

—*We do not accept anything whatsoever from our parents, friends, or benefactors for our personal use. Whatever is given to us is handed over to our superiors for the common use of the community or for the work.*

—*We shall eat the food of the people, of the country where we live, using what is cheapest. It should be sufficient and wholesome so as to maintain good health which is essential for the work of our vocation.*

—*Our Houses should be simple and modest, places where the poor feel at home.*

—*We shall walk whenever opportunity offers, in order to take the cheapest means of transport available.*

—*We shall sleep in common dormitories without privacy like the poor.*

—*We and our poor will depend entirely on Divine Providence both for our material and spiritual needs.*

*

Whenever it is necessary, we will do our begging willingly, in the spirit of poverty and cheerful trust—becoming beggars for the poor members of Christ who Himself lived on alms during his public life and whom we serve in the sick and the poor. We shall not store things nor shall we beg for more than what is necessary.

*

In our Society we must try to aim at a most perfect poverty. It is to be a wall of defence which has two effects:

—It excludes the enemy. As we know from the Spiritual Exercises, the first trick of the devil is to lead men to the love of wealth; the true love of evangelical poverty closes this avenue of our soul to the evil spirit.

—It secures peace and protection for those who dwell within the wall.

*

Our Lord on the Cross possessed nothing. He was on the cross which was given by Pilate. The nails and the crown were given Him by the soldiers. He was naked, and when he died, cross, nails, and crown were taken away from Him, and He was wrapped in a shroud given Him by a kind heart and buried in a tomb which was not his.

*

We must never get into the habit of being preoccupied with the future. There is no reason to do so. God is there. Once the longing for money comes, the longing also comes for what money can give: superfluities, nice rooms, luxuries at table, more clothes, fans, etc. Our needs will increase, for one thing brings another and the result will be endless dissatisfaction.

Poverty makes us free. That is why we can joke and smile and keep a happy heart for Jesus.

The first true poverty was when "Christ emptied Himself." For nine months He was lost in the little space of Mary's bosom: not even St. Joseph knew who He was. Having all things, yet possessing nothing. His birth was also like one of the poorest of the poor. Even our poor have someone to assist them. . . . Mary did not. At Nazareth even his people despised Him. It was not necessary for Jesus to practice this absolute poverty. There is only one reason: because He desired it. He wanted to be to the fullest "One" of us.

*

Poverty is necessary because we are working with the poor. When they complain about the food, we can say: we eat the same. They say, "It was so hot last night, we could not sleep." We can reply, "We also felt very hot." The poor have to wash for themselves, go barefoot; we do the same. We have to go down and lift them up. It opens the heart of the poor when we can say we live the same way they do. Sometimes they only have one bucket of water. It is the same with us. The poor have to stand in line; we do too. Food, clothing, everything must be like that of the poor. We have no fasting. Our fasting is to eat the food as we get it.

*

Christ being rich emptied Himself. This is where contradiction lies. If I want to be poor like Christ—who became poor even though he was rich—I must do the same. Nowadays people want to be poor and live with the poor, but they want to be free to dispose of things as they wish. To have this freedom is to be rich. They want both and they cannot have both. This is another kind of contradiction.

Our poverty is our freedom. This is our poverty—the giving up of our freedom to dispose of things, to choose, to possess. The moment I use and dispose of things as mine, that moment I cease to be poor.

We must strive to acquire the true spirit of poverty which manifests itself in a love for the practice of the virtue of poverty in imitation of Christ—in imitation of Him who chose it as the companion of his life on earth when He came to live among us. Christ did not have to lead a life of poverty. Thus He taught us how important it is for our sanctification.

*

We practice the virtue of poverty when we mend our clothes quickly and as beautifully as we can. To go about in a torn habit and sari is certainly not the sign of the virtue of poverty. For, remember, we do not profess the poverty of beggars, but the poverty of Christ. Let us also remember that our body is the temple of the Holy Spirit, and for that reason we must respect it always with neatly mended clothes. We would never dream of using dirty, torn cloth as a tabernacle veil to cover the door of the dwelling that Christ chose for Himself on earth since his Ascension into heaven. In the same way, we should never cover the temple of the Holy Spirit, which is our body, with torn, dirty, untidy clothes. Patched clothes are no disgrace. It is said of St. Francis of Assisi that when he died his habit had so many patches that the original cloth was no longer there.

*

The poor are great people and we owe them deep gratitude, for if they did not accept us then we would not exist as M.C.s. To be able to understand this, we look at Jesus. To be able to become man, He, being rich, became poor. He could have chosen the king's palace, but to be equal to us, He chose to be like us in all things except sin. To be equal to the poor, we choose to be poor like them in everything except destitution. Each of us has given our word to God to follow Christ in poverty.

*

When you make the vow of poverty, you say, "I have nothing." That is why you cannot destroy things or give them away without permission. By right, you can't even say, "This is my sari." For us, poverty is freedom. You are free to love God— free to love Jesus with an undivided heart.

*

The devil is very busy. The more our work involves bringing souls to God, the more he tries to take us away from God, to spoil the work. Poverty provides tremendous protection. I call it freedom. Nothing and nobody will separate me from the love of Christ.

You must experience the joy of poverty. Poverty is not only renunciation. Poverty is joy. Poverty is love. My reason for doing without is that "I love Jesus." Unless you experience for yourself this joy of poverty, you will never understand what I am saying. Have the courage to live that poverty. Jesus was born in Bethlehem. All He had was a piece of cloth, some straw. Picture the animals gathering around the child. There were no electric heaters. Our Lady must have taught Him to walk. He could have come down from heaven as a full grown man, but He came to us as an infant. Everything had to be done for Him. He became poor for love of us.

I will never forget something that happened when I was at Loreto. One of the children was very, very naughty. She was only six or seven years old. One day, when she was extremely naughty, I took her hand and said, "Come, we're going for a walk." She had some money with her. One hand held my hand and the other held tightly to the money. "I will buy this, I will buy that," she kept saying. Suddenly she saw a blind beggar, and at once she left the money with him. From that day she was a completely different child. She was so small and so naughty.

Yet that one decision changed her life. It is the same with you. Get rid of anything that's holding you back. If you want to be all for Jesus, the decision has to come from within you.

*

I want you to experience that joy of poverty which is really the perfect joy of St. Francis of Assisi. He called it Lady Poverty. St. Ignatius called it Mother Poverty. The more we have, the less we can give. So let us have less to be able to give all to Jesus.

*

Motherhouse, March 22, 1981

As our poor keep growing in poverty—due to the great rise in the cost of living—let us be more careful regarding the poverty of our houses. The daily needs that our poor cannot get—let us be more careful in the use of them—so that we also feel the hardship in food, clothing, water, electricity, soap—things which our poor often go without.

Chastity

Our vow of chastity is our response to the call of Christ. Our vow is made to God alone by which we commit ourselves:
—to live a celibate life in the fervor of charity and the perfection of chastity, for we are convinced that complete continence is neither impossible nor harmful to human development because, in the maturity and delicacy of our vocation as women, we love Christ with a deep and personal love, expressed in our love for our Sisters, our poor and the world in which we live.
—in a spirit of renunciation, not only to renounce marriage but also to engage ourselves to avoid every external or internal offence against chastity.

*

Our vow of chastity liberates us totally for the contemplation of God and the wholehearted and free service of the poorest of the poor. By it we cleave to Jesus with undivided love so as to:
—live in Him, for Him, by Him and with Him as our sole guide,

—be invaded by his own holiness and filled with his own spirit of love,
—show forth the luminous face of Jesus, radiant with purity and love for the Father and mankind,
—make reparation to God for all the sins of the flesh committed in the world today.

*

By our vow of chastity we do renounce God's natural gift to women to become mothers—for the greater gift—that of being virgins for Christ, of entering into a much more beautiful motherhood.

*

One day at a meeting, I was asked to give a message. So I told the people, "Husbands smile at your wives; wives smile at your husbands and your children." They could not understand how I was able to tell them this sort of thing. "Are you married?" one of them asked. "Yes," I replied, "and sometimes I find it difficult to smile at Jesus because He can be so demanding." And it is true. By our vow of chastity we are married to Jesus.

*

In my heart there is only one vacant seat. It is for God and nobody else. Temptation is like fire in which gold is purified. So we have to go through this fire. The temptations are allowed by God. The only thing we have to do is to refuse to give in. If I say I do not want it, I am safe. There may be temptations against purity, against faith, against my vocation. If we love our vocation, we will be tempted. But then we will also grow in sanctity. We have to fight temptation for the love of God.

*

By the vow of chastity, I not only renounce the married state of life, but I also consecrate to God the free use of my internal and external acts—my affections. I cannot in conscience love a creature with the love of a woman for a man. I no longer have the right to give that affection to any other creature but God.

What, then? Do we have to be stones, human beings without hearts? Do we simply say: "I don't care; to me all human beings are the same." No, not at all. We have to keep ourselves as we are, but keep it all for God, to whom we have consecrated all our external and internal acts.

*

Our Lord, at his dying moment, thought of his mother. That is the proof that He was human to the last. Therefore, if you have a loving nature, keep it and use it for God; if you have a smiling temperament, keep it and use it for God.

People in the world think that the vow of chastity makes us inhuman, makes us become like stones, without feelings. Each one of us can tell them it is not true. It is the vow of chastity that gives us the freedom to love everybody instead of simply becoming a mother to three or four children. A married woman can love but one man; we can love the whole world in God. The vow of chastity does not diminish us; it makes us live to the full if it is kept properly. The vow of chastity is not simply a list of don'ts—it is love. I give myself to God and I receive God. God becomes my own and I become his own. That is why I become completely dedicated to Him by the vow of chastity.

God does not want to impose a burden on us by the vow of chastity. We must love our consecration, which sets us apart for God alone. We must be free of things to be full of God. The vow of chastity sets us free to love with our whole heart and soul for God's sake.

*

By my vow of chastity I free myself for the kingdom of God. I become his property and He binds Himself to take care of me. I must then give wholehearted free service. What is this whole-hearted free service? It is the outcome of chastity, of binding myself to Christ. Therefore, I bind myself to give not half-hearted but wholehearted service. When we neglect to do our work well, this vow suffers most—our service to the poor—because we become preoccupied with whatever we are giving our affection to.

*

Don't allow anything to interfere with your love for Jesus. You belong to Him. *Nothing can separate you from Him.* That one sentence is important to remember. He will be your joy, your strength. If you hold onto that sentence, temptations and difficulties will come, but nothing will break you.

*

Receive the symbol of our crucified spouse. I have chosen to be the spouse of Jesus crucified. Follow his footsteps in search of souls by showing great love in small things. He comes down to proclaim the good news to the poor through our works of love. We are M.C.s for that one reason only Carry Him and his light into the homes of the poor.

*

"Remember always, beloved daughters in Christ, the value of your religious consecration. Through your consecration to the Lord Jesus you respond to his love and discover the needs of his brothers and sisters throughout the world. This consecration, expressed through your vows, is the source of your joy and fulfillment. It is the secret of your supernatural contribution to the kingdom of God. It is the measure of the effectiveness of your service to the poor, the guarantee that it will last.

"Yes, to belong to Christ Jesus is a great gift of God's love, and may the world always see this love in your smile. To all of you goes our Apostolic Blessing." (Pope Paul VI, Rome, June 5, 1978)

These are the Holy Father's last words to the Missionaries of Charity. Go to Jesus and repeat to Him what I've told you. "Jesus in my heart, I love you. I believe in your love for me."

*

Chastity does not simply mean that we are not married. It means that we love Christ with an undivided love. To be pure we need poverty. Is it wrong to have things? We vow poverty not because it is wrong to have things but we choose to do without these things.

*

The vow of chastity is to love Christ with undivided, loving chastity. It is not only that we cannot have a family, we cannot get married. But it is something deeper, something living, something real—it is to love Him with undivided, loving chastity through the freedom of poverty. We must be free to love—and to love Him with an undivided love. Nothing will separate us from the love of Christ—and that is our vow of chastity.

By this vow we are bound to remain faithful to the humble works of the society: to the poorest of the poor, the unwanted, the unloved, the uncared for. That means we depend solely on Divine Providence. After years of dealing with thousands and thousands of people, we have never yet had to send anybody away because we didn't have something to give them. There has always been one more plate of rice, one more bed. We have never had to say, "I'm sorry, I cannot take you in or I cannot give you anything."

*

I remember when I was leaving home fifty years ago—my mother was dead against me leaving home and becoming a Sister. In the end, when she realized that this was what God wanted from her and from me, she said something very strange: "Put your hand in his hand and walk all alone with Him." This is exactly our way of life. We may be surrounded by many people, yet our vocation is really lived out alone with Jesus.

*

What am I binding myself to? What am I giving my vow to God about?—I bind myself to God with undivided love. I tell Almighty God, "I can love all, but the only one I *will* love in particular is you, only you."

*

To be able to understand chastity we must know what poverty and obedience are. They are like the pillars. If we remove the pillars, the whole building will tip to one side and fall.

Obedience

"Behold I come to do your Will, O God" (Heb 12:7).
Submission for someone who is in love is more than a duty—it is a blessedness.

Jesus, Only Begotten Son of the Father, equal to his Father, God from God, Light from Light, did not feel it below his dignity to obey.

Therefore, we will:

—accept, love, and respect all our lawful superiors,

—sincerely pray for them,

—show joyful trust in, and loyalty to them,

—make our obedience cheerful, prompt, simple and constant without question or excuse.

We should obey the known wish of our superiors as well as their commands in a spirit of faith. They may make a mistake in commanding, but we are infallible in obeying.

*

Whenever our superiors think it desirable for the greater glory of God to give us a change of residence, work, or companions, we should welcome this change as the very will of God and show a humble and joyful obedience.

*

Let the superior remember that she is first for the sisters and next for the work. Therefore, let all her dealings with her sisters be motherly, never discouraging them, especially when they fail. Let her take special care of the old and the sick and of those who do not take due care of themselves. In the house work let her be always the first to put her hand to the work. Let her have nothing special or different in food, clothes, or lodging. Let her trust her sisters completely. Let her be generous when the sisters observe poverty fervently. Let her house be a house of love, joy, and peace.

*

True obedience is a genuine act of love. Obedience makes us practice the other virtues. It likens us to martyrs, for it is a much greater martyrdom to persevere in obedience all through life than to die in a moment by a stroke of the sword.

*

The superior is in the place of God. The position given to her is like a chair. The chair remains, but the person can change. Today I sit in the chair; tomorrow somebody else might be sitting there.

But the chair is the same. The chair may not fit some as well as others. Some are too short for it and others too tall, while yet others fit it perfectly. The chair is in the place of God who gave your superior this position. I have to obey if I want to go on in peace.

*

It is impossible that a Sister who is obedient will not become a saint.

Obedience gives us inward joy and peace. Obedience is the only condition for close union with God.

We want to become holy and therefore we have to be thoroughly obedient. God never takes from us what we are not willing to give. We must give it to Him with our own free will.

For our obedience to be cheerful and prompt, we have to be convinced that it is Jesus we obey. And how do we reach that conviction? By the practice of the heroic virtue of obedience— love for love. If you want to know whether you love God, ask yourselves the question: "Do I obey?" If I obey, everything is all right. Why? Because everything depends on my will. Whether I become a saint or a sinner depends on me. So you see how very important obedience is. Our sanctity, after the grace of God, depends upon our will. Don't waste time waiting for big things to do for God. You will not have the readiness to say yes to the great things if you do not train yourselves to say yes to the thousand-and-one occasions of obedience that come your way throughout the day.

Something happened to one of the Sisters who was sent to study. The day she was to receive her degree she died. When she was dying she asked, "Why did Jesus call me for such a short time?" And Mother answered, "Jesus wants you, not your works." She was perfectly happy after that.

Knowledge of God, love of God, service of God—that is the end of our lives—and obedience gives us the key to it all.

*

A certain priest loved the Chinese and wanted to do something for them. He became so involved in the work that it seemed that even his eyes became slanted, like the Chinese. If I live constantly in the company of Jesus, I will look like him and do as he did. Nothing pleases God more than when we obey. Let us love God not for what He gives but for what He deigns to take from us. Our little acts of obedience give us the occasion of proving our love for Him.

＊

It is much easier to conquer a country than to conquer ourselves. Every act of disobedience weakens my spiritual life. It is like a wound letting out every drop of one's blood. Nothing can cause this havoc in our spiritual life as quickly as disobedience.

In the gospel we find many proofs of Christ's obedience. If we were to go to Nazareth in spirit we would first hear Our Lady's answer to the angel, "Be it done to me according to thy word." Then we would hear this about Jesus: "He went down and was obedient to them"—to a carpenter and a simple village girl. Then we would hear Jesus say: "I have come to do the will of my Father, of Him who sent me." At last, we would see Jesus at his passion, obeying his executioners blindly.

We must build our obedience on the example of Jesus in the gospel. What is this obedience? By this vow of obedience I give to God something He cannot take from me without my consent: my will, of which I have full control.

＊

To strengthen ourselves to remain obedient, we must refrain from criticism. Anything that weakens my obedience, however small, I must keep away from. If we don't obey, we are like a building without cement. For us, obedience is like cement. Obedience is unreasonable for a proud soul, but there is no unreasonableness in obedience for a humble soul.

Obedience is something that makes me Christlike. What we give up through poverty is something that many people in the world can do. The same is true of chastity. But to love and esteem the privilege of living under obedience is for the few chosen ones. Why love and esteem it? Because it is not only a sure means of fulfilling the will of God but is also a very special grace and honor.

What does perfect obedience bring? It is an unfailing source of peace. Inward joy comes only from perfect obedience.

Close union with God is a natural result of perfect obedience.

If we want to do something great for the Church, we must first become obedient. Jesus is our model. He was poor, obedient, charitable. "In you, Jesus, I want to be pure; I want to obey; I want to be poor." I cannot say I will find the way. No, I have to give up even my own self so that only Jesus does it in me.

*

Poverty and obedience are very closely united. These complete each other. One cannot be without the other. That is why scripture says, "He, being rich, became poor." Also, "Behold, I come to do Thy will, O God." "My food is to do the will of Him who sent me." I don't think Jesus would have been able to live his life if He had not accepted this. He had to become poor and to obey his Father fully. He became both materially and spiritually poor. If we are proud and uncharitable, rather than empty, then we cannot really obey.

Obedience is more difficult than poverty. Our will is the only thing we can claim. In poverty nothing is ours. In obedience I have my will, the only thing God will not take by force. The more you love God the more you will obey.

*

Many congregations have discarded this vow of obedience. They don't have superiors anymore. Each member makes her own decisions. They have discarded obedience completely. Do you know what has happened because of that? In the U.S. alone 50,000 nuns have left the religious life. The destruction of religious life comes mainly from the lack of obedience. Sheer negligence destroys religious life completely.

*

Obedience is the most perfect act of love for God. I obey not because I am afraid, but because I love Jesus. Then only will I be able to progress very far in sanctity. If I neglect obedience, poverty will go. When poverty goes, chastity will go. Tradition says the angels were told to adore the Child. "I will not serve" was the first act of disobedience. They had the chance to choose.

*

"He, being rich, became poor." It is difficult for a proud person to obey. We do not like to bend, to be humble. To be holy we need obedience. The gospel is full of the humility of Mary. As spotless as she was, as holy as she was, she obeyed. "Humility of the heart of Jesus, fill my heart." Let us, during the day, pray this prayer often. If there has been resentment in our hearts or if we have not accepted humiliation, we will not learn humility. We cannot learn humility from books. Jesus accepted humiliation. Nothingness cannot disobey. In our lives as Missionaries of Charity, obedience is the greatest gift we can give to God. Jesus came to do the will of his Father, and He did it from the very beginning to the very end.

If we really want to know whether something is a temptation, let us examine our obedience. It is the best light in time of temptation, and we will know exactly where we are and what we are doing. It is the best light in that terrible darkness. Even for Jesus, the devil wanted to find out who he was. He was not sure. The devil will stoop to anything to find out where our weak point is. He will do anything to get us to accept that one wrong thought, to say that one unkind word, to do that one impure act, that one act of disobedience, that one instance of giving something away without permission, that one neglect of prayer—just that one thing. If there is an award to be given for patience it should be given to the devil. He has a lot of patience.

*

This strength we need and must learn from Jesus. That is why we need the Eucharist. See how the devil acted with Jesus. He went step by step; one temptation, then another. He failed, but he began again. That is why Jesus knew how much we need Him, and that is why we should pray. Watch the beginnings. Temptations—like temptations against purity when they come—are only there to help us reach a greater love for purity. Obedience is the protector of all the vows and virtues. That is why we make our vows according to obedience. The devil does not care what thing he tempts us to do as long as we are not preoccupied with Jesus.

*

One of the doorways to holiness is obedience. To be able to obey, we must be free. That is why we take a vow of poverty, having nothing. Jesus came down and was subject. We must go down in the depths of our hearts and see how to bring holiness into the Society.

*

Many times Jesus said: "I have come to do the will of my Father. I and the Father are one." In the Old Testament, when did God punish? When his people did not obey; when they did not keep their word to Him.

*

How long was Jesus subject? Thirty long years. He had come to give the good news, and yet He spent thirty years doing the work of a carpenter. He was called the "son of a carpenter."

*

Examine your poverty. Is it something joyful? Examine your obedience. Is your obedience total surrender? They are twins. Poverty is the sister and obedience is the brother. If you know poverty and obedience, you will love them. If you love them, you will keep them.

*

Difficult, yes. It's meant to be difficult. Jesus says: "If you want to be my disciple, pick up your cross and follow me." He doesn't force us. He says, "if you want." We are not the only ones that have to obey. Even taxi drivers have to obey. Red light, green light, that's also obedience.

I've never received so many graces as through obedience. You will receive many more graces if you surrender totally.

Love for obedience is love for the will of God.

And *all* the superiors of our society—be what our Holy Father said in public—the servant of the servants of God. You are to serve and not to be served; the word "co-worker" fits each one of you more than any other Sister. Remember, you are first for the Sisters. Help them to grow to be Christlike. Know each Sister better. Then you will love her and only then will you serve her with a devoted love, as Christ loved each one of us.

*

Obedience well lived frees us from selfishness and pride and so it helps us to find God and, in Him, the whole world. Obedience is a special grace, and it produces unfailing peace, inward joy, and close union with God.

Obedience transforms small, commonplace things and occupations into acts of living faith, and faith in action is love, and love in action is service of the loving God. Obedience lived with joy creates a living awareness of the Presence of God, and so fidelity to acts of obedience becomes like drops of oil that keep the light of Jesus aflame in our life.

Wholehearted, Free Service to the Poorest of the Poor

Our consecrated service to the poorest of the poor is Christ's call to us through his Church,

—to love Him wholeheartedly and freely in the poorest of the poor with whom He identifies Himself and makes his presence in them known, loved, and served by all.

—to make reparation for sins of hatred, coldness, lack of concern and love for Him in the world today, in one another and in the person of the poorest of the poor.

*

By this vow we bind ourselves to give wholehearted and free service to the poorest of the poor according to obedience.

—Wholehearted means: with hearts burning with zeal and love for souls, with singleminded devotion, wholly rooted in our deep union with God in prayer and fraternal love, that we give them not only our hands to serve, but also our hearts to love with kindness and humility, entirely at the disposal of the poor.

*

We give immediate and effective service to the poorest of the poor, as long as they have no one to help them, by:

—feeding the hungry: not only with food but also with the Word of God,

—giving drink to the thirsty: not only for water, but for knowledge, peace, truth, justice, and love,

—clothing the naked: not only with clothes, but also with human dignity,

—giving shelter to the homeless: not only a shelter made of bricks, but a heart that understands, that covers, that loves,

—nursing the sick and the dying: not only the body, but also the mind and spirit.

*

The poorest of the poor, irrespective of caste, creed or nationality are: The hungry, the thirsty, the naked, the homeless, the ignorant, the captives, the crippled, the leprosy sufferers, the alcoholics, the sick and dying destitutes, the unloved, the abandoned, the outcasts, all those who are a burden to human society, who have lost all hope and faith in life, and every Missionary of Charity by accepting to live the life of evangelical poverty and by the very fact of being sinners—and all hard-hearted, persistent sinners, those under the power of the evil one, those who are leading others to sin, error or confusion, the atheists, the erring, those in confusion and doubt, the tempted, the spiritually blind, weak, lax and ignorant, those not yet touched by the light of Christ, those hungry for the word and peace of God, the difficult, the repulsive, the rejected, the sorrowful, and the souls in purgatory.

*

Our vocation is to follow the lowliness of Christ. We remain right on the ground by living Christ's concern for the poorest and the lowliest and by being of immediate but effective service to them until they find some others who can help in a better and more lasting way.

*

As you love God you must love the poor: in their sufferings. The love of the poor overflows from your love for God. You must find the poor and serve them. When you have found them, you must take them to your heart. We owe our people the greatest gratitude because they allow us to touch Christ. We must love the poor like Him. A Hindu told me, "I know what you do in Nirmal Hriday, you take them from the streets and bring them to heaven."

*

The difference between our work and social work is that we give wholehearted, free service for the love of God. In the beginning, when the work started, I got a fever and had a dream about St. Peter. He said to me, "No, there is no place for you here. No slums in heaven." "All right," I answered him, "then I shall go on working. I'll bring the people from the slums to heaven."

*

Our vocation is not the work—the fidelity to humble works is our means to put our love into action.

*

"That they may all be one even as you, Father, are in Me and I in you: that they also may be one in Us, so that the world may believe that you have sent Me" (Jn 17:21).

God will take care of you, if you remain one.

*

As a religious community, modelled on the first Christian community, our first great responsibility is to be community, revealing first to one another something of God's own love, concern, and tenderness—what it means to know and to be known, to love and to be loved, and thus to be a sign witnessing to the deepest vocation of the Church, which is to gather people from every tribe and tongue, and people and nation, redeemed by the Blood of Christ, to form God's family of love. "See how they love each other."

As members of an international community, we will use English as our community language.

*

Just as Jesus sent his disciples out two by two, we will also go out two by two with permission and with a Sister as a companion. We will pray the rosary on the streets and help each other to fervor and zeal, and we will also protect each other.

*

The superior of each house, however, will remember that she is first for the Sisters and next for the work. Therefore:
—all her dealing with the Sisters will be motherly, never discouraging them, especially in failure,
—she will encourage and joyfully welcome each member to make a personal and valuable contribution to the well-being of the society and the Church. This will lead to wiser decisions that will prove beneficial to all.
—she will always be the first to devote herself to the housework,
—she will have nothing special or different in food, clothes, or lodging
—she will trust her Sisters completely and be generous always, especially when the Sisters observe poverty well,
—she will respect with utmost discretion all that the Sisters confide in her, and do not wish to be revealed, especially personal matters. She will never force secrets out of them,
—above all, by her own example of humility, obedience and oneness with her higher superiors, she will teach her Sisters the art of doing "always the things that please the Father."

*

We shall always keep in mind that our community is not composed of those who are already saints, but of those who are trying to become saints. Therefore we shall be extremely patient with each other's faults and failures.
Our love for one another will be:
—selfless, generous, tender, personal, and respectful,
—beyond likes and dislikes, friendship and enmity, worthiness or unworthiness,
—faithful, deep, and freeing,

Our Way of Life 301

*—not compromising because we care; compassionate and forgiving
because we understand,*
*—always inspiring, encouraging, trusting, wholehearted and sacri-
ficial unto the death of the cross.*

*

My vows bind me to my Sister because she is much poorer
than the poor outside. If I am not kind and do not smile to the
poor outside, someone else will. But for my Sister there is no one
else.

*

Motherhouse, October 4, 1969

In times of her weakness, your superior comes and appears
as Christ in his distressing disguise—she needs your love,
your humility, your trust. Trust her with loving trust, in spite
of herself, for Jesus in her has not changed. He is the same, as
there is only one Jesus.

Our society is still young. Our superiors are still without
much experience. Have compassion on them, be kind to
them. See the hand of the good God that is trying to write a
wonderful message of love to you personally using that bad
pencil, maybe even a broken pencil. Even so, it is the hand
and mind of God, and you must try to understand and refrain
from examining the pencil. Today He uses the pencil which is
rough and yet the loving message is there—always beautiful,
always true, always thoughtful—only for you. Christ will use
only that pencil in the place you are—for you. Therefore, kiss
the hand, but do not try to break the pencil.

Our Life Together

*As a sign of entrance into a new state of life by religious consecration
and as a sign of our desire for self-effacement:*
   —we receive a new religious name at the time of profession,
   —we call each other "Sister."
Out Religious dress consists of:

—*a simple and modest white cotton habit,*
—*a white cotton sari with blue border covering the head,*
—*a cincture made of rope,*
—*sandals,*
—*a crucifix and a rosary.*
These will be the sign of:
—*our consecrated love for God and the Church,*
—*our dedication to the world's poor, and*
—*a reminder of the edification expected from all those who wear it.*

*

Candidates desirous to join the Society must be:
—*at least eighteen years of age,*
—*free from impediments,*
—*guided by the right intention,*
—*healthy in body and mind, and hence able to bear the hardships of this special vocation,*
—*able to acquire knowledge (especially the language of the people they serve),*
—*of a cheerful disposition,*
—*able to exercise sound judgment.*

*

The Sisters shall wear a plain Indian dress, that is, a white habit, a white sari with blue par, a girdle made of rope, a crucifix and sandals.

The White Habit and a sari with blue border is the sign of Mary's modesty; it should remind me of my separation from the world and its vanities, of my baptismal robe and how pure I must keep my heart.

The Girdle made of rope is the sign of Mary's angelic Purity. It should remind me that I should aim at the same purity helped by the strong guardian, Holy Poverty.

Sandals are a sign of freedom; of our own free choice we follow Christ in search of souls.

The Crucifix is a sign of love—the sign we should know, love, and imitate. When I dress myself I should, with devotion, remember what each article of my religious habit means to me.

Therefore, I should say each prayer with great love.

Yes, our dress is a sign that we belong—that is why we must take great care. This habit is a protection for us, both bodily and spiritual protection. Be grateful for the habit.

*

The work we have to do requires a healthy body. Therefore, each sister is in her conscience bound to take care of her health. The amount of food, which is very wisely prescribed for us, must be taken faithfully. This we do, not for the satisfaction of the senses, but to show our Lord our desire to work for Him and with Him, that we may be able to live lives of penance and reparation.

*

It would be a defect to speak about food or to complain about what is served. To be occupied with such thoughts at any time is not edifying. If dishes taste well, thank God! If not, thank Him still, and thank Him even more because He has given you an opportunity to imitate Our Savior in his poverty. Christ certainly did not feast sumptuously during his life. His parents were poor, and the poor do not feast on the good things of the table. In fact, He often endured real want, as the multiplication of the loaves and fishes and the plucking of the ears of corn on walks through the fields teach us. These incidents should be salutary reminders to us when our meals are meager.

*

To join the congregation we need few things. We need health of mind and body. We need the ability to learn. We need plenty of common sense and a cheerful disposition. I think common sense and cheerfulness are very necessary for a work like this.

*

June 1, 1972

As travelling expenses are becoming very high, we have decided in future to take with us, besides our clothes—only our pillow, pillowcase, two sheets, one blanket, glass, cup, and big plate. The rest will be provided for you in each house.

(Things should be numbered 1, 2, 3, etc.—everything numbered number 1 will go to one Sister; number 2 will go to the next Sister; and so on. This means that each house should have things according to the number of members in the house.)

*

February 25, 1974

Once a month you must all help clean the godown where food and relief goods are kept. All the Sisters in the house must know what you have to give to the poor, but one Sister must be responsible for giving it rather than everyone giving at random. Also, it would be good for everyone, including the superior—to clean drains and toilets at least once a week and to give a helping hand in the kitchen. Wherever there is a plot of land, make sure you work in the garden and plant as many fruit trees as possible so that you can give food to the poor. This will help you return to the spirit of hard labor and sacrifice which has always characterized the society.

*

We have been called to give until it hurts. Our constitution says that "as a sign of our consecration we receive a new name." We vow to give ourselves to God completely, and our new name expresses that vow. Our name is called and we answer: "Lord, you have called me." The moment we stop hearing our name being called we will be separated from Him. We can recognize his voice calling our name only in the silence of our hearts. Changing our names shows that we belong not to ourselves but to Jesus.

*

Never lose the chance to become like Jesus. We profess before the world, "I am the spouse of Jesus crucified." Like the woman at the altar who professes before the world her marriage to one man, we, too, change our name to show that we belong to Jesus completely.

EIGHT

Our Life of Prayer and Contemplation

Lord, teach us to pray (Lk 11:1).

Jesus has drawn us to be souls of prayer.

*

Jesus is our prayer, and He is also the answer to all our prayer. He has chosen to be Himself in us the living song of love, praise, adoration, thanksgiving, intercession and reparation to the Father in the name of the whole creation, especially the poorest of the poor and those who do not pray, who do not know how to pray, who do not dare and do not want to pray.

*

Every Missionary of Charity will pray with absolute trust in God's loving care for us. Our prayer will be the prayer of little children, one of tender devotion, deep reverence, humility, serenity, and simplicity.

*

By daily feeding on the scriptures, particularly the New Testament, we shall grow in a deeper and more personal knowledge and love of Jesus Christ and his teachings, so as to be able to feed his children with his divine word.

We shall be painstaking and diligent in studying and memorizing selected passages, daily reading and meditating on the scriptures—to be able to know and love God personally.

One with the Church in her celebration of the mystery of our redemption, we also promote devotion in accordance with the liturgy and liturgical seasons.

—Devotion to the Sacred Heart of Jesus is closely linked with the Eucharist and has a special place in our society. We renew each year the Consecration of our Communities on the Feast of the Sacred Heart. Every First Friday of the month will be preceded by a novena.

—In gratitude to Jesus for his great love during his Passion which is being continued today in his suffering poor, we shall make the Stations of the Cross every Friday as a community. Other days it will be left to the choice of each Sister.

*

Singing is an important part of our life of prayer. We shall keep our singing simple and use a minimum of musical instruments when necessary.

*

We are called to be contemplatives in the heart of the world by:
—seeking the face of God in everything, everyone, everywhere, all the time, and his hand in every happening, and especially,
—seeing and adoring the Presence of Jesus in the lowly appearance of Bread, and in the distressing disguise of the poor, by praying the work, that is, by doing it with Jesus, for Jesus, and to Jesus.

*

Our life of contemplation shall retain the following characteristics:
—missionary: by going out physically or in spirit in search of souls all over the universe.
—contemplative: by gathering the whole universe at the very center of our hearts where the Lord of the Universe abides, and allowing the pure water of divine grace to flow plentifully and unceasingly from the source itself, on the whole of his creation.
—universal: by praying and contemplating with all and for all, especially with and for the spiritually poorest of the poor.

*

Jesus Christ has told us that we ought "always to pray and not to faint." St. Paul says, "pray without ceasing." God calls all men and women to this disposition of heart—to pray always. Let the love of God once take entire and absolute possession of a heart; let it become to that heart like a second nature; let that heart suffer nothing contrary to enter; let it apply itself continually to increase this love of God by seeking to please Him in all things and refusing Him nothing; let it accept as from his hand everything that happens to it; let it have a firm determination never to commit any fault deliberately and knowingly or, if it should fail, to be humbled and to rise up again at once, and such a heart will pray continually.

*

People today speak much about the poor, but they do not know or talk to the poor. So, too, we can talk much about prayer and yet not know how to pray.

We have to feed ourselves. We can die from spiritual starvation. We must be filled continually, like a machine. When one little thing in the machine is not working, then the whole machine is not working properly.

We need oil for the lamp.

Our lives must be connected with the living Christ in us. If we do not live in the presence of God, we cannot go on.

*

Does your mind and your heart go to Jesus as soon as you get up in the morning? This is prayer, that you turn your mind and heart to God. In your times of difficulties, in sorrows, in sufferings, in temptations, and in all things, where did your mind and heart turn first of all? How did you pray? Did you take the trouble to turn to Jesus and pray, or did you seek consolations?

Has your faith grown? If you do not pray, your faith will leave you. All those priests and religious who left, first stopped praying and then lacked faith to go on.

Ask the Holy Spirit to pray in you. Learn to pray, love to pray, and pray often. Feel the need to pray and to want to pray.

If you have learned how to pray, then I am not afraid for you. If you know how to pray, then you will love prayer—and if you love to pray, then you will pray. Knowledge will lead to love and love to service.

*

Where can I learn to pray? Jesus taught us: "Pray like this: Our Father. . . . Thy will be done. . . . Forgive us as we forgive." It is so simple yet so beautiful. If we pray the "Our Father" and live it, we will be holy. Everything is there: God, myself, my neighbor. If I forgive, then I can be holy and can pray . . . All this comes from a humble heart, and if we have this we will know how to love God, to love self and neighbor.

This is not complicated, and yet we complicate our lives so much, by so many additions. Just one thing counts: to be humble, to pray. The more you pray, the better you will pray. How do you pray? You should go to God like a little child. A child has no difficulty expressing his little mind in simple words which say so much. Jesus said to Nicodemus: "Become as a little child." If we pray the gospel, we will allow Christ to grow in us.

One thing is necessary for us—confession. Confession is nothing but humility in action. We called it penance, but really it is a sacrament of love, a sacrament of forgiveness. That is why confession should not be a place in which to talk for long hours about our difficulties. It is a place where I allow Jesus to take away from me everything that divides, that destroys. When there is a gap between me and Christ, when my love is divided, anything can come to fill the gap. We should be very simple and childlike in confession. "Here I am as a child going to her Father." If a child is not yet spoiled and has not learned to tell lies, he will tell everything. This is what I mean by being childlike. Confession is a beautiful act of great love. Only in confession can we go as sinners with sin and come out as sinners without sin.

*

If you don't pray, your presence will have no power, your words will have no power. If you pray, you will be able to overcome all the tricks of the devil. Don't believe all the thoughts that he puts into your mind.

*

Motherhouse, October 1978

"Blessed are those who suffer persecution": We do not suffer much persecution, except the persecution caused by the devil against chastity, poverty, obedience, and whole-hearted free service. To resist this persecution we need continual refilling of prayer and sacrifice—of the Bread of Life, of the Living Water, of my Sisters in community, and of the poor. We need Our Lady, Our Mother, to be with us always, to protect us and keep us only for Jesus.

*

Motherhouse, February 18, 1967

Prayer enlarges the heart until it is capable of containing God's gift of Himself. Ask and seek and your heart will grow big enough to receive Him and keep Him as your own.

Mary's Example

"Behold your Mother" (Jn 19:27).
Immaculate Heart of Mary, cause of our joy, bless your own Missionaries of Charity.

*

The Magnificat is Our Lady's prayer of thanks. She can help us to love Jesus best; she is the one who can show us the shortest way to Jesus. Mary was the one who forced Jesus to work the first miracle. "They have no wine," she said to Jesus. "Do whatever He tells you," she said to the servants. We take the part of the servants. Let us go to her with great love and trust. We are serving Jesus in the distressing disguise of the poor.

*

Through all the work we do for Jesus, with Jesus, to Jesus, we will ask Him to deepen our love for his Mother, to make it more personal and intimate, so as to:

—*love her as He loved her,*
—*be a cause of joy to her as He was,*
—*keep close to her as He kept close,*
—*share with her everything, even the Cross, as He did when she stood near him on Calvary.*

Silence

"Behold, I will allure her and will lead her into the wilderness and I will speak to her heart" (Hos 2:16, 18).
Souls of prayer are souls of great silence.

*

Each one of us will take it as our serious and sacred duty to collaborate with one another in our common effort to promote and maintain an atmosphere of deep silence and recollection in our own lives, conducive to the constant awareness of the Divine Presence everywhere and in everyone, especially in our own hearts and in the hearts of our Sisters with whom we live in the poorest of the poor.

*

To make possible true interior silence, we shall practice:
—*Silence of the eyes, by seeking always the beauty and goodness of God everywhere, closing it to the faults of others and to all that is sinful and disturbing to the soul.*
—*Silence of the ears, by listening always to the voice of God and to the cry of the poor and the needy, closing it to all the other voices that come from the evil one or from fallen human nature, e.g., gossip, tale-bearing, and uncharitable words.*
—*Silence of the tongue, by praising God and speaking the life-giving Word of God that is the Truth that enlightens and inspires, brings peace, hope, and joy and by refraining from self-defense and every word that causes darkness, turmoil, pain, and death.*
—*Silence of the mind, by opening it to the truth and knowledge of God in prayer and contemplation, like Mary who pondered the marvels of the Lord in her heart, and by closing it to all untruths, distractions,*

destructive thoughts, rash judgment, false suspicions of others, revengeful thoughts and desires.

—Silence of the heart, by loving God with our whole heart, soul, mind, and strength and one another as God loves, desiring God alone and avoiding all selfishness, hatred, envy, jealousy, and greed.

Our silence is a joyful and God-centered silence; it demands of us constant self-denial and plunges us into the deep silence of God where aloneness with God becomes a reality.

*

To foster and maintain a prayerful atmosphere of exterior silence we shall:

—respect certain times and places of more strict silence,

—move about and work prayerfully, quietly and gently,

—avoid at all costs all unnecessary speaking and notice,

—speak, when we have to, softly, gently, saying just what is necessary,

—look forward to profound silence as a holy and precious time, a withdrawal into the living silence of God.

*

If we will only learn silence, we will learn two things: to pray and to be humble. You cannot love unless you have humility, and you cannot be humble if you do not love. From the silence of the heart God speaks. There is no silence if there are things that have got inside.

*

Regarding purity, Jesus said, "Blessed are the clean of heart, for they shall see God." If our hearts are filled with uncharitableness and jealousy, we cannot see God. I can spend hours in church, but I will not see God if my heart is not pure. That is why we need silence. In the silence of the heart God speaks and in the purity of the heart God speaks.

Silence of our eyes

Silence of our ears

Silence of our mouths

Silence of our minds

Silence of our hearts

For in the silence of the heart God will speak. Give Jesus these five silences as a token of your gratitude. You wi" ever learn to pray until you keep silence.

The fruit of silence is faith
The fruit of faith is prayer
The fruit of prayer is love
The fruit of love is service
And the fruit of service is silence

The fourth vow is the fruit of silence. If you don't pray you cannot be a Missionary of Charity—you will be a social worker.

*

Silence of the *heart*, not only of the mouth—that too is necessary. Then you can hear God everywhere: in the closing of the door, in the person who needs you, in the birds that sing, in the flowers, the animals—that silence which is wonder and praise. Why? Because God is everywhere, and you can see and hear Him. That crow is praising God. That stupid crow—I can hear it well. We can see and hear God in that crow, but we cannot see and hear Him if our heart is not clean.

*

December 27, 1963

He who spoke with authority now spends his earthly life in silence. Let us adore Jesus in the Eucharistic silence. We need to find God, and He cannot be found in noise and restlessness. See how nature, the trees, the flowers, and the grass grow in perfect silence. See the stars, the moon, and the sun, how they move in silence. The Apostle said, "We will give ourselves continually at prayer and to the ministry of the Word." For the more we receive in silent prayer, the more we can give in our active life. We need silence to be able to touch souls. The essential thing is not what we say, but what God says to us.

*

Motherhouse, July 3, 1978

If we are careful of silence it will be easy to pray and to pray fervently. There is so much talk, so much repetition, so much carrying of tales in words and in writing. Our prayer life must suffer so much because our hearts are not silent, for as you know "only in the silence of the heart, God speaks." Only after we have listened can we speak from the fullness of our hearts.

*

Motherhouse, January 31, 1980

"God is the friend of silence. His language is silence." Be still and know that I am God. He requires us to be silent to discover Him. In the silence of the heart, He speaks to us.

Jesus spent forty days before beginning his public life in silence. He often retired alone, spent the night on the mountain in silence and prayer. He who spoke with authority spent his early life in silence.

We need silence to be alone with God, to speak to Him, to listen to him, to ponder his words deep in our hearts. We need to be alone with God in silence to be renewed and to be transformed. Silence gives us a new outlook on life. In it we are filled with the energy of God Himself, which makes us do all things with joy.

Praying the Work

"I pray not only for these but for those who through their words will believe in Me" (Jn 17:20).
Pray and work daily that all may become followers of Christ.

*

We shall pray our work but we may not substitute our prayer by work.
Besides praying for the whole world, especially for the spiritually poorest of the poor, each sister will be assigned a specific prayer mission on the level of the universal and local church, nations, our own society, the poor we serve all over the world, the families and individuals we visit locally (for the contemplative sisters).

*

Faith in action is service. We try to be holy because we believe. In this room you see a big bulb and a big switch. But, if there is no connection with the main power house, then there can be no light. Faith and prayer is the connection with God, and when that is there, there is service.

*

The only thing Jesus has asked us to be is meek and humble of heart, and to do this, He has taught us to pray. He has put "meek" first. From that one word comes gentleness, thoughtfulness, simplicity, generosity, truthfulness. For whom? For one another. Jesus put "humility" after meekness. We cannot love one another unless we hear the voice of God in our hearts.

*

If only we could understand what it is "to pray the work." If we could only deepen our faith. Prayer is not just time spent and words uttered. If only our faith were as big as a mustard seed, we would be able to tell this thing to move and it would move.... If our hearts are not pure we cannot see Jesus in others.

*

If we neglect prayer and if the branch is not connected with the vine, it will die. That connecting of branch with vine is prayer. If that connection is there then love is there, then joy is there, and we will be the sunshine of God's love, the hope of eternal happiness, the flame of burning love. Why? Because we are one with Jesus. If you sincerely want to learn to pray: keep silence.

*

What have we to learn? To be meek and humble; if we are meek and humble we will learn to pray. If we learn to pray, we will belong to Jesus. If we belong to Jesus we will learn to believe, and if we believe we will learn to love, and if we love we will learn to serve.

*

Be sincere in your prayers. Do you pray your prayers? Do you know how to pray? Do you love to pray? Sincerity is nothing but humility and you acquire humility only by accepting humiliations. All that has been said about humility is not enough to teach you humility. All that you have read about humility is not enough to teach you humility. You learn humility only by accepting humiliations. And you will meet humiliation all through your lives. The greatest humiliation is to know that you are nothing. This you come to know when you face God in prayer. When you come face to face with God, you cannot but know that you are nothing, that you have nothing. In the silence of the heart God speaks. If you face God in prayer and silence, God will speak to you. Then, only, you will know that you are nothing. It is only when you realize your nothingness, your emptiness, that God can fill you with Himself.

When you become full of God, you will do all your work well, all of it wholeheartedly. We have our fourth vow of whole-hearted service: it means to be full of God. And when you are full of God, you will do everything well. This you can do only if you pray, if you know how to pray, if you love prayer, and if you pray well.

*

Your vows are nothing but worship of God. If you are sincere in your prayers, then your vows have meaning; otherwise, they will mean nothing. The taking of your vows is also a prayer because it is worship of God. Your vows are between you and God alone. There is no one in between. It is all between Jesus and you.

Spend your time in prayer. If you pray you will have faith, and if you have faith you will naturally want to serve. The one who prays cannot but have faith, and when you have faith you want to put it into action. Faith in action is service. Faith in action becomes a delight because it gives you the opportunity of putting your love for Christ into action—it is meeting Christ, serving Christ.

*

You need especially to pray, for in our society, the work is only the fruit of prayer ... our love in action. If you are really in love with Christ, no matter how small the work, it will be done better; it will be wholehearted. If your work is slapdash, then your love for God is slapdash. Your work must prove your love.

Prayer is the very life of oneness, of being one with Christ. ... Therefore, prayer is as necessary as the air, as the blood in our body, as anything to keep us alive—to keep us alive to the grace of God.

It is impossible to engage in the apostolate without being a soul of prayer, without a conscious awareness of and submission to the divine will. We must be aware of our oneness with Christ, as He was aware of his oneness with his Father. Our activity is truly apostolic only in so far as we permit Him to work in and through us—with his power, his desire, his love. We must become holy, not because we want to *feel* holy but because Christ must be able to live his life fully in us.

Prayer must come from the heart and must be able to touch the heart of God. See how Jesus taught his disciples to pray: Call God your Father; praise and glorify his name; do his will as the saints do it in heaven; ask for daily bread, spiritual and temporal; ask for forgiveness of your own sins and for the grace to forgive others; ask for the grace to resist temptations and for the final grace to be delivered from the evil which is in you and around you.

*

These words of Jesus, "Love one another, even as I have loved you," should be not only a light to us, but they should also be a flame consuming the selfishness which prevents our growth in holiness. Jesus loved us to the end, "to the very limit of love, to the Cross." This love must come from within—from our union with Christ. It must be an outpouring of our love for God. Loving must be as normal to us as living and breathing, day after day until our death. To understand this and practice it we need much prayer, the kind that unites us with God and overflows continually upon others. Our works of charity are nothing but the overflow of our love of God from within. Therefore, the one who is most united to Him loves her neighbor most.

NINE

Our Life of Service and Evangelization

*Whatsoever you do to the least of my brethren,
you do it to me. (Mt 25:40)*

Faith in action is love. Love in action is service.

*

*No work should be introduced or accepted which is not in conformity
with the aim of the society. As the society and all its members must be free
to go in search of souls, to carry God's love among the poorest of the poor, it
follows that we will have no regular schools, no boarding schools, no
hospitals, no nursing homes except those homes needed for the homeless
destitutes and the unwanted.*

*

*In the slums the Sisters should find a place where they will gather little
street children, whoever they may be. Their very first concern is to make
them clean, feed them, and only then teach them, and prepare them for
admission into regular schools. The love of God must be proposed to them
in a simple, interesting, and attractive way.*

*

*The Sisters shall visit the destitute and the sick, going from house to
house or wherever these may be found, and they must render to all the
humblest services. They shall also visit the jails.*

We shall:

—*call sinners to repentance,*
—*instruct the ignorant,*
—*counsel the doubtful,*
—*sustain the tempted,*
—*befriend the friendless and comfort the sick and sorrowful,*
—*bear wrongs patiently: trusting in God for deliverance in his own good time,*
—*forgive injuries,*
—*bring prayer into the lives of the spiritually poorest of the poor.*

*

We need to be pure of heart to see Jesus in the person of the poorest of the poor. Therefore, the more repugnant the work, or the more disfigured or deformed the image of God in the person, the greater will be our faith and loving devotion in seeking the face of Jesus, and lovingly ministering to Him in the distressing disguise.

*

St. Theresa of Lisieux said, "Our Lord has need of our love. He has no need of our works. The same God who declares that he has no need to tell us if he be hungry, did not disdain to beg a little water from the Samaritan Woman. He was athirst, but when he said, 'Give me to drink,' He, the creator of the universe, asked for the love of his creature. He thirsted for Love."

*

The true interior life makes the active life burn forth and consume everything. It makes us find Jesus in the dark holes of the slums, in the most pitiful miseries of the poor, the God-Man naked on the Cross, mournful, despised by all, the man of suffering crushed like a worm by the scourging and the crucifixion. This interior life motivates the Missionary of Charity to serve Jesus in the poor.

*

We must work in great faith, steadily, efficiently, and above all with great love and cheerfulness, for without this our work will be only the work of slaves, serving a hard master.

It is Him we serve in the poor; it is for his sake that we become beggars. How great will be our joy when at the last judgment we will hear Our Lord address his Missionaries of Charity with these words, "Come ye blessed of my Father, inherit the kingdom prepared for you from the foundation of the world. For I was hungry and ye gave me to eat, thirsty and ye gave me to drink. I was a stranger and ye brought me within, naked and ye clothed me. I was sick and ye visited me, in prison and ye came unto me . . . in as much as ye did it to one of the least of these my brethren, ye did it to me."

*

However beautiful the work is, be detached from it—even ready to give it up. You may be doing great good in one place, but obedience calls you elsewhere. Be ready to leave. The work is not yours. You are working for Jesus. Obedience and humility are one and the same thing. If you want to know whether you are humble, ask yourself, "Do I obey because I see Christ in every command?" Poverty one can get used to, but every act of obedience is an act of the will, and it gets harder as we grow older because we get our own ideas. Every humiliation is a sacrifice.

*

You may be exhausted with work—you may even kill yourself—but unless your work is interwoven with love, it is useless.

*

Don't give in to discouragement. No more must you do so when you try to settle a marriage crisis or convert a sinner and don't succeed. If you are discouraged, it is a sign of pride because it shows you trust in your own powers. Never bother about people's opinions. Be humble and you will never be disturbed. It is very difficult in practice because we all want to see the result of our work. Leave it to Jesus.

*

Never do the work carelessly because you wish to hide your gifts. Remember, the work is his. You are his co-worker.

Therefore, He depends on you for that special work. Do the work with Him, and the work will be done for Him. The talents God has given you are not yours—they have been given to you for your use, for the glory of God. There can be no half-measures in the work. You may feel very bad, but feelings are not the measure of our love for Christ. It is our will and our work that matters. Be great and use everything in you for the Good Master.

*

Remember the work is not ours and we must not spoil it. That would be a great injustice to God because the work is his. It is better that the whole society be wiped out than that God's work be spoiled.

*

We love Him in the distressing disguise. Otherwise there is no meaning in being an M.C. Our society goes deeper. It is the hungry Christ I feed. Christ is really in the poor.

*

We have to love our vocation. I must really say: Christ lives in me. I must be able to say that. We have to keep on desiring. The desire will only be fulfilled when we are face to face with God. Here on earth we must have that desire to live with Christ in the poor. Jesus said, "I was hungry, you gave me to eat. I was thirsty and you gave me to drink. I was ignorant and you taught me. You took me to church." This is not simply something to excite our imagination. Jesus really said it. So He is the poor we meet everywhere.

*

We are the servants of the poor. We give wholehearted, free service to the poor. In the world the people are paid for their work. We are paid by God. We are bound by a vow to love and serve the poor, and to live as the poor with the poor.

*

St. Ignatius said, "I must do my work as if everything depends on me—and the result I leave to God." The people in the world take so much trouble—we also must do the same. They work for hours to make themselves attractive. We must make ourselves attractive to God.

*

We must do better than the people in the world because we do it for Jesus. If we find it difficult, we should ask Jesus to give us a drop from his precious blood.

There is a story of a little robin. He saw Jesus on the cross, saw the crown of thorns. The bird flew around and around until he found a way to remove a thorn—and in removing the thorn it struck him. Each one of us should be that bird. What have I done; what comfort have I given? Does my work really mean something?

The little robin tried to remove just one thorn. When I look at the cross, I think of that robin. Don't pass by the cross—it is a place of grace. The cross—hands seared with pain. Did I put compassion in my hands for one who was sick? How did I touch my patient?

*

For money the people do so much work in the world. I want you to do well for the greater glory of God. What does it matter whether the whole world knows of the M.C.s? That does not change anything. But Mother wants the poor to get the best things that others get for money.

*

I don't need numbers. I need M.C.s full of love, full of zeal. God has entrusted us with a very special thing: to be his love and compassion to the poorest of the poor. You can't do that if you are not holy.

*

No Missionary of Charity is called to do big things. Our work sounds big because there are so many little things, but when you look at it, there is nothing to show—nothing. I was so happy to see a Sister cleaning the toilets, because they were shining. She must have cleaned them with great love and done it in the presence of God.

If something belongs to me, I've got full power to use it as I want. I belong to Jesus; He can do to me whatever He wants. The work is not our vocation. I can do this work without being a religious. Can you tell me why we become M.C.s? The work is not our vocation. Our vocation is to belong to Him. Our profession is that we belong to Him. Therefore, I am ready to do anything: wash, scrub, clean. I am like a mother who gives birth to a child. The child belongs to her. All her washing, staying up at night, and so on is proving that the child belongs to her. She will not do this for any other child, but she will do anything for her own child. If I belong to Jesus, I will do anything for Jesus.

*

The child is the fruit of married love. How beautiful! God has said: "Let man and woman be created for that purpose."

The Church is the spouse of Jesus, and for us M.C.s the fruit of that oneness with Jesus is the poor. Just as the fruit of mother and father is the child, so the fruit of my relationship with Jesus and me is the poor. Today ask yourself: "What is the fruit of my vow of chastity?"

*

Mary said: "Let it be done according to thy word." Then she went in haste. See her total surrender. This is why Our Lady is a Missionary of Charity in the true sense of the word. Each morning I, too, must go in haste: I am going to have an audience with God. Each morning I receive Jesus: his blood, his body in my body. Then what happens? Our Lady spent nine months with Jesus; Jesus was in her . . . and what did she do? Scrub, clean, wash, but she really loved her total surrender. I have to do the same. In the street I must go in haste, burning with love and zeal to give Jesus to the poor.

*

Let the praise of people not destroy the peace in our hearts and make us restless. It has been given to us; let us give it back to Him with great love. They cannot give praise to all. It has been given to One—but it has been given to the lepers, the children, dying patients—all. All that work is only a drop in the ocean, but if we neglect to put in that drop, the ocean will be less.

*

As you know, we have got our Brothers also who are Missionaries of Charity. One of our Brothers loves the lepers. We are taking care of 49,000 lepers in India. This Brother really loves the lepers. He came one day after he had had some difficulties with his superior. He said to me, "I love the lepers; I want to be with them. I want to work for them. My vocation is to be with the lepers." I said to him, "Brother, you are making a mistake. Your vocation is not to work for the lepers. Your vocation is to belong to Jesus. The work for the lepers is only your love for Christ in action; and, therefore, it makes no difference to anyone as long as you are doing it to Him, as long as you are doing it with Him. That's all that matters. That is the completion of your vocation, of your belonging to Christ."

*

A Sister was telling me that just two or three weeks ago she and some other Sisters picked up a man from the streets in Bombay and brought him home. We have a big place donated to us which we have turned into a home for the dying. This man was brought there and the Sisters took care of him. They loved him and treated him with dignity. Right away they discovered that the whole of his back had no skin, no flesh. It was all eaten up. After they washed him they put him on his bed, and this Sister told me that she had never seen so much joy as she saw on the face of that man. Then I asked her, "What did you feel when you were removing those worms from his body; what did you feel?" And she looked at me and said, "I've never felt the presence of Christ; I've never really believed the word of Jesus saying, 'I was sick and you did it to me.' But his presence was there and I could see it on that man's face." This is the gift of God.

*

In India we have more and more Hindus, Muslims, and Buddhists getting involved in the work. Why are they coming?

Because they feel the presence of God. They want to serve God in their own way, and they've found that by sacrifice and by prayer they can do that. They come to be with the poorest of the poor, even though in India, it is very, very difficult to touch lepers, to touch the dying.

*

I insist on saying that we are not social workers. We are really contemplatives in the heart of the world.

*

The Missionaries of Charity is just a little instrument in the hands of God. We must try to keep it always like that—the small instrument. Very often I feel like a little pencil in God's hand. He does the writing; He does the thinking, He does the movement—I have only to be a pencil and nothing else.

*

—You are being sent, you have not chosen for yourself where you want to go, and you are *sent* just as Jesus was *sent* to us.

—You are sent not to teach but to learn: learn to be meek and humble of heart. That is just what Jesus has asked us to do: "Learn of me for I am meek and humble of heart."

—You are sent to serve and not to be served: Go to serve with a humble heart. Never escape the hard work. Be always the first one to do it.

—Go to be a cause of joy to your communities.

—Go with zeal and love for the poor.

—Go in haste, like Our Lady, to serve.

—Choose the hardest thing. Go with a humble heart, with a generous heart. Don't go with ideas that don't fit into our way of life: with big, big ideas about theology and what you would like to teach, but rather go to learn and to serve.

—Share what you have received, with a humble heart.

—Go to the poor with great tenderness. Serve the poor with tender, compassionate love.

—Say yes to peace with your tongue. Close your mouth rather than speaking a word which will hurt anyone.

—Go to give yourselves without any reservation. Give yourselves wholeheartedly, unreservedly.

*

Have I really learned to pray the work? Maybe I have never learned to pray the work because the whole time my mind is "work." Here are words that will help you: "With Jesus, for Jesus, to Jesus." If you want to know how much you love Jesus, there is no need to ask anybody to tell you. In the sincerity of your heart you will know, if you practice silence.

*

You have done a lot of work these days; it was nicely done, but did you give what was inside of you? What did that giving mean to you? Did you give with love, respect? If you did not pray that giving it was just a giving.

Did the people see you give with love and respect? Did you give the medicine with faith to the sick Christ? This is the difference between you and the social worker.

*

I will pick the roses. The sharper the thorns, the sweeter shall be my song. For the aim of joining is not to become social workers. Our work is not a profession, but a vocation chosen to satiate the thirst of Jesus by total surrender, without counting the cost.

*

We must know that we have not come here to be numbers. I want Missionaries of Charity and not just workers. With money I can get workers. I want each of us to be able to say, "I work for the poor because I love God."

"I was hungry and I waited for you but you did not come. I was homeless on the street. I waited for you but you did not come." Jesus will judge us on this. Somebody told me that we are the only ones in the whole church of God with this fourth vow of charity. We must be conscious of this, Sisters. We have a special responsibility to the Church to fulfill this special call.

Sisters, don't look for big things, just do small things with great love.

Feeding the hungry Christ.
Clothing the naked Christ.
Visiting the sick Christ.
Giving shelter to the homeless Christ.
Teaching the ignorant Christ.

We all long for heaven where God is, but we have it in our power to be in heaven with Him right now—to be happy with Him at this very moment. But being happy with Him now means loving like He loves, helping like He helps, giving as He gives, serving as He serves, rescuing as He rescues, being with Him twenty-four hours a day—touching Him in his distressing disguise.

We need to realize that we have the privilege of touching Jesus twenty-four hours. When I'm feeding that child, I'm feeding Jesus. Think a little. Elizabeth did not know—but the child in her womb jumped. The same thing should happen when our slum people meet us. "That Sister—she has compassion. She is giving Holy Communion, giving medicine as if she were giving Holy Communion."

*

Lent, 1975

Each time Jesus wanted to prove his love for us, He was rejected by mankind. Before his birth his parents asked for a simple dwelling place and they were given none because they were poor. The innkeeper probably looked at Joseph the carpenter and decided that he would not be able to pay. So he refused. But Mother Earth opened a cave and took in the Son of God.

Again, before the redemption and the resurrection, Jesus was rejected by his people. They did not want Him—they wanted Caesar; they did not want Him—they wanted Barabbas. At the end, it was as if his own Father did not want Him because He was covered with our sins. In his holiness He cried, "My God, my God why hast thou forsaken me?"

Yesterday is always today to God. Therefore, today in the world Jesus stands covered with our sins, in the distressing disguise of my Sister, my Brother. Do I want Him? If we are not careful, soon the riches of the worldly spirit will become an obstacle. We will not be able to see God, for Jesus has said: "Blessed are the clean of heart, for they shall see God."

People rejected Jesus because his poverty was hurting their riches. My Sisters, do our poor reject us because our riches hurt their poverty? Are they at ease with us because we are so like them in poverty? Can we look straight in the face of the poor and say with a sincere heart: "I know poverty; she is my companion: I love poverty; she is my mother." "I serve poverty; she is my mistress."

*

Motherhouse, July 3, 1978

Begin the leprosy and medical work with a prayer and put in a little more gentleness, a little more compasssion for the sick. It will help you to remember that you are touching the Body of Christ. He is hungry for that touch. Will you not give it?

*

To become a saint one must suffer much, and to love much we must suffer more. Suffering begets love, but it is also fruitful because it begets life for souls. How full of love we must be in order to be true to our name.

*

Yesterday has gone, tomorrow has not yet come and we have only today to make Him known, loved, and served.

The Poor We Serve

Our children may be only slum children, but for that very reason just anything will not do. Each Sister must find a way to attract, to capture the children. Don't think that you need not prepare the lessons because you know more than they. They must have the best, and their good must be uppermost in your mind. Don't get stale in your methods, like stagnant water. Keep on improving yourself. Try new ways and means. You may have the knowledge, but you must also know how to impart it.

Our children come to school with empty stomachs—don't waste their time. They must learn something—to be able to read and write a little and tell a little about the life of Our Lord. Make them happy. They have much to suffer already, and we cannot treat them as we would children going to a regular school.

*

Be kind, very kind, to the suffering poor. We little realize what they go through. The most difficult part is the feeling of not being wanted. This is the first hardship a leper experiences, even today. Show your love for them by being very kind—act kindly, speak kindly. I prefer our Sisters to make mistakes through kindness than to work miracles through harshness and unkindness.

*

In Addis Ababa, where the government is expelling missionaries a few hours on notice, the Governor said to me, "Even if I have to send away everyone else, yet I will not let your Sisters go, because I know and see that the Sisters love and care for our poor people."

*

All over the world people are saying that Mother Teresa is spoiling the poor by giving them things free. At a seminary in Bangalore, once a nun said to me, "Mother Teresa, you are spoiling the poor people by giving them things free. They are losing their human dignity." When everyone was quiet, I said calmly, "No one spoils as much as God Himself. See the wonderful gifts He has given us freely. All of you here have no glasses, yet you all can see. If God were to take money for your sight, what would happen? Continually we are breathing and living on oxygen that we do not pay for. What would happen if

God were to say, 'If you work four hours, you will get sunshine for two hours?' How many of us would then survive?" Then I also told them: "There are many congregations who spoil the rich; it is good to have one congregation in the name of the poor, to spoil the poor." There was profound silence; nobody said a word after that.

*

Do we treat the poor as our dustbins to give whatever we cannot use or eat? I cannot eat this food so I will give it to the poor. I cannot use this thing or that piece of cloth so I will give it to the poor. Am I then sharing the poverty of the poor? Do I *identify* myself with the poor I serve? Am I one with them? Do I share with them as Jesus shared with me?

This is the wonderful part of our vocation, that as M.C.s we have created an awareness of the poor in the whole world. Twenty years ago no one would believe that there were hungry, naked men and women around. Today the whole world knows our poor because of our work. Because they know they want to share.

The other day, a group of Hindu school children came from very far. They had won prizes in a contest at school and had asked the headmistress to give them money instead of the prizes. Then they said, "Now, take us to Mother Teresa. We want to give this money to her poor people." How wonderful it was that they did not use that money for themselves! Because we have created this awareness the whole world wants to share with the poor. Whenever I accept money or an award, I always take it in the name of the poor, whom they recognize in me. What am I? I am nothing. It is the poor whom they recognize in me and that they want to give to, because they see what we do. Today people in the world want *to see*. Why is our congregation spread all over the world today? It is because people see what we do: feeding the hungry Christ, clothing the naked Christ, taking care of the sick, the dying, the leprosy patients. Because they see, they believe. How sad it will be if we are not sincere in what we do.

Our poor people suffer much, and unless we go with joy we cannot help them. We will make them more miserable.

*

Among the poor we have the rich poor—children better gifted, patients who are cleaner, and so on. We must be careful not to pick and choose. There are children who are mentally dull who cannot respond to you and so you neglect those. This is where we have the duty of wholehearted, free service. The "rich" poor child can still have a place but it is the child so dull, stupid, and hungry, for whom I must especially work.

*

At home, we must love our Sisters. They too are—the poorest of the poor. Afterwards it will be easy outside.

*

Our poor people are becoming poorer day by day. Be a comfort to the poor and take every trouble to help them. Open your eyes to the needs of the poor. Put into reality the words "to give wholehearted, free service to the poor." Give to Christ in his distressing disguise. It is Jesus in the poor that you feed, clothe, and take in. Do it all with a great, undivided love.

*

Our Sisters are working in New York with the shut-ins. They see the terrible pain of our people, the pain of loneliness, of fear, of being unwanted and unloved. I think it is much greater pain, much greater than even cancer or T.B. The Sisters have often met people like that, people who are completely brokenhearted, desperate with feelings of hurt.

*

Sometime ago a man came to our house and said: "Mother, there is a Hindu family that has eight children. They have not eaten for a long time. Do something for them." So I took some rice and went. When I arrived at their house, I could see the hunger in the children's eyes. Their eyes were shining with hunger. I gave the rice to the mother. She took it and divided it into two, and then she went out. When she came back, I asked her, "Where did you go?" She said, "They are hungry also." Her neighbors were also hungry. What struck me most was not that she gave the rice but that she knew they were hungry. Because she knew, she shared. I did not bring more rice that night. I waited until the next morning so that they could experience the joy of sharing and loving.

Love, to be true, has to hurt, and this woman who was hungry—she knew that her neighbor was also hungry. That family happened to be a Mohammedan family. It was so touching, so real. This is where we are most unjust to our poor— we don't know them. We don't know how great they are, how lovable, how hungry for that understanding love. Today God loves the world through you and through me. Are we that love and that compassion? God proves that Christ loves us—that He has come to be his Father's compassion. Today God is loving the world through you and through me and through all those who are his love and compassion in the world.

*

God has been pouring many graces into the congregation, and I think we owe deep gratitude to the poor. Their life of suffering, their life of prayer, their life of tremendous forbearance obtains many graces for us. Also, there are all those thousands of people who have died in our hands. I am sure they pray much for us when they go to heaven. The whole thing is nothing extra-ordinary, nothing special. It has been just a simple surrender, a simple yes to Christ, allowing Him to do what He wants. That is why the work is his work. I'm just a little pencil in his hand. Tomorrow, if He finds somebody more helpless, more stupid, more hopeless, I think He will do still greater things with her and through her.

*

Jesus is reliving his Passion in our poor people. The poor are really going through the Passion of Christ. We should treat them with dignity. These poor people are Jesus suffering today. We must find ways and means of helping them; don't add to their sufferings. Poor people are living Jesus' Calvary today.

Our Life of Evangelization

The special aim of the society is to labor at the conversion and sanctification of the poor in the slums; that is by nursing the sick and the dying, by gathering and teaching little street children, by visiting and caring for beggars and their children, by giving shelter to the abandoned.

To labor at the conversion and sanctification of the poor in the slums involves hard, ceaseless toiling, without results, without counting the cost.... To convert and sanctify is the work of God, but God has chosen the M.C.s in his great mercy to help Him in his own work. It is a special grace granted to the M.C.s, without any merit of theirs, to carry the light of Christ into the dark holes of the slums.

"I have other food to eat that you know not of. Lift up your eyes and see the fields, white and ready for the harvest" (Jn 4:32-35). This is my food, the conversion and sanctification of souls.

＊

When we do "our work," visit the families, teach, nurse the sick, help the dying, gather the little children for church, we should do it with one aim in view: "the salvation of the poor." We want to bring them to Jesus and bring Jesus to them.

The knowledge we impart must be that of Jesus crucified. St. Augustine says: "Before allowing his tongue to speak, the apostle ought to raise his thirsting soul to God, and then give forth what he has drunk in and pour forth what he has been filled with."

Zeal for souls is the effect and the proof of true love of God. If we really love God, we cannot but be consumed with the desire of saving souls, the greatest and the dearest interest of Jesus. Therefore, zeal is the test of love and the test of zeal is devotedness to his cause—spending our life and energy in the work for souls.

We have to carry Our Lord to places where He has not walked before. Therefore the Sisters must be consumed with one desire: Jesus. Speak of no one but Him crucified. We must not be afraid to do the things He did—to go fearlessly through death and danger with Him and for Him.

A "missionary" carries the interest of Christ continually in her heart and mind. In her heart there must be the fire of divine love and of zeal for God's glory and for the salvation of souls. This love makes her spend herself without ceasing. This becomes her real object in life and her joy.

The missionary must die daily, if she wants to bring souls to God. She must be ready to pay the price He paid for souls, to walk in the way He walked.

Our holy faith is nothing but a gospel of love, revealing to us God's love for men and claiming in return men's love for God. "God is love." A missionary must be a missionary of love. We must spread God's love on earth if we want to make souls repent wholeheartedly for sin, strengthen them against temptation, increase their generosity and their desire to suffer for Christ. Let us "act Christ's love among men," remembering the words of the *Imitation of Christ*, "Love feels no burden, values no labours, would willingly do more than it can, complains not of impossibility because it conceives that it may and can do all things; when weary is not tired; when straightened is not constrained, when frightened is not disturbed; but like a lively flame and a torch all on fire, it mounts upwards and securely passes through all oppositions."

Love has a hem to her garment that reaches to the very dust. It sweeps the stains from the streets and lanes, and because it can, it must. The Missionaries of Charity, in order to be true to their name, must be full of charity in their own souls and spread that same charity in the souls of others—Christians and pagans.

*

If you give to the people a broken Christ, a lame Christ, a crooked Christ—deformed by you, that is all they will have. If you want them to love Him, they must know Him first. Therefore, give the whole Christ—to the Sisters, first, then to the people in the slums. Do I give the Christ who is full of zeal, love, joy, and sunshine? Do I come up to the mark? Or am I a dark light, a false light, a bulb without connection, having no current and therefore shedding no radiance? Put your heart into being a bright light. "Help me to shed thy fragrance everywhere I go."

Let the poor, seeing you, be drawn to Christ. Poverty makes people very bitter, and they speak and act without realizing what they do. But do they remember Christ when they see you—even if they get angry—because you remind them of Christ?

Draw them to God but never, never to yourself. If you are not drawing them to God, then you are seeking yourself, and people love you for yourself and not because you remind them of Christ.

*

The surest way to preach Christianity to the pagan is by our cheerfulness, our happiness. What would our life be if the Sisters were unhappy? It would be slavery and nothing else. We would do the work but we would attract nobody.

*

The Sister must have one thing clear: there is a soul to save, a soul to bring to God. The Sister has to be extremely kind and gentle; in touch of hand, in tone of voice, in her smile—for the work is very delicate. Nirmal Hriday is a treasure house; so is every hospital. An unkind word or look is enough to spoil the work. Such perfection of charity is not in us but we must acquire it—kindness in action. You will not learn kindness by looking after sick people unless you practice it on healthy people, because the sick are often trying and hard to please.

*

What is the good news? The good news is that God still loves the world through each one of you. You are God's good news, you are God's love in action. Through you, God is still loving the world.

Recently, one great Brazilian man, a man of high position, wrote to me that he had lost faith in God and man. He gave up his position and everything and only wanted to commit suicide. One day, as he was passing by a shop, his eyes suddenly fell on a TV in the window. There was the scene of Nirmal Hriday, the sisters looking after the sick and dying. He wrote to me that after seeing that scene, he knelt and prayed for the first time in many years. Now he has decided to turn back to God and have faith in humanity because he saw that *God still loves the world*—he saw this on TV.

*

A rich couple came to see me the other day. They had been to Nirmal Hriday. The man told me that when he saw the Sisters caring for the dying something clicked in his heart. He said that he would never be the same man again. What clicked? I do not know, but he met God's love in action and something clicked in his heart, so he cannot be the same man again.

*

Once a man came to Kalighat, right into the ward. I was there. After a little while he came back and said to me, "I came here with so much hate in my heart, hate for God and hate for man. I came here empty, faithless, embittered, and I saw a Sister giving her wholehearted attention to a patient, and I realized that God still loves. Now I go out a different man. I believe there is a God and that He loves us still." Often we do our work slapdash because we do not have enough faith. If we truly believe we are doing it to Jesus we will do our work well.

*

Once, someone asked me, "Why do you go abroad? Don't you have enough poor in India?" So I answered, "I think Jesus told us to go and preach to all the nations." That is why we go all over the world to preach his love and compassion.

When our Sisters were in Ceylon, a minister of state once told me something very surprising. He said, "You know, Mother, I love Christ but I hate Christians." So I asked him how that could be. He answered, "Because Christians do not give us Christ; they do not live their Christian lives to the full." Gandhi said something very similar, "If Christians were to live their Christian lives to the full, there would not be one Hindu left in India." Isn't it very true? This love of Christ should urge us to spend ourselves without ceasing.

A Mohammedan Mulvi was standing with Father Gabric and looking at a Sister bandaging the wound of a leper with so much love. She didn't say anything, but she did something. He turned to Father and said, "All these years I believed that Jesus was a prophet, but today I know He is God because He has given so much love into the hands of this Sister." Even today, that Sister does not know that her action brought Jesus into the life of that man.

*

The light, O Jesus, will be all from you—none of it will be mine. It will be you shining on others through me. Shine through me and be so in me that every soul I come in contact with may feel your presence in my soul. Let them look up and see Jesus.

*

The joy of Jesus will be my strength—it will be in my heart, in every person I meet. They will see it in my work, my walk, my prayer—in everything.

*

At the opening of Baroda a group of Hindus came to me and said: "You have come to convert us?" I looked at them and smiled and said, "Naturally, that's the treasure I have; I would like you to be Christian, but I will not force it on you. Even God cannot force Himself on anyone who does not want Him."

Faith is a gift. Let us not humiliate the Hindus by saying, "For a plate of rice you give up your religion." Christianity is a living reality. It is a search and we must desire it and find God.

*

Very often we pick up sick and dying destitutes from the streets of Calcutta. In twenty-five years we have picked up more than 36,000 people from the streets and more than 18,000 have died a most beautiful death. When we pick them up from the street like that, we give them a plate of rice. In no time we revive them. A few nights ago we picked up four people. One was in a most terrible condition, covered with wounds, her body full of maggots. I told the Sisters that I would take care of her while they attended to the other three. I really did all that my love could do for her. I put her in bed and then she took hold of my hand. She had such a beautiful smile on her face and she said one word only: "Thank you." Then she died. There was a greatness of love. She was hungry for love, and she received that love before she died. She spoke only one word, but her understanding love was expressed in that word. I have never seen a smile like that.

*

Yesterday, a Sister was telling me about some Sisters who go to the prison. They take the blessed sacrament, and the prison chaplain has started daily adoration for half an hour. To see those prisoners, young boys and men, adoring. They are preparing some of those boys for First Communion. They're hungry for God—they are very hungry for God. That man who we picked up from the streets said, "I have lived like an animal in the street but I'm going to die like an angel." I can tell you that of the 18,000 that have died in Calcutta alone, I've not seen one of them die in distress. Nobody has died in despair. We ask them: "Do you want a blessing by which you will see God and your sins will be forgiven?" Nobody says no. Up until now, nobody has refused to receive the blessing and go and be with God. It is so beautiful. We feel this is the fruit of our vocation, of our oneness with Christ. We need that continual feeding; that is why we begin the day at half past four in the morning and then we have mass, Holy Communion, and meditation.

*

May, 1964

To children and to the poor, to all those who suffer and are lonely—give them always a happy smile; give them not only your care but also your heart.

Kindness has converted more people than zeal, science, or eloquence. We take a vow to give wholehearted service to the poor. Does this not mean love of the poor? The poor are not at our service. If we want the poor to see Christ in us, we must first see Christ in the poor.

*

Motherhouse, January 10, 1968

Let us preach the peace of Christ like He did; He went about doing good. He did not stop his works of charity because the Pharisees and others hated Him or tried to spoil his Father's work. He just went about doing good. Cardinal Newman wrote: "Help me to spread thy fragrance everywhere I go; let me preach thee without preaching, not by words but by my example—by the catching force, the sympathetic influence of what I do, the evident fullness of the love my heart bears to thee." Our works of love are nothing but works of peace. Let us do them with greater love and efficiency. It is always the same Christ who says:

I was hungry—not only for food, but for peace that comes from a pure heart.

I was thirsty—not for water, but for peace that satiates the passionate thirst of passion for war.

I was naked—not for clothes, but for the beautiful dignity of men and women for their bodies.

I was homeless—not for a shelter made of bricks, but for a heart that understands, that covers, that loves.

*

Motherhouse, May 1975

Often you see small and big wires, new and old, cheap and expensive lined up. Until the current passes through them there will be no light. That wire is you and me. The current is God. We have the power to let the current pass through us, use us, produce the light of the world—Jesus, or refuse to be used and allow darkness to spread.

Our Lady was the most wonderful wire. She allowed God to

fill her to the brim. By her surrender, "Be it done to me according to Thy word," she became "full of grace." The moment she was filled by this current, by the grace of God, she went in haste to Elizabeth's house to connect the wire, John, to the current, Jesus. As his mother said, "This child, John, leapt up with joy at your voice." Let us ask Our Lady to come into our lives also and make the current, Jesus, use us to go round the world, especially in our own communities, and so that we can continue connecting wires of hearts of men with the current, Jesus.

Charity Must Cost Us

The more repugnant the work, the greater the effect of love and cheerful service. If Mother had not first picked up that woman who was eaten up by rats—her face, and legs, and so on, I could not have been an M.C. But I returned, picked her up, and took her to Camphel Hospital. If I had not, the society would have died. Feelings of repugnance are human. If we give our wholehearted, free service in spite of such feelings, we will become holy. St. Francis of Assisi hated lepers but he overcame his hatred. He died; but Christ lives.

*

There was a queen who was a holy person, but her husband was rather cruel. Yet she treated him as she would treat Christ. She had a mother-in-law who was jealous of the love her son bore his wife. One day Queen Elizabeth offered hospitality to a leper and even gave him her husband's bed to lie on. The mother-in-law, seeing this, seized the opportunity to set her son against his wife. The husband dashed angrily into the room but to his surprise he saw the figure of Christ on the bed. Elizabeth could have acted thus only because she was convinced she was doing it to Christ Himself. We must therefore be proud of our vocation which gives us the opportunity to serve Christ in his poorest. It is in the slums that we must seek to go and serve Christ.

At the altar how gently and tenderly the priest touches the consecrated host, with what love he looks at it. The priest believes that the host is the disguise of Jesus. In the slums Jesus chooses as his disguise the miseries and poverty of our people. You cannot have the vow of charity if you have not got the faith to see Jesus in the people we contact. Otherwise our work is no more than social work. . . : What if you feel a disgust and run away? Feelings don't count. Run away but come back without delay.

Charity, to be fruitful, must cost us. Actually, we hear so much about charity. Yet we never give it its full importance: God put the commandment of loving our neighbor on the same footing as the first commandment. God's love is infinite. God has prepared us for service, so He expects this from us. He has given each of us something that in one way or another will enable Him to shine through us.

We want to be something for Almighty God, and since we cannot reach God and do it directly to Him, we serve Him in the poor people of India. We are here purely for the love of God. Our charity must be true. We must feel in our very bones that we are doing it—we should be living fires of love. Every M.C. must be like a burning bush. Love to be true must hurt. It must be something I want to give—cost what it may.

*

Today, in the words of our Holy Father, each one of us must be able "to cleanse what is dirty, to warm what is lukewarm, to strengthen what is weak, to enlighten what is dark." We must not be afraid to proclaim Christ's love and to love as He loved. In the work we have to do, no matter how small and humble it may be, we must make it Christ's love in action. Do not be afraid to proclaim his poverty. Do not be afraid to go with Christ and be subject to those who have authority from above and so declare Christ's obedience unto death. Rejoice that once more Christ is walking through the world, in you and through you, going about doing good.

When He showed his heart to Margaret Mary, Jesus said again and again, "Love me as I have loved you." "Impossible," she said, "the only way I can do it is if you take my heart and give me yours." Let us ask Jesus sincerely, "Let me share your loneliness, your being unloved, uncared for." Do something today to share in the Passion. Maybe Jesus is asking something of you in a special way, maybe something small. If He is not asking you, it might be because you are holding very tightly to something. He will never force it out of you. Maybe He wants you just to smile, to say "May I," to be on time, or to give up an unhealthy friendship.

*

"My child, receive the symbol of our crucified spouse. Follow his footsteps in search of souls. Carry Him and his light into the homes of the poor, especially to the souls most in need. Spread the charity of his heart wherever you go and so satiate his thirst for souls." These words express beautifully the whole of our life. If we just live this, we will be holy; we will be spouses of Jesus crucified.

We must not imagine that we will be crucified with nails. Crucifixion, Sisters, is when something hurts me and I hurt back. I say the word and I put a nail into somebody's heart. Nobody knows how big the nails were, but we know that Jesus was crucified. If you are in pain, see in your pain that pain of Jesus, your loneliness in his loneliness. Spread the charity of his heart wherever you go.

*

Suffering will come, trouble will come—that's part of life; a sign that you are alive. If you have no suffering and no trouble, the devil is taking it easy. You are in his hand.

If I am the spouse of Jesus crucified, He has to kiss me. Naturally, the nails will hurt me. If I come close to the crown of thorns, it will hurt me. If a man leaves his father and mother and clings to his wife, they become one. Cleave to each other. If I am one with Jesus, it must hurt when I share his sorrow.

*

Rome, October 10, 1980

What delicate love God has had for the poor of the world to have created the M.C.s. You and I have been called by our name because He loved us. Because you and I are somebody special to Him—to be his Heart to love Him in the poor, his Hands to serve Him in the poorest of the poor. My children, how much love and care we must take of Him—if only we were in love with Him. Let us learn to pray the work to be able to be twenty-four hours with Jesus, to do it for Jesus and to Jesus. We need a pure heart, a heart that is filled with nothing but Jesus.

*

To be a co-worker means to work along with someone, to share together in tiredness, humiliations, and shame, not only in success. Those who share everything are partners, giving love for love, suffering for suffering. Jesus, You have died, You have given everything, your life blood, all. Now it is my turn. I put everything into the field also. The common soldier fights in the way, but the devoted one tries to be near the captain to share his fate. This is the only truth. . . . The only thing that matters—for it is the spirit of Christ.

He wants to live his life in you, to look through your eyes, walk with your feet, love with your heart. In Christ and through Christ. Hear Jesus, your co-worker, speak to you. "I want you to be my fire of love among the poor, the sick, the dying, and the little children—the poor I want you to bring to me."

APPENDIX A

Rule of Life and Covenant
of the
Universal Brothers of the Word

"To Me to Live Is Christ."

"There is a very great need among young people for the Brothers of the Word—contemplatives in the heart of the world—by their life of prayer, adoration, contemplation, penance and total surrender to God and by their presence and the spoken Word of God for two to three hours daily to the poorest of the poor. By so doing they will proclaim Christ to all nations and make the Church fully present in the world of today."

(Mother's letter to Pope Paul VI, 12/21/77)

*Association of
Christian Faithful
Founded by
Mother Teresa
of Calcutta*

1. Our Call
Our brotherhood, known as the Universal Brothers of the Word, is an "association of the Christian faithful" founded by Mother Teresa of Calcutta with life commitments of chastity, poverty, obedience, and wholehearted free service to the spiritually poorest of the poor.

*International
Character*

2. By its international character, our brotherhood partakes of that special mission of the Church: To shed on the whole world the radiance of the gospel message and to unify under one spirit all men of whatever nation, race, or culture, standing forth as a sign of that brotherliness which allows honest dialogue and is invigorated by it.

Community of Brothers in Jesus the Lord

3. We believe that we have been called by the Father in the likeness of the first Christians to be a community of brothers in Jesus, the Lord; to follow Him through the inspiration, teachings, and example of Mother Teresa of Calcutta; and to be of one heart and mind: in a community of goods, in humble submission to one another and to the Servant Leader, remaining single for the Lord, daily persevering in prayer, adoration, and the "breaking of the Bread," and also being available as carriers of his Word to the spiritually poorest of the poor in season and out of season to the extremity of the world.

Contemplatives in the Heart of the World

4. Our vocation is to be Universal Brothers, carriers of God's love, contemplatives in the heart of the world, monks and missionaries, committed to bring with our life, the Word to the world in the spirit of ecumenism promoted by Vatican Council II.

Universal Brothers of the Word

5. *Our Name*
To evidence our vocation rooted in the universality of the Catholic Church, we will be called "Universal Brothers of the Word." This means that, for Jesus' sake,

we want to be Brothers to each and every human being, regardless of color, culture, or creed and for that purpose we want to remain humble, little, and vulnerable, to love until it hurts.

The "Word" is the "Logos" of the Father in his pure divinity in pre-history, and the Word Incarnate on earth, in the history of salvation. He is the Lord Jesus Christ, alive and real today among us, speaking to us and guiding us—we gather in his Name. We covenant ourselves to Him and to each other, to follow in his way, with a joyful and undivided heart by the power of the Holy Spirit.

"I Thirst"

6. *Our aim*

> "I will give saints to Mother Church."
> (Mother)

Our aim is to quench the thirsting Jesus on the cross for love of souls and the hunger of souls for Him, the Word and Bread of Life, by the profession of the evangelical counsels and wholehearted free service to the spiritually poorest of the poor, so to make the Church fully present in the world today. Our specific mission is to labour for the salvation and sanctification of the spiritually poorest of the poor all over the world, wherever they may be, by:

Our Mission: "To Proclaim Jesus, Saviour to All Nations"

Knowing the word of God through daily meditation, study, and sharing of Scriptures;

Living the Word of God in prayer and action in a life marked by the simplicity of the gospel;

Loving the Word of God Incarnated: under the appearance of Bread, to satisfy mankind's hunger through our daily adoration and Spirit-filled celebration of the Holy Eucharist;

Speaking the Word of God to the spiritually poorest of the poor in whose distress Jesus is disguised so that they may be restored to the lost image and relationship with the Father. This apostolate of prayer, contemplation, and action shall be our specific vocation: that Jesus Christ be proclaimed "Saviour" to all nations.

Total Surrender, Loving Trust, and Cheerfulness

7. *Our Spirit*

"Our ideal is no one but Jesus." (Mother) Our spirit is one of total surrender to God, loving trust in each other, and cheerfulness to everyone as was lived by the Holy Family in Nazareth. "Make your family another Nazareth where Jesus can come and rest awhile" (Mother's letter to the Brothers, June 7, 1979). Christ was entirely at the disposal of his Father for the ransom of many. Though He was God, He did not count equality with God a thing to be grasped, but emptied Himself taking the form of a servant, being born in the likeness of men (Phil 2:5-8).

Total Surrender

8. To be possessed by him so that we

may possess Him, to take whatever he gives and to give whatever He takes with a big smile; to be used by Him as it pleases Him without being consulted; to offer Him our free will, our reason, our whole life in pure faith, so that He may think his thoughts in our minds, do his work through our hands, and love with our hearts.

Our total surrender consists also in being totally available to God and his Church through our availability to our Servant Leader, our Brothers and the peoples we serve. It is thus we will be all powerful with Him who strengthens us.

Loving Trust

9. Jesus trusted his Father with an unshakable trust. His trust was the fruit of his intimate knowledge and love of the Father. He trusted his Father so completely that he entrusted his whole life and the mission for which he was sent into the hands of his Father. He was fully confident that his Father would work out his plan of salvation in spite of the ineffectual means used and the apparent failure.

Cheerfulness

10. Joy is indeed the fruit of the Holy Spirit and a characteristic mark of the kingdom of God, for God is joy. Christ wanted to share his joy with his apostles, "That my joy may be in you and that your joy may be full" (Jn 15:11). Our joy is a sign of our generosity, selflessness, and close and continual union with God. A joyful heart is the normal result

of a heart burning with love, for he gives
most who gives with joy, and God loves
a cheerful giver.

A Brother filled with joy preaches
without preaching. Joy is a need and a
power for us even physically, for it
makes us always ready to go about
doing good.

Therefore we shall accept: to live the
life of poverty in cheerful trust, to offer
cheerful obedience from inward joy, to
minister to Christ in his distressing
disguise with cheerful devotion. This
cheerfulness will be the best way to
show our gratitude to God and to
people.

Reborn in Christ

11. *Means*
Reborn in Christ by water and the Spirit
and established in the Church as a
community of life in faith, hope, and
charity, we who enter into the mysteries
of Christ's life ought to be molded into
his image "until He is formed in us"
(Gal 4:1).

Faith

12. Faith, a gift of God, introduces us
into the spiritual reality of the Kingdom,
whose coming was announced by
Christ. It grows in obedience to his law
and expresses itself by fraternal charity.
Finally, it is sealed by fidelity and confidence, "for we know in whom we have
placed our faith" (2 Tm 1:11). It is He
who grants to those that believe in Him,
to do greater things even than those He
Himself did on earth.

With an interior conviction, we live and do things which we would never have dreamed of doing. As Universal Brothers of the Word, we are especially called upon to see Christ in the appearance of bread and to touch Him in the brokenness of the spiritually poor.

Hope

13. In hope we rely utterly on the omnipotence of Him who said: "Without me you can do nothing." Persuaded of our nothingness and with the blessing of obedience, we attempt all things, doubting nothing, for with God all things are possible. We will allow the good Lord to make plans for the future, for yesterday has gone, tomorrow has not yet come, and we have only *today* to make Him known, loved, and served. Grateful for the thousands of opportunities Jesus gives us to bring hope into a multitude of lives by our concern for the individual sufferer, we will help our troubled world at the brink of despair to discover a new reason to live or to die with a smile of contentment on its lips.

Charity

14. God is love: Charity has its source in the eternal love of the Father and the Son in the Spirit. We allow the Spirit of love to take possession of us, to break all barriers to love, to make us open to others at the very depths of our being, capable of receiving both God and mankind.

Christ when He took bread said: "Take and eat, this is my Body delivered for you." By giving Himself, He invites us to grow in the power of his love to do what He has done. Christ's love for us will give us strength and urge us to spend ourselves for Him. "Let the Brothers and the people eat you up." We have no right to refuse our lives to others in whom we contact Christ.

Meek and Humble of Heart

15. Jesus, anxious that we learn from Him that one lesson to be meek and humble of heart, allowed his heart to be opened. We must become small to be able to enter his heart. Christ, our way to humility, asks us to live in Him and by Him. Convinced that by ourselves we can do nothing and have nothing but sin, weakness, and misery, we acknowledge all gifts of nature and of grace as gifts of God. We do not allow ourselves to be disheartened by any failure as long as we have done our best; neither do we glory in our success but refer all to God in deepest thankfulness. We will meditate frequently on the humility of Christ and pray to the Holy Spirit for light, to know ourselves better, since self-knowledge leads to humility. Towards our Brothers we will be tender and forgiving and count ourselves the least among the brethren. With our poor we will be gentle and compassionate. With Jesus our Saviour, "Lamb led to the slaughter," and with our poor, we

will accept cheerfully and in the spirit of faith all the opportunities He makes especially for us to share in the silence, loneliness and agony of his passion in our life, due to misunderstanding, false blame, rejections, temptation, incapability, lack of virtue, correction, sickness, old age, and death.

Conclusion:
Brothers of
the Silence

To be true Brothers of the Word, we must also be true Brothers of the Silence: God spoke only one Word and he spoke it in an eternal silence. We must hide within it if we want to understand it: this Word is his Son Jesus Christ.

Missionary of Charity Addresses

Motherhouse of the Missionary
of Charity Sisters
54 A Lower Circular Road
Calcutta 700016
INDIA

Missionary of Charity Sisters
335 East 145th St.
South Bronx, New York 10451
U.S.A.

Missionary of Charity Sisters
(contemplatives)
34 Aberdeen St.
Brooklyn, New York 11207
U.S.A.

National Link—U.S.A.
Mrs. Vi Collins
5106 Battery Lane
Bethesda, Maryland 20814
U.S.A.

Motherhouse of the Missionary
of Charity Brothers
7 Mansatala Row
Kidderpore
Calcutta 700023
INDIA

International Co-Workers of
Mother Teresa
Mrs. Ann Blaikie
Stone Cottage
Wonersh, Near Guildford
Surrey GU5 0PE
ENGLAND

Sick and Suffering Co-Workers
Mlle. Jacqueline de Decker
Karmel Ooms St. 14
2018 Antwerp
BELGIUM

Motherhouse of the Universal
Brothers of the Word
P.O. Box 13288 Delmas
Port Au Prince, Haiti
WEST INDIES

Universal Brothers of the Word
7506 North West Second Ave.
Miami, Florida
33150
U.S.A.